The Life of an Economist

The Life of an Economist

AN AUTOBIOGRAPHY

Charles P. Kindleberger

BASIL BLACKWELL

Copyright © Charles P. Kindleberger, 1991

First published 1991
First published in USA 1991

Basil Blackwell, Inc.
3 Cambridge Center
Cambridge, Massachusetts 02142, USA

Basil Blackwell Ltd
108 Cowley Road, Oxford, OX4 1JF, UK

All rights reserved. Except for the quotation of short passages for the purposes of criticism and review, no part of this publication may be reproduced, stored in a retrieval system, or transmitted, in any form or by any means, electronic, mechanical, photocopying, recording or otherwise, without the prior permission of the publisher.

Except in the United States of America, this book is sold subject to the condition that it shall not, by way of trade or otherwise, be lent, re-sold, hired out, or otherwise circulated without the publisher's prior consent in any form of binding or cover other than that in which it is published and without a similar condition including this condition being imposed on the subsequent purchaser.

Library of Congress Cataloging in Publication Data

Kindleberger, Charles Poor, 1910–
  The life of an economist: an autobiography / Charles P. Kindleberger.
      p.   cm.
  Includes index.
  ISBN 1-55786-109-9 (hardback)
  1. Kindleberger, Charles Poor, 1910– . 2. Economists – United States – Biography.   I. Title.
  HB119.K56A3   1991
  330'.092 – dc20
  [B]   90-42899
                                                                      CIP

British Library Cataloguing in Publication Data
A CIP catalogue record for this book is available from the British Library.

Typeset in 10½ on 12½ pt Sabon
by Colset Private Limited, Singapore
Printed in Great Britain by Billing & Sons Ltd, Worcester

*For my teachers and students
(from whom I also learned)
and for the comrades-at-arms
of EOU*

Contents

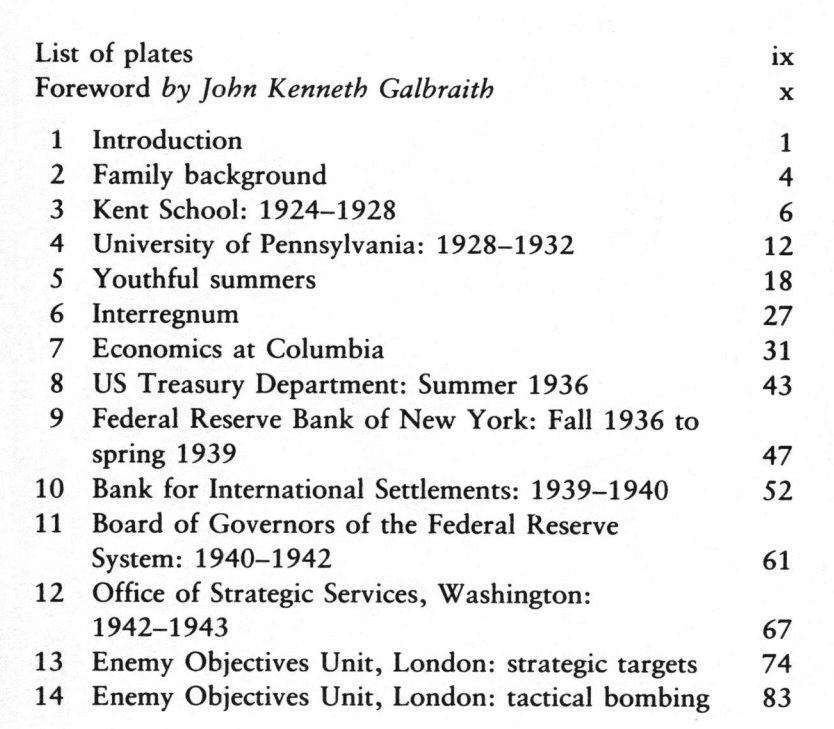

List of plates		ix
Foreword *by John Kenneth Galbraith*		x
1	Introduction	1
2	Family background	4
3	Kent School: 1924–1928	6
4	University of Pennsylvania: 1928–1932	12
5	Youthful summers	18
6	Interregnum	27
7	Economics at Columbia	31
8	US Treasury Department: Summer 1936	43
9	Federal Reserve Bank of New York: Fall 1936 to spring 1939	47
10	Bank for International Settlements: 1939–1940	52
11	Board of Governors of the Federal Reserve System: 1940–1942	61
12	Office of Strategic Services, Washington: 1942–1943	67
13	Enemy Objectives Unit, London: strategic targets	74
14	Enemy Objectives Unit, London: tactical bombing	83

Contents

15	G-2, Twelfth Army Group	90
16	Office of Finance and Development, Department of State: Summer and early fall 1945	103
17	Seminary Hill and the car pool	106
18	Division of German and Austrian Economic Affairs, Department of State: 1945–1947	112
19	The Marshall Plan, Department of State: 1947–1948	121
20	Goodbye Washington, hello Academia	128
21	MIT and Lincoln: The forties and fifties	132
22	Geneva: 1953–1954	145
23	MIT again in the fifties	149
24	Oxford and Paris: 1960–1961	160
25	MIT administration	167
26	Research: The sixties	174
27	Atlanta: 1967–1968	182
28	Kiel and Rome: 1970–1971	188
29	Professor of Economics Emeritus and Senior Lecturer	193
30	Retirement	206

Appendix A: Curriculum Vitae	211
Appendix B: Bibliography	216
Index	219

Plates

Between pages 148 and 149

1. CPK as deck-boy, on SS *Bird City*, 1930.
2. CPK with Sarah in Davos, Switzerland, 1940.
3. CPK with uncle and son, 1941.
4. Award of Bronze Star by General Bradley, 1944.
5. Emile Despres and Werner Knoke, 1938.
6. Ragnar Nurkse, 1954.
7. Dinner in honor of Professor Haberler, 1954.
8. Department of Economics and Social Science, MIT, 1950.
9. The Kindleberger family in Lincoln, late 1960s.
10. Celebration of the retirement of Professor Albert Kervyn de Lettenhove, 1986.
11. Symposium in honor of Bertil Ohlin, 1976.
12. CPK with Lord Franks, 1977.
13. Department of Economics, MIT, 1976.
14. CPK in garden toolhouse, Lincoln, about 1970.

Foreword
John Kenneth Galbraith

Charles Kindleberger, known to academic colleagues for a near half-century as Charlie, is one of the truly distinguished and notably productive economic historians of the years since the Second World War. He is also, more than incidentally, a lifelong friend – a friendship, I might add, that for me has been refreshed and reinforced by his guidance and, on occasion, forthright instruction on matters of shared interest and concern.

I have just identified Kindleberger as an economic historian. That, as he notes in the pages following, is an inadequate characterization. He has always gone beyond history *qua* history to identify, especially as regards the great and continuing sequence of speculative boom and disenchantment that often portends more general economic disaster, what is important in the economic and wider human experience and to tell what has continuing relevance. It is history in this larger dimension that has placed us in his debt.

There are some of us in university and professional life who, in our writing, reach wisely or unwisely, successfully or otherwise, for an audience beyond the academic walls. This, as Kindleberger tells in his introduction, he eschews. His is a book by a scholar for scholars. Let no one admire it less for that.

There was, in fact, much in Kindleberger's life and experience

Foreword

that would have had a more general appeal. He played an influential role in the Office of Strategic Services (OSS), during the Second World War. Then, in the latter months of the war, he played a central part in providing intelligence and guidance to the most intelligent and responsive of the generals of the war, Omar Bradley. In the early months of the peace he had an important hand in shaping policy, particularly on economic matters, in post-war Germany. On this task we worked together for some months, not always with too great a feeling of accomplishment. Even the most obvious and urgent courses of action had to make their way through the State Department bureaucracy, through that of the Joint Chiefs of Staff and on to our proconsul, General Lucius Clay in Berlin. Not always did we feel that all that was necessary and good survived. There is a sense of companionship in shared success but also in shared frustration.

Not much of this, as the author tells, appears in this book. This is not surprising; on the contrary, it is wholly in character. For a great part of his life Kindleberger has been a central and universally respected figure in the economic work and life of the Massachusetts Institute of Technology, the larger Cambridge economic community, and the economics profession generally, his role in the last reflected in his eventual and richly earned presidency of the American Economic Association. It is to this audience and interest and its larger penumbra that this book is deliberately addressed.

There is another feature of this memoir that calls for mention. Academic life is known, along with much else, for the conflicts that more than occasionally erupt, the honest differences of thought and view that are fought out and, not rarely, the other differences and conflicts that reside in personal jealousy or dislike. There is little of that here. Kindleberger is not a person who suffers fools gladly. But he suffers them in tolerant silence, and not less those with whom he is thrown into scholarly disagreement. In consequence, in his academic life he had few, if any, enemies, and few, indeed, are celebrated here. It is, perhaps, a disadvantage to be a memoirist who is respected, even

Foreword

loved, by all. But that is the case of Kindleberger. It is a literary handicap for which all of us should yearn.

I am pleased, indeed proud, to have had the opportunity to write these words of introduction. My pleasure in this, however, is decidedly less than it was from the opportunity to read the manuscript in its original form, fresh from the old-fashioned mechanical typewriter of which the author tells and which, I must note, is one step on from the ball-point pen to which I am addicted. I invite all who have an interest, however marginal, in economics and the history that in the sequence of speculative euphoria and collapse we are so reliably doomed to repeat to share my pleasure and my instruction.

1

Introduction

This is professional autobiography of a disappearing breed. I am an old-fashioned economist, who finished his training in the 1930s, spent twelve years in banks, the military and government, and in starting to teach in 1948 made the conscious and perhaps mistaken decision not to undertake the daunting task of retraining in modern analytical, largely mathematical, techniques. Insofar as I am classified as an economic historian – I prefer to think of myself as an historical economist – I am not, repeat *not*, a Cliometrician, that is, an economic historian who uses a great deal of econometrics. People of my stripe are sometimes referred to derisively as "literary economists." *Tant pis*, as the French say – so much the worse.

Another disability, I guess, is that I still write with a mechanical typewriter rather than with a word processor and a laser printer. But then I know how to spell. People continue to profess astonishment when they see my study or my office. But again, old dogs . . . I have been writing at length, as will be observed in the sequelae, with an acute case of hypergraphia that has produced twenty-five books, more or less, since 1937, the first drafts in all cases typed with two index fingers, one on each hand. In the summer of 1986 at the World Institute of Development Economic Research (WIDER) in Helsinki, Finland, I asked

Introduction

for a mechanical typewriter for the office to which I was assigned, and learned that WIDER had none. For a few days I tried to manage an electric machine, but it proved not to be user-friendly, at least not friendly to this user. As I brushed the wrong key and tried to pull back, it would push ahead in error. I finally suggested to WIDER that it buy a mechanical machine, and that if necessary I would pay for it. In the event, there was not one available for sale in the city. Finally a local secretary rescued me by remembering that her husband had a mechanical typewriter stored in their attic. With that I wrote a couple of papers in five weeks.

As an account of the professional life of an economist, there is little in the book on my good marriage, now of fifty-three years – another old-fashioned trait – my family of four children, three children-in-law, five grandchildren, and the good times at home and abroad. An occasional digression into these non-professional paths has proved inescapable. I have strayed from the confines of pure professionalism, too, in recording some of the memorable stories collected in the sixty years along the way.

Autobiography, of course, is an exercise in narcissism, and one that a few years ago I was prepared to mock. One evening at the American Academy of Arts and Sciences, I amused myself by asking a number of the white-haired in attendance, "How is your autobiography coming along?" I am not clear at this remove whether the stress of the question was on "your" or on "autobiography." The late beloved Harold ("Doc") Edgerton, the MIT stroboscopic camera engineer–inventor, took me somewhat aback by saying, "It's half finished." But the best answer, and one that stopped me in my tracks, was that of John K. Fairbank of Chinese history fame, who replied: "It has been chosen for the Book-of-the-Month Club for next month."

I mention twenty-five books. Their titles are listed in sequence in an appendix at the end of this book. But twenty-five books overstates the evidence of hypergraphia. Three are merely published sets of lectures, on the whole slim volumes. One is a 128-page pamphlet, perhaps not a book at all, another a facsimile reproduction of old State Department letters on

Introduction

occupation problems in Germany immediately after the Second World War. Seven more are collections of papers for the most part previously published in scattered periodicals or symposia. This comes close to selling the same horse twice. On a number of occasions, the late Harry G. Johnson, who taught at the University of Chicago and the London School of Economics, used to publish the same article once in the West (the Western Hemisphere, or Europe) and again in Southeast Asia as a help in spreading the word in areas where subscriptions to major journals were hard to come by. In reviewing one of his books, I observed that the jacket flap noted that he had published almost 400 papers, and asked whether the figure was gross or net. In my own case, the monographic or synthetic literature on the list – real books – comes down to about ten items.

The professional life of the economist in question consisted of sixteen years of formation or education – investment in human capital as it is now called – twelve years in central banking, the military and government, and thirty-eight years in academic research and teaching. I asked my friend Kenneth Galbraith, who has wide experience in such matters, whether he thought the manuscript would make a "trade" book for the general reader. He advised cutting down on the background and educational chapters, and on the later academic portion, and beefing up the middle years, paying more attention everywhere to the more interesting personalities – economists, generals, and high government officials. Good advice, no doubt, but on reflection I thought it wiser to give up the notion of writing a bestseller, and concentrate on what I knew. I am grateful to Ken Galbraith for his kindness in reading the manuscript and for writing his generous foreword. Thanks also go to David Warsh, the economics columnist of *The Boston Globe*, who encouraged me to pursue this exercise in vainglory.

2

Family background

Mine is an Eastern seaboard family. I was born in New York, spent summers in Rhode Island, went to school in Connecticut, college in Pennsylvania, live in Massachusetts, and prefer for vacations above all else, to go sailing in Maine. My father was born in Washington, DC, my mother in Annapolis. The former lived in a number of places, as his father, and his brother, were naval doctors who were moved about in the service. My mother grew up in Philadelphia. My parents were married in 1906 and lived in New York in Greenwich Village in a brownstone "railroad flat," an apartment that occupied a whole floor of a narrow, deep house. When that proved too small for a family with five children, all born at home, we moved to Flushing, then an attractive suburb on Long Island. This was in 1919.

It was a middle-class family, comfortable until the depression of the 1930s deepened, but far from rich. There was enough income in the 1920s to send the three younger children away to school, me to boarding school, my younger sisters to private school in New York City. Father was a lawyer in a small firm of his own with two partners. He had had polio as an infant, and consequently wore a brace and walked with a cane all his life. As a child, he met Hetty Green and her son Colonel John

Family background

Green, the latter with the same affliction, as they sat waiting with parents in doctors' offices.

The name Kindleberger came from Germany, but probably before that from the narrow valleys of Switzerland near Berne that resorted to emigration because of insufficient land to hold their peasant children. It is believed that my patronymic ancestor arrived in Philadelphia from the Palatinate in Germany in 1749. My great-grandfather, T.J. Kindleberger, was probably born in this country and named after Thomas Jefferson. His son, my grandfather, was born in Ohio in 1835, married my grandmother, the daughter of a naval officer stationed in Norfolk, Virginia. The naval officer was Charles Poor, after whom my uncle and I were named. He was the captain of the *Brooklyn*, which let the blockade-runner *Alabama* slip out of Norfolk in the Civil War, asked for a court martial to clear himself of treason as a possible Southern sympathizer, and was exonerated. My grandfather operated as a surgeon on Admiral Farragut's flagship in the battle of Mobile Bay ("Damn the torpedos: full speed ahead.") And my uncle Charlie was present at the battle of Manila Bay fought by Admiral Dewey. The other seven great-grandparent names were English or Scottish. One, William Wirt, was Attorney-General under President James Madison, and even ran for the presidency in 1832 on the Anti-Masonic ticket. He lost to Andrew Jackson, and is said in William Preston Vaughn's book *The Anti-Masonic Party* to have been "a pitiful candidate."

3

Kent School
1924–1928

Father and mother were Episcopalians. My first cousin, Roger Williams Jr, attended Kent School, so that when it was decided after one and a half years at the Flushing High School that I be sent away, it was natural enough that they should choose Kent. At age thirteen I took the train from Grand Central Station up the Pittsfield line, took my examinations and was admitted. Two others on that train were Hugh Handsfield, subsequently a McGraw-Hill textbook editor, and John Scott Mabon, who was an editor for a time with Appleton-Century and then with the University of Michigan Press.

The class of 1928 at Kent did not stand high in the eyes of the headmaster, Frederick H. Sill, an ordained minister and celibate monk in the Episcopalian Order of the Holy Cross. Sill had been a coxwain on the Columbia crew in the 1890s, and coached both crew and hockey. Our class was more intellectual than sporting, in contrast with the values of the place. If I am not mistaken, of the forty-two boys who graduated in June 1928, five earned Phi Beta Kappa keys in college, and five or six PhDs. Another was a mathematician and head of research in Bell Helicopter, still another wrote on paleontology with Richard Leakey after having been a Time–Life science books editor. Of the four who went into secondary school teaching, only one, an autodidact geographer and biographer–explorer, can be said to have been intellectually creative. But it was an off-beat group. I played second-team football, class hockey – unable to make either the first or second team – and became manager of the tennis team, was number two on the *Kent School News* and number one on the chess team (until my final year when a fourteen-year-old came along and beat us all out for the position).

Some of my classmates hated school. I happened to love it, whether from lack of imagination or merely a good digestive tract that predisposes one to like whatever happens along. The 1920s was a period of the dominant headmaster: Drury at St Paul's, Peabody at Groton, Taft at Taft, Batchelder at Loomis, St John at Choate, Boyden at Deerfield. Sill was certainly no exception. When I later met General George Patton he reminded me of Sill; both of them were men under not very strong emotional control who were apt to go on rampages, such as when Patton slapped a malingering soldier in a hospital in Sicily. Sill would rant and rave when something went wrong, and send a form, or the whole school, out to do penance, sometimes running around the big pond several times, occasionally working on a job such as cleaning up a construction site. Our class was doing the latter one day under instructions to pile combustible material in one place, and the rest in another, when Sill sneaked up on us on his hands and knees on the infirmary porch, lifted his head over the rail and shrieked at some miscreant: "What are you piling it there for? *That* won't burn." It became our class watchword. On one occasion I happened to be in the northeast room of the old Main Building when Sill came in and saw two boys playing ping-pong with books, spine up, for a net. This enraged him and he rushed across the room, and kicked one of them in the rear as he bent over to pick up a ping-pong ball, sending him sprawling. The boy was Draper Kaufman, who grew up to become a midshipman, frogman in the Second World War, and ultimately an admiral and commandant of the Naval Academy.

I suspect that Sill was a thoroughly repressed latent homosexual, under considerable tension. These Victorian headmasters were frequently poor administrators, quixotic, not too

Kent School

well organized, but they were fascinating characters none the less. Loved by some of their students, hated by others, all youth knew they were in contact with a real personality. I cannot reassemble the evidence but I believe I am right in saying that most of their successors were fired by alumni, trustees, parents, whomever, after a short tenure, because they were unable to fill out the shoes of the "great men." They did, however, break up the pattern and clear the path of *their* successors.

In the subsequent sixty-one years I have been interested in the intellectual profiles of the top of my class. Students were given numerical grades, which were averaged, an average of over eighty being the qualification for the honor roll. I was number four in my class with an eighty-four average. Ethelbert Talbot Donaldson, the grandson of Bishop Talbot, a one-time presiding bishop of the church, was number one with an average of ninety-two. (The highest average I remember was that of Philip H. Rhinelander in the class of 1925, who weighed in at ninety-six, and went on to a brilliant career as a professor of philosophy at Stanford University.) Following Donaldson was Palmer Futcher, son of a Baltimore doctor who had been a student of the great Dr William Osler in Canada. Futcher had an average of about eighty-seven. Then came Edward Cussler, average about eighty-five, who went into chemistry after college with the DuPont company. Donaldson and Futcher both went to Harvard, where Donaldson discovered excitement and gin, and Futcher studied. From being number two in a class of forty-two at Kent, Futcher ended up first at Harvard, out of a class of six or seven hundred. Second in that 1932 Harvard class was a great athlete, Barry Wood. Wood and Futcher went on to the Johns Hopkins Medical School, where, as I understand it, Wood was first and Futcher second. Later Futcher taught medicine at Hopkins and the University of Pennsylvania and was a good doctor, while Wood became the head of Washington University Medical School in St Louis and a great figure in national medicine. My own case has been characterized as that of an aging over-achiever.

Donaldson's career profile was a bit bizarre. After Harvard,

Kent School

he returned to Kent and taught for a number of years; I am not sure what, but probably English and Latin. Then at one stage he found himself fully disengaged. Some student had been stupid. He bawled the student out, threw chalk at him and perhaps a blackboard eraser, all the time thinking of something else. This made him realize that teaching school was not his *métier*. He enrolled in graduate studies in English at Yale, wrote a thesis on *Piers Plowman*, Text B, and ultimately became at Yale a leading professor of Middle English, notably Chaucer. At one stage he found himself enamored of a student, divorced his wife, married the student, but became enraged when the Yale department would not give her tenure as a professor, and left for the University of Indiana, which would hire the pair, finishing his days there. A parallel resignation from the Harvard department of history befell H. Stuart Hughes, an Office of Strategic Services (OSS) colleague and a leading American intellectual historian. The process is known as flunking one's mid-years. Professor Hughes and his new wife ended up together on the West Coast somewhere.

A close and nameless friend of mine was first in his class at a different school, first in his class at a top-ranking university, first in his class at law school, made a brilliant career as a policy adviser in public life, and is a marvellous critic, but has a mediocre record in intellectual creativity. These profiles are puzzling. Two of the most creative members of our class at Kent were Maitland Armstrong Edey, the collaborator with Leakey, and Prentice Downes, an explorer, self-taught geographer, and school-teacher. Neither scholastic record remains in my memory. Edey wrote a memoir for our 50th reunion that I wanted him to submit to a national magazine, a most evocative picture of the 1920s at a high-minded, austerely simple school. Downes was perhaps the outstanding teacher at Belmont Hill School, west of Cambridge, Massachusetts, until his early death, highly original with a capacity continuously to surprise. I learned in the 1950s that he hated Kent despite his successes at football, hockey, and baseball.

I was second string at Kent, not only in football and on the

Kent School

Kent School News, but in following Donaldson in both Latin and Greek. He chose to take the Greek prize, so I ended up with the Latin. If I remember well, I also won an essay contest.

In the class ahead of me at Kent was one Robert T. Miller, with whom I later had multiple contacts: cousin of my wife's brother-in-law, William H. Walker, Department of State colleague – he in public relations by way of Nelson Rockefeller's group on Latin America – and a person whose name was continuously brought up by investigators in loyalty questions, because he had been denounced as a Communist by Elizabeth Bentley. While one of his cousins, Hamilton Robinson in the State Department, turned his back on Miller, none of the rest of us did, including my brother-in-law, Francis T. Miles, his Princeton classmate. Miller had made some money in the stock market in 1933, and went to Russia to see what it was about. There he wrote for a newspaper as a stringer, and married an American woman who may have been interested in Marxism. His conservative Baltimore family was not pleased by all this, and he waited in Europe until his twins were born, meanwhile working in Paris for the Spanish loyalists. My wife and I see him from time to time, especially in connection with the Walkers, and find him and his wife delightful friends.

I am not sure that charges of "disloyalty" and associating with undesirable people belong in the life of an average economist. Unfortunately they do for one who went through the 1930s, 1940s, and the early 1950s. More relevant to economics, however, is another Kent episode. In the spring of 1928, March I believe, the school was struck with an epidemic of pneumonia. These were days before the advent of penicillin and sulfa-drugs, and at least three of the three hundred boys died. Owing to the emergency Father Sill decreed an early and prolonged spring vacation, and we were all sent home. At home there was little to do. My local friends were in class from nine to three; the few who went away to school were properly away. I asked my father for advice – perhaps one of the last times I did so – and he suggested that I might take a job with his broker, Blair and Company. This was arranged, and for two weeks I was a runner in Wall Street, in the first four-million-share days in history. The back offices were swamped. It was necessary to stay past six o'clock to deliver and collect securities. One got an extra dollar for supper money for staying after six, and if I could hold off dinner until I got back to Flushing by subway to the Long Island station and train to Main Street, Flushing, that was free and clear, and a sizeable percentage of my weekly salary – a number I fear I have forgotten.

Unforgotten as a number, however, is the size of the check I used to carry in my pocket to repay the National City Bank, as it was then, the brokers' loan of Blair and Company contracted the day before – $1,000,000. In the sixty-one years since those days, I have never had so much money in my pocket. The four-million-share days were fateful, in my present view, in cutting off foreign lending in bonds by the United States, causing stringency in Germany, Latin America, and Australia – though Anna Jacobson Schwartz does not think so – and starting the euphoric bubble in the stock market that was to burst in October 1929.

4

University of Pennsylvania
1928–1932

Most of my 1928 classmates at school went to Harvard, Yale, or Princeton, except for the several who could not get into those places even in those days of relaxed college admission. I went to the University of Pennsylvania, where my father and uncle Charlie had gone. Father was a member of the class of 1894, in the decade of perhaps the most intense college spirit. When I was born it was decided I would be named after my uncle (he disliked his own name, borrowed from outside the family from a friend of his father), that I would go to Penn, and that I would be a lawyer. I managed to escape the last fate, but had no chance of choosing a college for myself. It worked out well.

Let me start with Latin and Greek. Having had two years of Greek at Kent, I decided to go on at Penn, and enrolled in a course in Homer. I cannot now recall whether it was the fall or spring of the freshman year. The class was taught by a Professor Kent, with a game leg which he put to good use in acting out the god Hephaestus. He was a scholar of linguistics. In the class, beside me, were two graduate students, a senior and a sophomore. The graduate students were Selig Harris, studying Hebrew, who later became a professor of linguistics, I believe, and the teacher of the renowned Noam Chomsky, and one

Seifert studying German. The senior was Bernard Cataldo, later first in his class at law school, and a professor of law, who would then translate Homer at sight into blank verse. Two 1989 letters in the *Pennsylvania Gazette* extolled both Cataldo's teaching ability in law and his charm. The sophomore was a member of the DuPont clan who gave very little competition to the older members of the class. It was an experience.

My freshman course in philosophy in the spring of 1929 has twice come into play in my economics. For one, it taught me about necessary and sufficient conditions, *causa proxima*, *causa remota*, and *causa causans*. A throws a damp squib at B, who passes it along to C, and so on until finally Y throws it to Z in whose face it explodes. A is *causa remota*, Y is *causa proxima*. B to X are necessary causes, but there is no *causa causans* or sufficient condition. When all conditions are necessary, and none sufficient, causality becomes very dicey.

The other useful bit in this course in logic was the story of the young man and the old sophist, which I have told a number of times when I have found myself on a platform in debate with one of my former students. A young man in Athens went to the agora, met an old sophist and said he wanted to study sophistry, but unhappily had no money (talents before the days of drachmae). The old sophist said that this was not an insuperable barrier, that he would give the lessons, and the young man could pay him when he won his first case. Such was agreed. But the young man failed to practice sophistry. One day the old man needed money, as old men will, and haled the young man into court, saying, "Learned judge, if I win, I win, and he must pay, and if you judge he wins, he will have won his first case, and therefore must pay." I use this to urge my skill as either debater or teacher. Unhappily, the young sophist had been a brilliant student, and countered: "Learned judge, if you say I win, I win, and don't have to pay. And if you say I lose, I shall have lost my first case, and under the terms of the contract, do not have to pay." To this day, I do not know who had the better argument.

At Penn I was perhaps hyperactive. In the fall, I went out for the 150 lb freshman crew, heeled for the *Daily Pennsylvanian*, and joined a literary and debating society called Philomathian. Among the members were Sidney Sufrin, later Professor of Labor Economics at Syracuse, a young socialist of the Ypsils (Young Peoples' Socialist League), Arthur Fletcher, a senior named Michael Blankfort (I think), who went on to Hollywood and was attacked as a Communist, plus a most agreeable Southerner who later was a reporter for the *New York Times*, named Arthur Loeb. My wife and I kept up with Loeb for a time in New York.

The biggest excitement, however, arrived in the presence of Andrew Biemiller, a graduate student in history who came on campus late and ended up sharing rooms with the senior living in the freshman dormitory as an adviser, directly across the hall from my single room. Biemiller's views and sophistication were heady stuff. He had studied the year before with Harry Elmer Barnes, the revisionist historian at Clark University in Worcester, and thought with Barnes that the Germans had not started the First World War. When I tried to peddle this view to my grandmother McIlvaine, who still lived in Philadelphia, she almost had apoplexy. Biemiller had many other advanced views, which I cannot recollect. He made a friend of Herbert Keith Fitzroy, a lawyer studying for a doctorate in legal history, and I used to see something of them both, ending up wide-eyed. Biemiller left history for politics, especially labor politics, serving for a time as secretary to the Socialist Mayor Hoan of Milwaukee, going on to become the Congressman from a precinct in that city, and ending after his defeat for re-election as chief Congressional lobbyist for the American Federation of Labor – Congress of Industrial Organization (AFL–CIO) in Washington.

Fraternity rushing occurred only in the second term of the academic year. My father had not been asked to join a fraternity, perhaps because of his lameness, and he was most anxious for me to join one. I finally was chosen by and chose Delta Psi, sometimes known as St Anthony Hall, and benefited enormously from it, not only in the financing of my graduate training, discussed below, but because I enjoyed the small support-group of congenial men. The members for the most part had ties to

University of Pennsylvania

Philadelphia, which restrained their campus partying, and were fairly mature, which eliminated hazing (the harassment of novitiates), which is occasionally cruel and physically dangerous. It recruited graduate students who came from colleges where no fraternities had existed, notably Princeton and Haverford, which meant that one consorted to a degree with medical and law students.

By my sophomore year I was beginning to get tired of Latin and Greek. As I rationalized it at the time, I detested the professor in Horace, who seemed a shallow show-off. As I saw it later, my real interest in economics was of a kind that matures only after about twenty years of age. It surely was not the inspiration of my teachers. My first course was taken from a graduate student, little older than I, named Ralph Young, who later headed the Research Division of the Federal Reserve Board. At the time, he was an uninterested and uninteresting teacher, concerned I now assume, mostly with his own studies. Other members of the department were S. H. Patterson, Weldon Hoot, Karl Scholtz, and, in the Wharton School, instructors in banking named Harr and Harris. S. H. Patterson used to bang the desk and say, "I am not a Socialist, but I believe that babies are more important than dollars." I did not know enough cost–benefit analysis at the time to ask what the price of a baby was in his calculus. But economics was interesting, especially after the stock market crash of 1929, and the decline in my family's income. The professor from whom I took a course in banking – whether Harr or Harris I cannot recall – was a wily character. Concerned that he would start a run if he simply took his deposit out of his bank, he borrowed a similar amount and transferred it to a different and stronger bank. Then when his original bank closed its doors, he asked for and obtained an offset of his loan against his deposit. He may have exaggerated the impact of his banking actions on the world at large, but his somewhat devious behavior made an impression on this student.

Over the years I have developed a couple of theories about recruitment into economics. First, I hypothesize that except for a few cases, most economists start off in college majoring in some other field. Today the first major is typically mathematics or physics. It is easy to plan for a career in the physical sciences, engineering, or medicine at an early age, because one is exposed to the realities of those fields early. Somewhat later an interest in history may develop. In the social sciences, however, it is almost invariably necessary to wait until the age of about twenty. Children grow up in homogeneous environments, and are unaware of the complexity of the typical social situation until they have been exposed to a series of them in the city, the university, or both.

An exception must be made for sons of social scientists, which may account for John Stuart Mill, John Maynard Keynes, John Maurice Clark, and others. But the father–son career relationship is a tricky one, and can work either way, or both. At MIT we have had sons of lawyers, bright, who thought they wanted to be economists while under the spell of some charismatic teacher, but then after a year or two of graduate school decided that they wanted after all to follow in father's footsteps. I admired my father, but was turned off the law on the ground that most of it was fighting over spilled milk, so to speak, rather than dealing with current problems. In college I once went to Washington to hear my father plead a case in the Supreme Court, dealing with a decision of the Alien Property Custodian in the First World War, this about fifteen years after the event.

One ironic note about my college grades is that the only C I got in any course was in William Lingelbach's lectures on European history from 1870 to 1914 – a field in which I now work to a considerable degree. The reason is not uninteresting. I worked too hard, tried to answer at too great length, and was insufficiently mature to produce graceful, parsimonious answers. One member of my fraternity, William Busser, who ended up as a Foreign Service officer, would study for the examination by covering only one aspect of the course – say the Franco-Prussian war or the carving up of Africa after 1885 – and write for the whole three hours on that, overwhelming the poor graduate-student grader, and getting an A, whereas I had far too much knowledge for a beginner to package well, and pulled the lower grade.

University of Pennsylvania

In my capacity as an editorial writer for *The Pennsylvanian* in my junior year, I came to know the provost, George McClelland, with whom I also took a course in Scottish poets. This served me in good stead when the university was invited to select a junior to compete for a place in a program of summer study in Geneva, Switzerland. In the spring of 1931, too, I participated as a member of the Pennsylvania group, headed by Herbert Keith Fitzroy (known as "Fitz"), in a model League of Nations held at Princeton. Another participant was Carolyn Thompson of Bryn Mawr, through whom I met Francis T. Miles, who ultimately became my brother-in-law. As I contemplate today's problem of disarming, even in post-Berlin-Wall times, I fear that the Pennsylvania group's delegation to disarmament in 1931 was simple-minded.

Further on *The Pennsylvanian*. The staff was presumably paid, but mostly in goods exchanged for advertisements from local haberdashers. A top hat acquired in this fashion has now devolved on my kindergarten-teacher daughter, who uses it in her quondam role as circus ring-master. In the fall of 1931, I took advantage of a due-bill of American Airlines to fly to Washington and back on a weekend to call on Miss Thompson, who had graduated from Bryn Mawr. It was this infatuation which prompted me to graduate in February 1932, having failed through political maneuvering to win the editorship of *The Pennsylvanian* and ending up as merely managing editor. February 1932, I quickly realized, was not a propitious time to launch oneself on a lifetime career. But before I come to those difficult days, a few words on undergraduate summers.

5

Youthful summers

Most *summers before* 1928 were spent at the family cottage in Jamestown, Rhode Island, where my father had been brought up. When the Atlantic fleet moved from its winter quarters in Norfolk, Virginia, to Narragansett Bay in Rhode Island, well-to-do naval officers spent the summer in Newport. Those less well endowed summered in Jamestown on Conanicut Island. Two ferries joined the island west and east, and their replacement by bridges has ruined the place for me. So many of the places my family knew have gone downhill, and in one case, the section of Washington where my father was raised, come up again. West Philadelphia and Flushing still await gentrification. Jamestown is pleasant enough, but far more developed than in the days of the ferries and the rush from one to the other in the ten minutes spent in dock. Those were halcyon days, from which I began to break away in August 1927 when I went away to Citizens Military Training Camp (CMTC) on Great Diamond Island, off Portland, Maine, my introduction to those icy but lovely waters. This was at the insistence of my father whose boyhood friend, Colonel John Wright, was the Fort McKinley commandant.

In the summer of 1928 I took a job surveying Kent School, learning to use the tape, stadia rod, transit, and triangulation.

Youthful summers

It was memorable especially for one trip to New York with my fifth form colleague (I was a newly minted graduate), Evan Blanchard, in his Model T Ford. In the 180 miles to New York and back we had nine flat tires. At one stage we had to buy a new vulcanizing kit to repair the punctures, after the first had been used up. One scratched the rubber, put on some goo, affixed a cap that one lighted to vulcanize the leak, and then pumped the tire up by hand.

International economics began in 1929. My uncle, Roger Williams, married to my mother's sister, Frances, was vice-president of the Panama Pacific line and got me a job for the summer as a cadet on the bridge of the SS *California*, presumably as an apprentice for a career as a merchant-ship officer. The *California* plied to San Francisco and back, with stops at Havana, the Panama Canal, and San Pedro in each direction. The crew did not disembark in Havana, as it was a requirement that we stay sober enough to help the passengers up the gangplank when the tenders brought them back to the ship. We did, however, buy fruit and rum from bumboats which flocked to the anchorage, lowering the money over the side and hauling up the trade goods. For those without a vivid memory of those days who wonder why the passengers needed help coming back aboard, I would remind them that these were still the days of that noble experiment, Prohibition, which lasted until November 1933.

My recollections of that summer are mostly of placidity. The one striking memory is of an Italian dinner, arranged by one of the sailors, in Jungletown in San Francisco, the Italian quarter, where for some derisory sum, such as $1.50, we ate literally buckets of spaghetti, or at least one large amount of spaghetti cooked in and served from a bucket, plus salad, olives, and the like. The room was in a small apartment whose walls had been covered with used mats discarded from printing-press rolls, and painted over. About the room one could read headlines such as "Babe Ruth Hits Homer No. 56," and "Harding Cortege Moves East."

At one point, in San Diego, a couple of us took the bus to Tijuana in Mexico to add another country to what was then a small life-list – the United States, Cuba (territorial waters, if not dry land), and Canada, where on her seven-year sabbaticals, my mother would take the family back to North Hatley, Quebec, where she had gone in her youth, staying in a hotel, the Connaught Inn, rather than keeping house in Jamestown. All this time, however, and until I was twenty-one, I had never been south or west of Washington over land.

A footnote to the nepotism that got me the cadet and later two more jobs: I mentioned when I first came to MIT that I had worked on ships, and a graduate student in meteorology with whom I car-pooled said he had done so too, ten years after me. I noted that my uncle had gotten me the job; so, he said, had his. I mentioned that my uncle was vice-president of a shipping company; his, he said, was vice-president of a union. The transformation of the character of nepotism tells something about what was happening to labor–management relations in the 1930s.

In 1929 I told my family that I would like to work on ships again, and my father discovered a friend or an acquaintance – I do not now know who – who got me a job as an ordinary seaman on the MV *Australia*, at the time the largest tanker in the world at some 11,000 tons, as compared with today's 200,000 or more tonners. We sailed from Bayonne, a dirty, tough, stinking city on the Jersey shore across from Staten Island, and made for San Pedro, California, to make my fifth and sixth time through the Panama Canal. On the return trip, the ship was laden with gasoline, a dangerous cargo, which the Texas Company was moving from the west to the east coast – and selling for a penny a gallon – to hold the price up in California. Most memorable was a three-week poker game, played with white dried beans as chips, worth a nickel each. The central figure was a sailor who would now be known as a gambling addict. He had played for the house in casinos in the west, to fill out tables that were shy of appropriate numbers, with the house paying all his losses, and letting him keep half his winnings. The game started usually at four, after the twelve to four watch, and went on until something like two in the morning. Players would drop out to

Youthful summers

go on watch, drop back in when they were relieved, or even in their coffee-break. I have the feeling I was on the four to eight watch – the one I liked best, as one could savor sunsets and sunrises – and would play mostly from eight to midnight. The game started small and grew. The semi-professional won all the time and ended up a couple of hundred dollars ahead. Others who started early lost at first and gradually recovered as they became more skilled, and plucked the newly joining neophytes. One Swede did badly in stud poker, unable to say "Jack" instead of "Yack" when he had a good hole card. I believe I ended up some $20 ahead.

Returning to New York in midsummer, I signed off because of strongly diminishing returns from going through the Panama Canal, and Uncle Roger came to the rescue. He got me a job as a "deck-boy," at $20 a month, on the SS *Bird City*, a Hog Islander, or standard-type freighter built during the First World War at Hog Island in the Delaware River, owned by the Moore–McCormack line and bound for the Baltic. The itinerary was Copenhagen, Danzig, Helsinki (then Helsingfors), Leningrad, Kotka, Raumo, and Kemi – three pulp-and-paper ports in Finland – Copenhagen again, and then Portland, where I got paid off to hurry back to college a couple of days late.

The ship sailed from Avenue D and about 9th Street in Manhattan, a very tough part of town – so tough that in walking back to the ship at midnight I stayed in the middle of 14th Street, out of the shadows. A number of the crew were locals, and would not hesitate to pick up a board in a fight and use it as a bludgeon. One sailor claimed – perhaps only boasting – that he had participated in a hijacking of the first cargo of rubber to come into New York harbor in 1925 or 1926 when the price had risen to $3.40 a pound (because of the export restrictions in British Malaya of the Stevenson rubber plan) and before it fell to under a dollar in 1927 and to 20 cents by June 1929. Among the other seamen I recall best Whitey, Pete, Rudi, and Blackie. (All had nicknames, mostly descriptive; I was "Slim," and the other deck-boy, a high-school student from Brooklyn, was "Red.") Whitey was Paul Wedseltoft, a Dane from Bornholm (the "Pearl of the Baltic") who wanted to see his family again. I kept up with him during the 1930s to my very great benefit when he turned up in Philadelphia as a junior officer on a cruise ship, and provided a gallon of rum that I smuggled ashore under a borrowed coonskin coat. Pete held a purchased Swedish passport under the name of Petersen. He was a Russian sailor who had been present in 1917 at the revolt at Kronstadt, the naval base off Leningrad, and while he was a Communist sympathizer, he went into exile because he could not prove that he had not been on the side of the rebels. He was badly educated, but with a wonderful ear for languages, and could swear, curse, blaspheme, and use foul talk in eighteen languages, he said – at least Russian, Swedish, Norwegian, Finnish, French, German, English, Spanish, Italian, and especially Portuguese, for he had been working on a Brazilian run. He also wanted to see his family. So did Rudi, a White Russian. Pete and Rudi were planning to smuggle large quantities of American stuff ashore, including a gramophone which Rudi dropped over the side in Leningrad into a rowboat manned by a relative or friend.

Blackie was an American (a white man with very black hair). An excellent sailor, he was an alcoholic who drank up his pay and ended each voyage owing the ship money, so that he could not quit without being blacklisted. He had been radicalized by a Communist sailor on the previous trip. One evening, drunk, in the lower bunk next to mine in the fo'c'sle that housed about ten of us in the deck gang, he grabbed a broom – falling out of his bunk – swept the group as if the broom were a gun, and asked: "If your father and mother were over there, J.P. Morgan there, and the Russian army over there, who [sic] would you shoot?" I believe the question belongs to the fallacy of the undistributed middle, since it fails to allow for answers such as "All (or none) of the above," but it revealed that he was bothered. He was sober from New York to Copenhagen, as the slop-chest was dry for that passage. Thereafter, one could drink against one's pay, and it was not unknown in the Baltic portion of the run, for the deck gang to work with a paintbrush in one hand and a bottle of beer in the other. The purser favored Tuborg over

Youthful summers

Carlsberg, and the crew drank cases of it.

In Copenhagen the ship changed berths on the morning after arrival. Of the deck crew only four of us were aboard, the rest ashore drunk or still in bordellos. I was drafted to go aloft in the rain with the eighty-one-year-old Lithuanian "Pops," to rig the main boom. Ordinarily deck-boys were confined to the deck. Later I made my first visit to the town, including a tour of Tivoli, and still vividly recall a large group of unsmiling children hugely enjoying themselves on a turntable as they fought to stay on against centrifugal force.

We loaded as deck cargo in Copenhagen two huge cement-mixer drums that were guyed down across the after-hatches and made the crew duck, even dropping to one knee, as we went forward or aft from midships. They were bound for the Soviet Union as imported capital equipment. I especially resented them as the deck-gang messboy failed to make it back to the ship as we left Danzig and as his drafted substitute, I had to maneuver the canisters of hot food and coffee under them.

In Helsingfors, where we had only a couple of hours ashore, I astounded myself, buying what I thought was gingerbread, a huge amount for very little money. It turned out to be black bread, made from rye, the kind that left a sour breath in the 1920s and 1930s before rye bread was denatured.

The high point of the trip was Leningrad, with the long haul past Kronstadt up the Neva. We were four days in port, enough for a certain amount of sightseeing: the Winter Palace, Saint Stephens, the fortress Peter and Paul across the Neva; visits to the Seaman's Soviet where we were proselytized; visits aboard by union organizers, who tailored the story of their experience to the audience, one telling us that he broke his leg in the Passaic silk strike of 1919, and telling a British ship that the incident occurred in a Liverpool ship strike of the same year. The same man spoke one evening at the Seaman's Soviet, with an audience of attractive young women sitting in the back of the hall, hoping to learn English. Whitey Wedseltoft and I took pleasure in addressing the ladies to make the point that the organizer's English was execrable and should not be looked to as a model.

Youthful summers

As a tenderfoot – if that metaphor is appropriate for sailors – I had brought a topcoat aboard. Pete and Rudi each borrowed it to smuggle ashore goods tied around their middles. Pete was caught on one occasion, and heard the customs guards discussing his fate, saying that they could do nothing with a Swede. He played possum in pretending not to understand Russian, was released, and I got the coat back.

Turning westward, we picked up pulp and paper at Kotka, Raumo, and Kemi, three tiny wooded ports with streams bringing logs down to mills on shore. Kemi is at the top of the Gulf of Finland, close to the Arctic Circle. I did not get ashore there as we anchored off the port because of shoal draft, and were discouraged from trying to go ashore by tender. A day in Copenhagen and then we headed for home via the Pentland Firth to the north of Scotland. In an episode prescient of the troubles of the Exxon tanker in Alaskan waters in April 1989, the captain was drunk one night and scraped bottom in the approach to the Firth. I prayed we would have to put in to Glasgow for repairs, but the SS *Bird City* made very little water and we headed for Portland and New York. I asked to be paid off in Portland, to get back to Philadelphia and the university. Six weeks' pay at $20 a month plus my starting balance less expenditure at the slopchest for beer and tax-free cigarettes left me with something like $12.50. At the railroad station I asked how much it cost to take the train to New York. The answer was close to $15. I went all night by bus.

In the spring of 1931 I was chosen among perhaps twenty other Americans to receive a scholarship at the Students International Union in Geneva, Switzerland. The scholarship did not cover the steamer fare, but my family dug that up. The project was the work of a wealthy New York socialite, Mrs Maude Hadden, and she had arranged for Salvador de Madariaga, the Spanish political scientist in international relations, to run a summer-long seminar. As it turned out, Madariaga had just been designated as Spanish ambassador to the United States and was not available, so that the Union was melded into a larger organization, the Graduate School of International Relations, run by

Youthful summers

Sir Alfred Zimmern, professor of international relations at Oxford University, and his French wife. The economics leaders were H. W. Richardson of the University of Leeds, I believe, and Pat Sloan, a nephew of Alfred Marshall, who was a Communist by ideology, but – perhaps I should say "and" – a good technical economist. (One of the high points of the summer was to see Sloan, preparing to go to the Soviet Union for an extended stay, packing such unusual items of luggage as toilet paper and needles.) There was a long series of visiting lecturers, of whom I remember – my memory possibly refreshed by seeing a notebook of the summer years later – Paul Douglas, Douglas Copland of Australia, and Moritz Bonn of Germany. Sir Alfred was an interesting lecturer, with a proclivity for saying over and over again, "Je ne critique pas; je constate" ("I am not criticizing; I am telling you how it is.")

I am afraid that I did not reflect much glory on University of Pennsylvania training in economics that summer. I can't remember what project I took on – something about unemployment. F. Taylor Ostrander, the Williams College junior, was far more sophisticated than I, discussing learnedly the Keynes–Ohlin controversy over reparations when I was not quite sure who Keynes and Ohlin were. I was sublimely unconscious of the foreign-exchange troubles of Austria, Germany, and Britain that I wrote about some forty years later. The Bank for International Settlements was known to me as the employer of a somewhat older fellow, Charles Darlington, later an official of the Mobil Oil Company, who would come from Basle to Geneva to spark one of the many attractive American college women. The social life – swimming, climbing, partying in the cafés – was delightful. A visit of the school by bus over the Mount Cenis pass to a Fascist Youth camp under the Monte Rosa involved a certain amount of patrolling by American men to safeguard the flanks of the American girls from pinching Italian hands. One crisis occurred when a Belgian listening to a lecture that dealt in some fashion with Italy muttered ostensibly to himself, "A bas, Mussolini," only to be overheard by an Italian sitting behind him who created an uproar by demanding an apology. It is hard for

Youthful summers

me, looking back, to judge what the summer did for me as a would-be economist. It did perhaps what good teachers can best do, which is to stimulate appetite and create enthusiasm. Students teach themselves (and each other). The role of experience and teachers is to encourage and to motivate. The summer of 1931 did that for me.

6

Interregnum

In the fall of 1931 I thought I was in love, despite receiving no encouragement, and decided to graduate from the University of Pennsylvania at the earliest opportunity – February 1932 – to get a job, and prepare myself to support a family. All this showed a remarkable absence of realism. I returned from Philadelphia and started pounding the pavement. One road led to the Federal Reserve Bank of New York, whose president, George L. Harrison, had been befriended by my great aunt in Washington, Mrs Charles C. Glover. I was interested in building a career in foreign exchange. The New York Fed was a good place to do that. My father wrote a letter to Mr Harrison asking him to see me. He was most polite and completely negative. The Fed had no use for the likes of me, with a simple bachelor's degree and no experience. And besides, there was a depression.

After six weeks of looking, of which I recall only the visit to Mr Harrison, my father learned of a new lobbying group, the National Economy League, headed by, among others, Archibald Roosevelt, son of President Theodore Roosevelt. Father's friend Colonel Arthur Cosby, who occasionally came to our house for Sunday dinner, was going to be the office manager. I was offered and accepted a job as an office boy. The National Economy League was a conservative group, pushing for balancing the

Interregnum

budget, something of which I later, as a Keynesian, learned I should have thoroughly disapproved. My task was to assemble bits of literature and stuff it into envelopes to be mailed out to the faithful. When something even slightly better came along, I moved on.

With two summers of working on deck on merchant-marine vessels, and a love of the water that had begun long before that, I thought of a job in marine insurance. Again Uncle Roger Williams came to the rescue. As vice-president of a steamship line, he had connections, and one was with the marine-insurance brokerage, Johnson and Higgins. Again the opening found was that of office boy. In the marine department, the work consisted of moving papers around, and in particular of getting two vice-presidents to sign mountains of checks that passed back and forth, from broker to underwriters, and when policies paid off, from broker to the insured. Enormous piles of checks stapled to invoices had to be signed, by two officers, and the trick was to find a vice-president – I remember the names of Messrs Keegan, Sexton, and Cauchois, but there were doubtless others in the marine department – who looked up for long enough, so that in heaping the checks on his desk you were not disturbing him. I enrolled in a course on marine insurance in some insurance institute with classes in Wall Street, and read a book by a distant cousin of mine, Wharton Poor, an admiralty lawyer, with the enticing title *Charter Parties and Bills of Lading*. I did well in the course, too.

Office boys were continuously at war in those days with a breed that has died out, elevator operators. An elevator operator detested an office boy who was unwilling to climb one floor or descend two by the stairs, and who insisted on a ride. It was not an interesting war.

In my capacity as office boy I experienced an example of elasticity of demand. When the US Post Office raised the rate of first-class postage from the base rate of 2 cents to 3 cents, Johnson and Higgins decided to take its business away, and deliver the mail itself. This is also an example of a well-known accounting problem, "Make or buy." In this case Johnson and

Interregnum

Higgins decided to make, that is, deliver by hand, all communications for the insurance district that ran from Wall Street, up William, to Maiden Lane and Liberty Streets. The office manager was a man of pleasant disposition but limited analytic powers, and after watching him stumble over the problem for a day or two, I established the three equal routes that the three office boys would rotate in – a makeshift job of dynamic programming.

This was hardly a thrilling experience, and when an opportunity came along to go to graduate school in economics, I grabbed it. It came by almost pure chance.

The fraternity to which I belonged at Pennsylvania had then but nine chapters at various universities, of which the founding chapter was that at Columbia. This had fallen on evil days. Like many big city universities at the time, the middle-class group that my fraternity drew upon was dwindling, and other well-known fraternities, such as Alpha Delta Phi, were recruiting the cream of the crop. The alumni of St Anthony Hall at Columbia, especially those who had been there in the 1890s and who were now, some of them, successful in professions and business, were saddened to see the group's decline, and willing to spend some money to prevent it. It was thought that if a couple of members from other chapters could be induced to transfer to Columbia, the chapter might build back a critical mass. They recruited an undergraduate from Virginia who was on the verge of dropping out of college for financial reasons. And they asked me if I would like to go, with their support, to Columbia Law School. I said, "Law school, no; graduate school in economics, yes," and they accepted.

I started in the spring of 1933 by taking one evening course taught by Ralph W. Robey, who was also financial editor of the *New York Post*. He would follow the March 1933 banking crisis by day, and tell us about it in the evening, leaving virtually no time to get to the syllabus that I assume the course possessed. I later heard a great deal about the event from my good friend, Emile Despres, who stayed in the Federal Reserve Bank of New York (at 33 Liberty Street in downtown New York) for perhaps

Interregnum

a week, sleeping in the infirmary, as the bank staff tried to solve the problem of reopening the banks, closed in Roosevelt's bank holiday of March 3, and at the same time avoid the reporters that were circling the building like piranhas.

I continued to live at home in Flushing and work at Johnson and Higgins until the fall of 1933, when I went to Columbia full time and lived at St Anthony Hall on Riverside Drive. One piece of paper, now lost, stated that my salary was being raised from $13 a week to $15, because of the National Recovery Act; reading between the lines I could discern "And for no other reason." In the summer of 1933 Gerald Lowe Jr, a young vice-president, told me that my purgatory as an office boy was coming to an end and that I could now start to learn the business, especially the complex branch of marine adjustment or settling claims. I declined, and said I was quitting.

7

Economics at Columbia

Economics education at Columbia in the 1930s was not terribly exciting. In the first place there were too many students: hundreds of candidates for the master's degree, who took up room in classes, inhibited discussion, served as the bread and butter of the department in terms of revenue but were intellectually a diversion. It is a little arrogant, perhaps, but a department like that of MIT does not admit economics students for the master's degree, and uses it only as a consolation prize for those few who are deemed unable to qualify for the PhD. Secondly, the faculty spent a great deal of time off campus: Wesley C. Mitchell, Arthur F. Burns, and others at the National Bureau of Economic Research downtown; my thesis adviser, James W. Angell, working at home in Riverdale, north of Manhattan. Thirdly, banking was taught in the business school, not the economics department, which made for reduced interaction. There was no core of economic theory: Mitchell taught the history of economic thought in a manner that the students liked – connecting theory with economic history – but his lectures were later regarded as pedestrian when he gave them in England. John Maurice Clark taught bits of theory, but was a dull lecturer. An instructor from New Zealand, Ralph Souder, taught an advanced and abstract course that I have completely forgotten.

Economics at Columbia

One weekend I brought the book home and left it on my bureau. My mother came into the room at one point, looked at the title page, saw the words "an elementary study," and started to read. In the top line of the text was a footnote to which her eye dropped; it read: "It must be remembered that an exclusionist positivism is of itself methodological . . ."; my mother thought her son must really be smart if this was elementary. The book's title was *Prolegomena to Relativity Economics: An Elementary Study in the Mechanics and Dynamics of an Expanding Economic Universe.*

Interaction between faculty and students outside the classroom was limited, and the student body was not sufficiently cohesive and small to provide the intense intellectual interaction that is the essence of advanced learning. Moses Abramovitz went off in the second year for a stay at Harvard, but that desertion was compensated for by Milton Friedman and Allen Wallis coming for a year from the University of Chicago to work with Professors Mitchell and Burns.

In the fall of 1934 Henry H. Villard came to Columbia from Cambridge University, England, where he had spent two years, bringing with him the excitement of the Keynes seminar, working through *The General Theory*, which was to be published in 1936. Walter S. Salant shifted from Cambridge to Harvard at the same time with similar impact. Our course in money had been taught by James W. Angell, whose work in the field has not survived. In 1935–6 Villard and I organized a seminar that met in the evenings at the apartment of Professors Arthur R. and Eveline Burns, he in industrial organization and she in social-security economics. This proved to be as stimulating as any formal seminar listed in the catalogue. W. Randolph Burgess, a vice-president of the Federal Reserve Bank of New York, attended one meeting, and when I expressed an interest in working on foreign-exchange problems at the Bank, invited me to apply. I later got the job.

I cannot claim that my ultimate interest in economic history was much stimulated by the course taken with Professor Vladimir Simkovitch. He was of Russian origin, as may be deduced from his name, the husband of Mary Curtis, who was the director of Greenwich House, the settlement house in New York, and a man who pinched female students who failed to protect themselves by sitting in the middle seats in the classroom, well away from the aisles he roamed. Professor Simkovitch belonged to the horse-collar school of economic history: that is, the view that the horse-collar was one of the great inventions of all time because it allowed horses to plow instead of oxen, and increased the speed and extent of spring plowing. (I happen to favor the general idea behind the school, but with respect to the invention of the rudder to replace the steering oar, and the lateen sail to replace the square sail, making it possible for bigger ships to sail closer to the wind, and thus opening up the Age of Discovery.) Simkovitch had us read his article on "Hay and history," holding that Rome fell because of depletion of the soil, before hay made it possible to overwinter draft animals in good condition for early spring plowing – a theory which may or may not be respected today. His real contribution, however, was a series of stories, told in a thick Russian accent, with which I later regaled generations of young instructors at MIT.

Eli Shapiro, later a colleague at MIT, was visiting Mihail Florinsky, with whom Simkovitch shared an office. After the conversation had gone on for some minutes Florinsky got restless, and said, "Excuse me, Mr Shapiro, I have to stop now to prepare for my class." At this point Simkovitch leaned over from his desk and said, "No, Mihail. It's a mistake. Let me tell you about teachink. Take one cup ideas, one bucket of water, meex. Give the students one drop an hour."

In one lecture, he mentioned social progress. "I tell you about social progress. It's winter, evening, a swamp. Is a heron standing on one leg, with the other tucked up under its wink. The leg it's standing on is colt. It takes the leg out from under its wink, puts it down in the colt sand, and takes other leg and tucks it up under udder wink. Ladies and gentlemen, that's social progress."

To complete the collection, we were led to believe that there was a captain of the air force, who was studying for a PhD, and who took the general examinations. He had on his board, say, Mitchell in theory, Angell in money, Chaddock in statistics, and Simkovitch in economic history. When the results had been determined, he had failed theory, failed money, failed statistics, and passed economic history. At that time, if a candidate failed a subject on generals, he or she was allowed to take them again, without having to include any subject passed. In due time the candidate tried again, with Clark in theory, Chaddock in statistics, and Simkovitch in socialism. This time he failed theory, failed statistics, and passed socialism. On a still later occasion, if the story be true – which is doubtful – he took the examination for the third time, when Mitchell, Clark, Souder *et al.* were away, and had Simkovitch in theory and Chaddock in statistics. This time he passed theory, but failed statistics. Simkovitch is then said to have cried to Chaddock: "Professor Chaddock, boy wants PhD. Give him PhD. We have *planty* PhDs."

I enjoyed the courses in banking in the School of Business. Professor H. Parker Willis, one of the many authors of the Federal Reserve Act of 1913, along with Carter Glass, was memorable less for his ideas – with his teacher, Laurence Loughlin of the University of Chicago, he believed in the real-bills doctrine, that any expansion of credit used to finance trade was *ipso facto* legitimate and non-inflationary – than for his polished lectures. The polish, I am sure, came from long years of dictating. Willis wrote a weekly column for *Agence Economique* in Paris, which he dictated. He also wrote frequently for the *Journal of Commerce*. He dictated all his articles and books, as well as letters. The result was a literary style of lectures and talks, with topic sentences and shapely paragraphs, that those of us who work directly with the typewriter can envy but not emulate.

In my first full term I took a course with Benjamin Haggott Beckhart, in foreign banking if I remember correctly, and wrote a term paper on "Competitive exchange depreciation between Denmark and New Zealand." I cannot recall how I happened to light on the subject, and it seems to have been well before I learned any statistics, because I failed to take the marked seasonals out of the data. The focus of the paper was on the British butter market in which the two countries competed. Monthly figures for imports of butter into Britain I dug out of *Monthly Accounts of the United Kingdom relating to Trade and Navigation*, a publication in the Columbia collection (but not that of the MIT Dewey Library). The paper concluded that the competition had mostly benefited Britain, which got its butter more and more cheaply. Beckhart liked the paper and suggested I submit it for publication to the *Harvard Business Review*. This I did. It was accepted – heady stuff for a first-year graduate student. What is more, the *New York Herald Tribune* wrote a lead editorial in its praise, probably because it thought I was condemning the action of Roosevelt in going off gold half a year earlier.

Parker B. Willis, Professor Willis's son, was a friend of mine. I dined once or twice at the Willis house in St George, on the northern tip of Staten Island, and was impressed by what an old-fashioned father Professor Willis was, dominating the dinner-table conversation. His three grown sons and daughter, even his wife, hesitated to volunteer bits of conversation, waiting for him to initiate a topic. He was by no means tyrannical or malevolent, merely what I understood to be Victorian. During the bank holiday, I was told, having anticipated the worst, he had drawn a substantial amount of cash out of the bank, and, while disapproving of his graduate assistants and junior faculty not having anticipated what happened, as he had, provided them with cash as they needed it, albeit secretly one from another.

Willis had as his chief assistant another Russian, Vladimir Kazekevitch, a dour, gaunt, blue-bearded soul, who wore a threadbare blue-serge suit with its shoulders covered with dandruff. Kazekevitch somehow won a lottery and a trip to Bermuda. He wore his lugubrious academic clothes, and sat on deck reading what was obviously a red-cover book by Marx, causing the other passengers to make wide circles around him as they paraded. On arrival in Hamilton Harbor for a six-hour stay, he saw a British warship. Ashore he made for the public library to find out who paid for the maintenance of the ship that was there to suppress the natives, and was overjoyed to learn, as he suspected, that the Bermudians paid for it with regressive taxation, largely from the backs of the blacks. A delightful Marxian holiday. Kazekevitch later returned to Moscow and worked in the American intelligence section of the government. I tried to see him in 1947 but failed. One read his name on infrequent occasions thereafter. I liked him a lot.

There were only two respectable fellowships in economics, one in the economics department and one in the business school. Moses Abramovitz had the economics one in my first year, and Arthur Hersey had it in my second. I applied after two years of living off my fraternity's generosity, but was awarded one instead in the business school. Arthur Hersey, the older brother of the novelist, John Hersey, took a job in the Federal Reserve Board in Washington where I later worked in 1940–2. Some years later, when I was making a consulting trip to the Board, I arrived on the overnight train, breakfasted, and repaired to the facilities before the meeting began. Having concluded my business in a cabinet, I tried to leave but found I could not open the door. The door came down so low as to make escape under it problematic. I was looking over the top to explore that as an avenue of egress, when in walked Arthur Hersey. We had not seen each other for perhaps fifteen years. I said, "Arthur, get me out of here." He was astonished. Then from further down the row came the voice of an unseen person, saying, "I have been stuck in that one. Reach down under the door and lift up." It worked.

In my last year of residence as a graduate student at Columbia, in receipt of the bounty of the university with a fellowship, I was required to live in university quarters, so that it might get some of the money back. This is the sort of tied-in sale against which Adam Smith fulminated, calling it "the sneaking arts of underling tradesmen." And yet there were external economies. I roomed across the hall from Carl McGowan, now deceased, a law-school fellowship holder, who went on to become the legal adviser to Governor Adlai Stevenson in Illinois, the eulogist at Stevenson's memorial service, and judge of the

Economics at Columbia

Second Circuit Court of Appeals in Washington.

Another scholarly colleague from Penn was Herbert Keith Fitzroy, working on a doctorate in legal history which I think he never finished. He wrote one paper on "The punishment of crime in provincial Pennsylvania," inscribed a reprint to me "To Charlie, who taught me all I know about crime," and one to Sarah Miles reading "To Sarah who taught me how delightful crime can be."

Harry Butler of St Anthony Hall was a graduate student working on a PhD in English, who supported himself by playing the piano in nightclubs. Something of a wit, he was full of rather off-color mixed clichés: "Water like Grandma used to make," "There wasn't a dry seat in the house," "A bird in the hand makes Jack a dull boy," and, telescoping bedrock and hardpan, "Let's get down to bedpan."

Still another interesting personality was Frank E. ("Jim") Kilroe, again a St Anthony resident, and a graduate student in the Allan Nevins American history factory. His father was a doctor, of Irish extraction, who had attended Pierre Lorillard at some point and won his confidence. When Lorillard was looking for a disinterested person to head the New York Jockey Club, he asked Dr Kilroe, who then gave up medicine for horse-racing. His sons, Edward and Jim, had other major interests but were attracted on the side to horse-racing. Jim was writing a master's thesis on Charles Evans Hughes and the insurance scandal of 1905, but in working through the newspapers of that period found it impossible to skip over the racing results, in order to see how the forebears of the current colts and fillies had done in their day. He was also diverted from research over a number of days by the gripping account of a court case in which Enrico Caruso, the operatic tenor, was accused of pinching a matron in the monkey house of the Central Park Zoo. In due course Jim finished his master's degree, gradually drifted into horse-racing and ended as the handicapper at the Santa Anita racetrack in California. Unfortunately my intimacy with this colorful man was not kept up.

Dr Kilroe was once asked by Winslow Ames, who had come

Economics at Columbia

for a year to New York to practice ballet with Lincoln Kirstein, what to do about a sore back. "Stop, Winslow," he said, "stop this jumpin' around."

It was time by now to abandon the undergraduate society of 434 Riverside Drive, and I was busy courting Ms Miles, who was tutoring two girls out on Long Island. It is a matter of some tax interest that Sarah Miles was puzzled about my finances. To distinguish fellowships, which are not taxed, from wages, which are, they had to be paid in lump sums, half each term, which, after subtraction of room rent, amounted to $550 paid at the end of October and the end of February. For the first month or two of the term I was relatively affluent, for the last weeks impecunious. Ms Miles was quite unable to tell from my courtship expenditure whether I was rich or poor, failing, as a non-economist, to recognize cyclical fluctuations.

I have no recollection how I spent the summer of 1935. In 1934, however, I got a job selling an economic forecasting service on commission. The territory was the whole world – outside of New York city, which had been allocated to others. The service cost something like $125 a year, the commission was substantial – perhaps 40 percent or $50 per sale – but demand was unbrisk. My weekly advance was $20, which made it difficult to live high, but I stayed at my fraternity houses in Philadelphia and Cambridge (MIT), with my great-aunt in Washington, and my aunt, Mrs John M. Nelson, in Baltimore. The latter was acquainted with the Mileses, which allowed me to invest some spare time, when financial offices were closed, on what proved to be my ultimate marital payoff. In Washington, there was a heat wave, with eggs fried on sidewalks and the like. Having no office to repair to, I spent from 11:45 a.m. to 2:00 p.m., when the chance of finding a prospect in his office was limited, in air-conditioned movie houses, without much regard to the quality of the film being shown. At the end of the summer I received a letter from Jules Bachman, later a professor of economics at New York University, enclosing a check for something like $1.47 and congratulating me as the first and only salesman ever to have earned in commissions his total advance.

Economics at Columbia

After passing my general examinations in the spring of 1935, I proposed to write a dissertation under James Angell on international short-term capital movements. Angell lacked a warm nature, and called me Mr Kindleberger all through the process of supervision. He did, however, respond fully to the separate chapters of the thesis, as I submitted them to him in 1935–6 at Columbia, and later as I mailed them to him from Washington, DC, and Flushing, writing two- and three-page single-spaced letters of criticism and suggestions. In the end we disagreed on the main point of the thesis, whether disequilibrium in a balance of payments should be measured by gold flows alone, as he thought, or gold flows plus or minus short-term capital movements, as I maintained. I have been grateful to him for his dedication to the task of thesis supervision, frequently neglected in the academy, and for his tolerance in letting me depart from his erroneous ways. Because of his coolness, however, I took great pleasure later in 1945, from my lofty position in the Department of State, in getting him an appointment as the minister-representative of the United States at the Inter-Allied Reparations Agency.

I became engaged to be married on September 26, 1936, the date, as I later learned, of the Tripartite Monetary Agreement between France, Britain, and the United States, later joined by Belgium, the Netherlands, and Switzerland. My prospective father-in-law, a professor of English at Johns Hopkins University (and a winner of the Congressional Medal of Honor in the First World War, in which he lost a leg), L. Wardlaw Miles, thought it would be well when I asked for the hand of his daughter that I should finish my dissertation before getting married. How old-fashioned that all seems today! I did, however, finish the thesis in time to get married on May 1, 1937, and managed to work the date of engagement – which, as I mentioned earlier, coincided with the negotiation of the Tripartite Monetary Agreement – and of our marriage – when the Federal Reserve System raised reserve requirements – into the text of my thesis. When it was published, I slipped an arbitrary name, S. Murgatroyd, into the index, keyed to the pages where

Economics at Columbia

the two dates appear. I have subsequently told somewhat dumbfounded students that it serves as an aid to remembering those dates as long as one bears in mind that one becomes engaged before getting married – at least it was so in that era.

Before the Second World War Columbia University continued the European practice of requiring a candidate for the doctorate to turn in seventy-five printed copies of the dissertation, which it would exchange for similar works from European universities that belonged to the cartel. There were two ways this could be done. The dissertation could be bound together with four or five other theses in social science, in which case it would never come to light again, or the candidate could arrange for a separate publication, in almost all cases heavily subsidized by him- or herself. Luckily, my new wife brought a dowry of about $6,000 to our union, and I took half of it to give to Columbia University Press. A Mr Wiggins, my editor, urged strongly that I print no more than 400 copies (at our expense). I begged for more, and he grudgingly agreed on 600. Seventy-five went to Columbia, as noted, a few to professors and friends. The rest were sold under an arrangement whereby I got half the gross price, and Columbia University Press the rest for its marketing effort. The Press insisted that it be sold for $3 a copy. Three dollars times, say, 500 copies is $1,500, half of which is $750. Three thousand dollars less $750 is a net cost to Mrs K. of $2,250. Luckily I asked my lawyer father how to handle the gross receipts that merely diminished the certain loss, so as not to pay tax on them as income. He suggested that I write the thesis on my books as an asset, depreciate it each year by the amount of gross receipts, so that no tax would be due, and when and if all copies were sold, write the rest off as a capital loss. This we did, the loss being postponed until the high wartime tax rates. When the original edition sold out and copies went to more than $20 in the secondhand market, the Columbia Press invited me to put up some more money for a second printing. I declined with heavily sarcastic thanks. Ultimately, Augustus M. Kelley, Inc., a reprint house, bought the copyright from me for $150, and issued its own printing.

Economics at Columbia

The writing of the dissertation began only after I had left Columbia in June 1936. Before that time I had been collecting material. One useful technique to acquire new material was to review it. I approached the *Political Science Quarterly*, published under Columbia University sponsorship, offering to review three books on international capital movements, by Malpas (in French), Nurkse (in German, a language I studied for two years at Penn), and Iversen (in English). In this manner, I got access to this literature free long before I could have hoped to have it acquired by the library.

One major step was taken while I was at Columbia: that of curing my stuttering, or at least getting it under control. As a child, at school and at college, I had stuttered badly. In graduate school, a friend of whom I saw a good deal, Eileen O'Daniel (later Eileen Eddy, president of her Smith class of 1932 and a participant with me in the Students International Union in Geneva in the summer of 1931), took the initiative in finding the National Hospital for Speech Disorders, on Fifth Avenue about 104th Street, in the facilities of some non-profit institution such as the Russell Sage Foundation. There were classes several nights a week, but I attended on Friday nights for perhaps twenty weeks in 1934–5. The place was run by one Dr James Sonnett Greene, who held to the theory that stuttering came about not from anything to do with the mouth, lips, tongue, vocal chords, etc., but from poor breath control. Stutterers, he held, were sensitive souls who got tense and cut off their breath. He made us recite vowels with separate consonants, for example, "Pee, pay, pie, po, pu; me, may, my, mo, mu; lee . . ." and so on, and persuaded me, and perhaps most of the class, that any imagined difficulty with a particular letter was illusory. I recalled that as a choirboy in Flushing, when I talked to the choirmaster over the telephone and stuttered, he would order me to "Sing it," because one does not stutter in singing with controlled breath. The other members of the group were for the most part simple folk, who wanted to overcome their inability to go to the grocery store before the days of supermarkets and order a "pppppound of bbbbutter." The tuition was $10 for the period I attended, and surely the best investment I ever made. I have stuttered since from time to time, on my general examinations in the spring of 1935, for example, and occasionally even now in pronouncing my name over the telephone. But not to stutter in teaching, or in a big public lecture before as many, on some occasions, as a thousand people, reminds me of my deliverance. Resolution to attend was assisted by the embarrassing fact that at the second lecture to a class at the American Institute of Banking, that Professor Willis had arranged for me, 90 percent of the class had moved across the hall to the room of the other instructor in the course, from which they had to be brought back by fiat.

The worst $10 I have ever spent – or at least the one that most embarrassed me – was the amount contributed to the committee to defend Dirk J. Struik, an MIT professor of mathematics who was charged with disloyalty. In sending it, sometime in 1950, I wrote that I did not know what his affiliations or political views were, but wanted to help him defend himself against attack. In my FBI files, one obtained under the Freedom of Information Act and the second under appeal, as provided by the Act, there are perhaps twenty mentions of my support for Struik, the alleged Communist, and no mention of my disclaimer.

8

US Treasury Department
Summer 1936

It is difficult now to recall the state of the academic job market in the 1930s. There was almost no chance of getting an academic job, although Villard was offered a job at Yale, his alma mater, took it, resigned in a huff after receiving a letter telling him what he should teach, and then got a job at Amherst. His contact with the Keynes seminar may have made a difference. I once drove Aaron Gordon, the well-known business-cycle analyst from the University of California at Berkeley, from Cambridge to New Haven, which we both were visiting, and he told me that at Harvard only one job came on the market in 1934. Edgar M. ("Bump") Hoover Jr was first in line and he got it and went to Michigan. The next year there was one more, and Gordon took it in Berkeley. Before that time he had been a teaching assistant and tended furnaces in Cambridge. The income from one job he sent home to his parents.

With the help of Randolph Burgess, whom I later grew to dislike, I was offered a job at the Federal Reserve Bank of New York, but to begin on October 1, 1936. In the meantime, there was a temporary opening at the international section of the Research Division of the US Treasury Department, working with V. Frank Coe. He had come to the Treasury for the summer from the University of Toronto, to calculate purchasing-power parities, a way of estimating what the exchange rate of a currency should be (within a fairly wide range of error). Particular interest attached to the French franc, that had been devalued in 1926 but was now overvalued after the depreciation of the pound sterling, the Japanese yen, and the dollar. Ultimate depreciation of the franc occurred, as indicated earlier, in the Tripartite Monetary Agreement of September 26. I calculated by day, went back to an apartment on Connecticut Avenue and K Streets in the evening to work on my thesis, and, as already related, finished two and a half chapters by the middle of August. My salary was $200 a month, the same sum that I was offered and had accepted for the fall at the Fed in New York. At one point the head of the Division, Harry Dexter White, asked me whether I would like to stay on in the Treasury. I said I would consider it if he were to offer me a position at the P-2 level, paying $2,600 a year, or $200 more a year than I was then paid. He said "No."

Harry Dexter White was an able economist who had written a thesis at Harvard under Professor Frank W. Taussig on the French International Accounts from 1880 to 1913, but he was very unpleasant. Emile Despres later told me he was the only economist he can remember that he ever wanted to punch in the nose. Laughlin Currie and White would argue on social occasions, embarrassing everyone as they shouted at each other. White and Coe were later widely judged to have been Communists, and White is said by Whitaker Chambers to have contributed to the secret documents, mostly from Alger Hiss, that were stored for a time in his nephew's chimney and ended up in a pumpkin. He may or may not have been a Marxist – nothing I have ever witnessed directly would point in that direction – but he was a conspirator. He wanted to run the world. I have been told that he would send memoranda during the war to friends in other agencies, telling them what they ought to do. It is related that when Secretary of State Byrnes heard of the pumpkin papers he expostulated that White was trying to run a separate US foreign policy independently of the Department of State. Although it has been denied in the biography by his brother, I suspect he committed suicide after returning to

US Treasury Department

New Hampshire from having testified in the Congress and fighting off accusations. That would fit his conspiratorial character.

In any event, the fact that I had worked for three months for White and Coe in 1936 led the FBI to monitor my telephone calls in the Department of State ten years later, and to peddle gossip from those calls to its sycophantic columnists such as George Sokolsky. A further result was that when I resigned from the Department of State in 1948 of my own volition, I could not get cleared to get back into government even for consulting until the Kennedy years brought McCarthyism to an end.

Coe may well have been a Marxist. He did his graduate work at Chicago where few people could get a PhD in those days because if they could pass Frank Knight they could not pass Jacob Viner, and vice versa. At the University of Chicago, according to the tale, he met his future wife, whose name escapes me, there from England on a Harkness fellowship. He suggested that they could live more cheaply in the coal-fields of Kentucky. They moved there from Chicago, and became radicalized in observing the conditions of the miners. I liked Coe, and kept in touch with him for a while, sending him a copy of my thesis in 1937. When I came back to Washington in 1940 I saw a little of him, but at no time was I a Trilby to the Svengali of White or Coe. Poor Coe: when the McCarthy heat was on there was so much he could not explain that he left, first for Mexico and then for Communist China. When Galbraith saw him in China on a trip for the American Economic Association, Coe expressed an interest in seeing more current books, and I sent some.

Another economist left the Treasury department to come to the Fed in New York at the same time as I did: Emilio Gabriel ("Pete") Collado, born in Cuba, grown up in the United States – Andover, MIT (BS) and Harvard (PhD in economics). His path and mine ran parallel to one another until he left the Department of State for the World Bank, the articles of agreement of which he helped negotiate at Bretton Woods. In due course, when Eugene Meyer became president of the World

Bank, he made it a condition of his acceptance that Collado be asked to resign, because Meyer feared him as a most effective bureaucrat. Collado proved he was more than a governmental bureaucrat in going to Esso, as Exxon was then known, and working his way up the finance and governmental relations ladder until he became a senior executive vice-president. Emile Despres once said that if Collado only had Despres advise him at every step, he would go far on the score of his energy and bureaucratic adroitness. It turned out that Collado went far without Despres's help.

Friedman bet me in the spring of 1936 that I would not write a chapter a month of my dissertation while working in the US Treasury for the summer; I was tidily ahead after two months, with two and a half chapters written, when Sarah Miles returned to Baltimore from her summer travels, and diverted my attention from economics. We became engaged on September 26, and I lost the bet. Allen Wallis was also in Washington in the summer of 1936, and lent me his model T Ford convertible to go to a party in Baltimore for Jeanie Miles, my future sister-in-law. I have a vivid memory of chugging along the road to Baltimore in evening clothes, in this rather primitive automobile, and having a locomotive engineer in a train running parallel to the road, waving and laughing at the incongruous sight.

It was my great good luck that White would not pay me $200 a year more, as I might have stayed in Washington and been drawn deeper into the quagmire that surrounded Treasury economic research and the Morgenthau vindictive attitude to Germany. Instead I lived at home in Flushing while working at the Federal Reserve Bank of New York, slaving away on the thesis at night and every other weekend, the alternate weekend going to Baltimore or my fiancée coming to New York. A hard life in some respects, but a fulfilling one.

9

Federal Reserve Bank of New York

Fall 1936 to spring 1939

My assignment in New York was twofold: I spent half my time in the Foreign Exchange Section of the Foreign Department, and the other half in Foreign Research, led by Lewis Galantiere, and working under George Willis, who followed economic conditions in Britain and the sterling area. The Foreign Exchange Section consisted of Emile Despres, who had come directly from Harvard with a BS in 1930, and a somewhat elderly banker, Robert Raymond, who had been squeezed out of the Chemical Bank and Trust Company in the depth of the depression, worked for a time as a bank examiner, and was an expert on bank numbers. The task of the section was to gather weekly reports from banks and brokers and quarterly reports of non-financial firms on foreign assets and liabilities, from which international capital flows could be calculated. Weekly letters were written to the secretary of the Treasury, with copies to the Federal Reserve Board, analyzing foreign-exchange markets and international capital flows. The Foreign Department was headed by Horace Stanford, was under Vice-President Harold Roelse, but we worked mostly for Vice-President Werner Knoke, a foreign-exchange trader, Vice-President Randolph Burgess on the central-bank domestic side, and Allan Sproul, the first vice-president, later the president of the Bank after George Harrison. Knoke was a serious technician with little flair. Burgess I have already commented upon. Allan Sproul, brother of Robert Sproul, the chancellor of the University of California at the time, was a wonderful man to work for, understanding, sympathetic, and helpful. He is a member of a pantheon of four great men under whom I have worked – far under, I hasten to say – Sproul, General Omar N. Bradley of Twelfth Army Group, William L. Clayton, the undersecretary of state for Economic Affairs after the war, and Secretary of State George Catlett Marshall. Long after I was at MIT Sproul, in retirement, noticed something of mine – a letter to the *New York Times*, if I remember well – wrote me a note and started a correspondence which lasted about five years until his death. With Emile Despres's widow, Joanna, I once went to see him in Marin County. He wrote a blurb for my book *Manias, Panics, and Crashes*.

I was more interested in the foreign-exchange section of the job than in area research, partly because of my academic interests, and partly because of the association with Emile Despres, who became a close friend. Despres was brilliant, made a great name for himself in government, in a narrow academic circle at Williams College and Stanford University, but published very little. His collected papers, edited by G. M. Meier after Despres had had a stroke, include memoranda written at the Federal Reserve Bank of New York, testimony before Congress, papers edited from tapes of lectures, and those written with others, including me. I was mildly annoyed that one paper we wrote together led some people to suspect that the ideas were his and the writing mine, when in fact some of the ideas had emanated from me. Another paper written also with Walter Salant, published in *The Economist* in 1966, in his collected papers and elsewhere, saw the light of day primarily because I refused, after a time, to let Despres and Salant continue to revise it, as each wanted to do. Both were perfectionists, in contrast to my "quick and dirty" predisposition. At school Despres had had a recorded IQ of 192, which fell in half on one occasion, bringing the psychologists streaming from Teachers College to

Riverdale in New York to see what was the matter. After stalling as long as his patience held out, he finally confessed that he had become tired of being a genius and had answered only every other question. The pundits were relieved that the stability of their measurements had been sustained.

My career paralleled that of Despres for a long period. After the Federal Reserve Bank of New York he went to the Board in Washington, to which he arranged for me to come from the Bank for International Settlements after the fall of Paris in June 1940. He went thence to the Office of Strategic Services (OSS), and I followed. After the war he was for a while in the Department of State, as was I. He left State early to go to Williamstown, and Williams offered me a job after I had spent a year or two at MIT. I turned it down. It was intellectually debilitating to be too long a colleague of Despres, as it was often easier to ask him his solution to a problem than to work it out for oneself. I decided it would be better to stay somewhat at a distance, although we corresponded a lot and saw one another fairly frequently.

In 1937–8 the Littauer School at Harvard was getting started and Alvin Hansen invited Despres to go there as a Littauer scholar on leave from the New York Fed. This gave me more responsibility, full-time in the Foreign Exchange Reports section, or whatever its official designation was. Despres was a sophisticated economist with no formal graduate training, and made the unfortunate mistake of signing up for his general examinations after having been at Harvard in 1937 for only two months. Professor Edward Chamberlin was so incensed by this effrontery that when his time came to question the candidate, he pushed a line of questioning into smaller and smaller corners, largely on his own work on imperfect competition, that Despres ultimately was unable to answer, and failed the examination. He thus had no PhD. When Stanford University considered him for a position in 1961, I was asked to write a letter, and luckily, as I was later told, struck the appropriate note by comparing him with Allyn Young, a great economist of the 1920s who left Stanford for Harvard and ultimately London, but whose published work was limited. Young was known as a superb teacher at Harvard, and a great inspirer of economics dissertations.

There were other interesting personalities in the New York Fed. John H. Williams was vice-president and economist, half of the time, the other half being spent as a professor of money and banking at Harvard. He patronized the overnight sleeper, the *Owl*, to such an extent that some of us thought he had hung pictures in his lower berth – this in the days before the New York, New Haven, and Hartford railroad had roomettes, and of course well before interurban travel had moved to airplanes. I saw more of Professor Williams later when I was at MIT and he at Harvard, and found myself slowly and partly unconsciously more and more impressed with his notion of "key currencies," on which more later. George Eddy was a distinctive character in economic research; a guard who once forbade him to go out of a certain entrance was told "Shoot me," by Eddy as he walked out. When my wife and I were abroad, he met and married Eileen O'Daniel, and we saw a good bit of them later on Seminary Hill, outside Washington. Pete Collado worked with Eric Lamb on Latin American affairs. George Willis was a capable, methodical economic analyst who later played a major role in Treasury Department international research after the days of White, Coe, Glasser *et al*.

In 1938 I met Paul Samuelson, who stopped in at the bank to see Despres after the latter's return from Harvard. Samuelson was twenty-three years old, and made a remark that I thought brilliant at the time: "I suppose a capable investor would know at what price he would buy, and at what price he would sell, every security in the world." Only years later did it strike me that the information costs would be so heavy that a truly rational man would restrict the securities he monitored for their worth to a selected few.

In the fall of 1938 or the winter of 1939, Mr Sproul asked whether I would be interested in a job at the Bank for International Settlements (BIS) at Basle, Switzerland. I said that I would. He arranged then for me to call on Leon Frazer at the

Federal Reserve Bank of New York

First National Bank of New York. Frazer had been president of the BIS. The First National Bank was an old-fashioned one at 2 Wall Street, if I recall correctly. Officers sat on the "platform," a huge open space with a great number of roll-top desks. If his hat was on the top of an officer's desk, then that officer was in the bank even though he might not be at his desk. Frazer was a man of evident sensibility, who had been a conscientious objector in the First World War, and ultimately committed suicide, but I recall the hats more than the personality. I got the job, and gave an informal undertaking to stay for three years, the bank moving my wife and me plus our furniture, all this agreed before the German takeover of Czechoslovakia in March 1939.

Per Jacobsson, the economist of the BIS, suggested that I spend a month in Washington at the Board before coming to Basle, and this we did in June 1939. One of the pleasures of that month was finally to meet in the flesh Chandler Morse of the Board's International Research Division. We had become good friends on the telephone over a period of two years as I called him weekly with the foreign-exchange reports and the highlights of the weekly letter written to Secretary of the Treasury Morgenthau and signed by Sproul, or Knoke, or in the joint absence Burgess. The Morses and Kindlebergers became lifelong friends. He was my boss in OSS in Washington, and I succeeded him in charge of the Enemy Objectives Unit (EOU) of the Economic Warfare Division (EWD) of the US Embassy, London, in March 1943.

10

Bank for International Settlements
1939–1940

My wife and I sailed to Europe on July 3, 1939, first class on the United States line SS *America*. We were first class because the Bank shipped a lot of gold, mostly from Europe to the United States during the "Golden Avalanche" after the price of gold had been raised from $20.67 an ounce to $35, and the world thought it might be lowered again. Any friend of the New York Fed was a friend of the United States lines, and with a word from someone, we were raised from tourist to first class, with a table twelve feet away from the captain's. On the same ship was the sorrowful Eduard Benes, who had been president of Czechoslovakia from 1935 to 1938. We failed to make his acquaintance. One munitions-maker we did meet – name lost, possibly Harrington – was the owner of the Harmon factory somewhere in Indiana that used to make automobiles, and was now engaged in building tanks. He spotted my name, and asked if I was connected with the well-known "Dutch" Kindelberger, of North American Aviation, later Douglas aircraft. I had to admit I was not. My uncle, Admiral Charles P. Kindelberger, had met Dutch, and they had agreed that they might be connected distantly in the Palatinate, but that Dutch's forebears had come to West Virginia in 1888, ours to Philadelphia somewhat earlier. Harrington, if that was his

Bank for International Settlements

name, was bothered by the fact that the German stewards padded about his cabin when he was at dinner, so said his child of a tender unknown age; perhaps they were spies, looking for intelligence on tank-making.

My father-in-law suffered from eczema, and one doctor guessed that some part of the problem might lie in the presence of my wife's dog, Mr Whimperton, which we had left in Baltimore after our marriage. We brought him to Europe. In 1931, when the visa to land in England cost $10, I had skipped that country, and was interested in visiting it *en route* to Basle. Whimps presented a problem because the rules demanded that a representative of Spratts be brought to Southampton to take the dog in sterile fashion to quarantine in London; later, we would have to pay for the dog to be taken, by his custodian, to the port of debarkation. I suggested to the purser that he debark (no pun intended) the dog in Cherbourg, put him in kennels, and we would pick him up later. The purser countered with the cogent suggestion that he take him all the way to Paris, since Cherbourg did not lie on the London–Paris route. This was agreed. When we arrived in Paris and called on the United States line to regain our ward, the agent said: "You have no dog. He's French now. When the boat-train got to Paris, we worked late, and there was no time to put the dog in a kennel. I took him home. He liked my aunt and my aunt liked him, and he also made friends with our monkey. I took him walking daily in the Bois du Boulogne. He barks in French now" – all this with a broad smile, as he handed Whimps back.

We started life in Basle in a modest hotel, the Bernerhof, and ultimately moved to Casinostrasse 14, across from a park and the Casino, which was then being used to house refugees from Nazi Germany. Life at the Bank was quiet in the summer – the heads of central banks met there monthly as a rule from October to May. I became acquainted with my boss, Per Jacobsson, my colleagues in the economics section, Fred Connally and Antonino Zecchi, the one formerly of the Bank of England, the latter on assignment from the Bank of Italy. Connally was a wonderful man with figures. After the war he almost singlehandedly did the

Bank for International Settlements

monthly accounting for the European Payments Union. He and his wife Pearl once came to dinner at our house in Lincoln, when he fascinated Paul Samuelson, another guest with his wife, Marian, by saying what a great relief in life it was to come finally to the realization that one was second-rate. The Connallys had a good life, skiing in winter, long holidays at home in England or on the Riviera in summer.

We liked the Zecchis. There was a considerable language problem: Signora Zecchi had Italian, French, German, and no English; my wife English and German; Nino Zecchi Italian, French, and English, but no German; and I English with a smattering of French and German. In the end, on our pleasant outings, we left Nino, the best linguist, as odd man out, talking German, with Novella Zecchi translating into Italian or me into English. Zecchi was a better violinist, I suspect, than economist, and played in the string quartet organized by the Bank president, J. W. Beyen, a Dutch banker, who played the cello. Beyen was a great wit; he called the group, which included as pianist the legal adviser from Vienna, Dr Wieser, the "International Financial Society for the Issuance of False Notes," a double or triple pun valid also in French and German. Beyen was later, as Dutch member of the board of the International Monetary Fund (IMF), famous for his remark about the first two managing directors: "The trouble with Camille Gutt [pronounced Goot] was that he had no roots, and with Ivar Rooth [pronounced Root] that he had no guts." Some take the view that the witticism cost him the job of Rooth's successor.

President Beyen was out of town when we first arrived in Basle, and I missed a chance to pay him a formal call at the office. A few days later at a luncheon party held by the secretary of the Bank, Signor Pilotti, I saw an effervescent youngish man to whom we had not been introduced, and it took me some moments to realize that this was my new boss. Beyen left the Bank some time in the winter of 1939–40 to take over the management of Unilever's properties in Germany, but was cut off on May 10, 1940, while visiting an intimate friend in Basle. He made his way to London, joined the Dutch government in exile, first as

Bank for International Settlements

finance minister, later as foreign minister, and then, as far as my knowledge extends, as Dutch director of the IMF in Washington.

Per Jacobsson was a fascinating personality. He could dictate economics in Swedish, English, French, or German, had worked with the League of Nations debt mission in Austria in the early 1920s, but was, as his daughter's biography poignantly reveals, a little unsure of his status as an economist in comparison with the great Swedish figures, Wicksell, Lindahl, Myrdal, and Ohlin, or such a luminary as Keynes. He was an overwhelming personality. One might start talking to him in the center of a room, and find oneself after a time backed into a corner with his large frame and thick glasses still in attack. He was far too much of a monetarist for me. I liked him, but did not much approve of his economics, and still think, without having made a recent test, that the 10th Annual Report of the Bank to which I contributed a great deal was modestly better than those it followed. Jacobsson went to the IMF as managing director in about 1958; whether because of his ebullient personality or the changing times, the institution took on new life and he became, as the cliché goes, a living legend. I am mildly irritated that I, who knew him fairly well, have never been asked to deliver one of the annual Per Jacobsson Memorial Lectures since his death. It may be just as well, as my review of his daughter's biography was not appreciated by her. It says something about his personality that he took me more seriously after the war when he had seen a line by D.H. Robertson, the English economist, appreciative of something I had written.

One saw little of Roger Auboin, the leading French representative at the BIS either in the summer of 1939 or after the war started in September. A French economist named Rodenbach was called up early into the French army, had to sell off his possessions with perhaps no place to move them to in France, and we acquired a few pieces to fill our overlarge apartment. Marcel van Zealand, brother of the former Belgian prime minister, Paul van Zealand, and a most agreeable man, saw my wife and me exploring a secondhand shop looking for furnishings, and bought and gave us a charming pewter coffee pot. At least three of my children have acquired items of furniture that we picked up then: Sally, the slate-top peasant table; Dick the Rodenbach rosewood country breakfront; and Randall, the repainted and hence not valuable Swiss armoire inscribed "Diese Kasten gehört Elizabethen Breiten Moserinnen, 1767."

The wartime American colony in Basle was small. We saw something of the consul, one Parker Buhrman, of a retired opera singer, Senta Erd, of the Handleys, he the head of the Firestone plant in Switzerland, who made a name for himself in rubber circles by managing to steal a barrel of Buna-S from a German plant of I.G. Farben so that his company could get a head start in learning how to make tires from it. He came from parents with twelve or thirteen siblings each and had ninety-six first cousins.

On one occasion in the fall, a reporter from the *Chicago Tribune* came to town. He had no foreign languages, and used to go to the office of a local newspaper and pay staff to tell him what the stories were about and translate those of interest. There was no need even for restaurant French or German. A man could get by splendidly with two words: Whiskey and Steak.

The Bank practically died after the outbreak of war. There were no monthly meetings, the lifeblood of the institution earlier that had attracted me. We did a bit of touring, having been caught in Lauterbrunnen when war broke out with my father-, mother-, and sister-in-law, who hurried back to Basle, took the train to Rotterdam, and just made the boat. There was skiing in winter, except that Sarah had to hang up her skis because of pregnancy, a fact not lost on her mother when she saw a postcard from Davos with me carrying skis and Sarah walking in a coat. When the Germans attacked in May, the Bank got the wind up and moved to Château d'Oex; some of the staff were Jewish, such as Dr Wieser, who had a son in the RAF, and slept nightly in the weeks before, on the other side of a pass from Basle. Château d'Oex was a beautiful resort, with fields of narcissus that made their way up the mountainside as the season advanced. (My friend, Ragnar Nurkse, died of a heart attack, plunging headlong into a field of narcissus on the Rochers de

Bank for International Settlements

Naye above Montreux – a nice way to go, but the wrong time.) On one lonely walk with Mr Whimperton, we trudged over the Col des Mosses, perhaps to Le Sepey, and took the postal bus back. *En route* homeward, a couple stopped the bus, and the man helped his sister aboard as she stopped hiking and he walked on. They both came to our hotel in Château d'Oex that evening, and proved to be Gero von Schultz Gaevernitz, and his sister, who was married to a Stinnes of the German steel family. Gaevernitz said he was living on arbitrage in US banknotes, having a friend in New York send him five $100 bills each week which he would sell for $650 or so, and then buy a check for $500 from a Swiss bank to mail back to New York. The premium on banknotes reflected the panic of the period. After the war, I learned that Gaevernitz worked later with Allen W. Dulles in the Swiss headquarters of OSS, in touch with the elements of the German resistance to Hitler. He published a book in 1947 about the various attempts to assassinate Der Führer, entitled *They Almost Killed Hitler*.

With the fall of Paris on June 17, I decided that if it were safe enough for my wife to travel in her condition, we should return to the United States, our three-year understanding with the BIS having been nullified by *force majeur*. I had been corresponding with Emile Despres at the Federal Reserve Board, and he began to cable the BIS, saying that Kindleberger was needed in Washington for the defense of the United States, getting the cables signed by Marriner S. Eccles, chairman of the Board. We consulted two obstetricians in Montreux: the elder said it was not safe to travel with my wife seven and a half months pregnant; his younger nephew said it was safe. We took the latter's advice. I made a hurried trip alone to Basle to put our furniture in storage; on the way back, changing trains in Zurich, I bought two rubber cushions, one a small pillow, the other a doughnut-shaped ring, for sitting on. On July 3, at five a.m., we set off from Geneva in the first American Express bus for Barcelona, counting on proceeding thence to Madrid and Lisbon to take the *Manhattan*, which the Department of State had sent to pick up the American citizens leaving Paris. The small bus had taken out two rows of seats at the back to make room for a large tank of gasoline, enough to get to Barcelona and back. It was unclear where the line had been drawn between occupied and unoccupied France. As we got on the bus, one passenger gave a $100 bill to the American Express representative in charge of the trip, saying that if he or the driver spotted Germans they should stop immediately, turn around and flee. The passengers were a few Americans and other citizens of then neutral countries; most of them were German, Austrian, or Swiss Jews, fearful that their Swiss refuge would be overrun. We sat in the first right-hand seat in the front, with our dog under the seat. I wanted the window open to give Sarah air. In the seat behind us were a couple, the man evidently unwell, and being cared for by his wife. We learned at the Spanish border that they were Professor Ludwig von Mises, the distinguished and very conservative Austrian economist, and his wife. Mrs von Mises wanted the window closed on her husband's behalf.

The bus avoided the direct route through Lyons and went through the mountains to get as rapidly as possible into unoccupied France. Along the road we saw bedraggled French army units, stranded automobiles that had run out of gasoline, refugees on foot. We stopped for the night at Orange, went through Nîmes, and reached the Spanish border at Port Bou in the late afternoon. There all was chaos. The Spanish would not allow anyone in without a visa for Portugal, and the Portuguese would not issue visas to anyone unless that person had a passport or a visa for elsewhere. Our dog could run back and forth across the border, but people like von Mises could not. Other buses from Geneva overtook us. At eleven that night, with a different assortment of passengers, we started from Port Bou for Barcelona. The road was full of holes from the shelling that the Loyalists had suffered in their losing retreat into France. The bus bounced about. After a time I noted that the hormones prevented Sarah from feeling uncomfortable, and that I was sitting on the cushions bought for her. I was considerably annoyed after we got on board the ship in Lisbon to learn that one of the new passengers was an obstetrician, a young man from New York

Bank for International Settlements

who had failed to get into medical school in the United States and gone to the University of Lausanne for his medical degree, internship, and residency in obstetrics. If he had been sensitive enough to imagine my concern, he could have told of his training and saved me a great deal of agony.

We arrived at the hotel in Barcelona at about five in the morning, and at nine I set off with Whimps to a travel agency to arrange for transport to Madrid. On the walk back, a whistle blew, the populace stopped and gave the Fascist salute. I am ashamed to say that I raised my arm in an ambiguous gesture so as to stay out of trouble.

We had a sleeper to Madrid. As we waited next morning in a van for a trip to the hotel, we saw Loyalist prisoners being marched off from the station in rags, their faces white and drawn. At the hotel there was tea-dancing in the afternoon, a macabre activity given our mood. We were unable to get sleeping accommodations for the ride to Lisbon, but did manage to get into a first-class carriage. With us was a family of three Poles – woman, brother-in-law, and the woman's son. They had been on the run since September. She did not know where her husband and the boy's father was. The passage over the mountains into Hungary, into Yugoslavia, Italy, then France, Spain, and now Lisbon, headed, with visas, for Brazil, was made possible by a substantial supply of jewelry and the brother-in-law's account of a couple of thousand pounds in London. It was a gripping story, which was written up months later in the *New York Times* when the woman and her son made their way from Brazil to the United States. The story was exactly as it had been told to us, with one exception: there was no mention of the brother-in-law, and all was related as if the woman had done it all herself.

One annoyance was a woman economist from a League of Nations bus who came by, saw Sarah's condition, and said that Sarah should not be sitting up all night, but should sleep in a *wagon-lit*. She did not offer hers.

In Lisbon in the morning, we took a taxi to a hotel, and, on finding that no room was to be had, I settled Sarah and the dog in a park, and went to fifteen more hotels before finding a room.

Bank for International Settlements

Three days later we were on the ship, with a doctor and nurses, and I relaxed into a spate of bridge-playing.

Aboard the *Manhattan*, I mingled with some of the American expatriates leaving Paris. One somewhat elegant young man said that he had been having tea on the veranda of the Grand Hotel in Estoril when a friend appeared, rejoicing, and said, "I just gave $200 to the clerk in the Pan Am office, and he got me on tomorrow's Clipper for New York." A few minutes later, another person in the group was paged and called to the telephone, returning shortly in some anger, saying, "I have just been told that I can't have my seat on the Clipper going to New York tomorrow."

The same man also mentioned *à propos* the prospects of getting our furniture out of Switzerland and Europe, that he envisaged no trouble. He had given one of his post-impressionists to the Museum of Modern Art, and it had arranged to crate and ship all the other paintings; and he had given a Louis XV escritoire or some such to the Metropolitan, and in recompense it was taking care of the delivery of his furniture to New York. Like vultures after carnage, the museums seemed to be hovering over the wreckage of a way of life.

In due course we arrived in New York, were met, and were brought to Baltimore. Nine days later my son and heir was born.

11

Board of Governors of the Federal Reserve System
1940–1942

I had better start this chapter by emphasizing that I was not a member of the Board of Governors, but a research economist who worked for it. The punctuation in *Who's Who* has given me trouble about that, and for a later period in my life, about my position in the Army. There I was a major, in the General Staff Corps, though some read it as if I had been a major-general in the Staff Corps.

The Board of Governors had no great responsibilities during a period of preparation for war, but maintained an inventory of economists that could be diverted to various tasks as they emerged, much as later the Office of Strategic Services played a vacuum-filling role, undertaking intelligence tasks that the armed services had generally overlooked. I was in the International Division of the Research Department, under a very New England type of person, Walter R. Gardner. Gardner was a stickler for exact designation of column and row headings on a table, something that graduate schools are for the most part too grand to teach. He was a rational man, who, when he saw a sign that said "Don't Walk on the Grass," knew it meant that the authorities did not want paths made across the grass, but that a random saunter would be acceptable. Equally a "Stop" sign

Federal Reserve System

meant that one should be careful, but there was no real need to bring a car to a complete stop. These attitudes may have been rational but they were hard on occasion to explain to policemen.

For a time I collected items of odd behavior, or perhaps more accurately of imaginative behavior, such as James Meade fishing a used manuscript out of Ronald Edwards's wastebasket at the London School of Economics, observing that nothing had been written on the back, and writing *The Balance of Payments* on the reverse side – to the palpable saving of paper for Britain. Gardner was such an idiosyncratic type. When the Fed was at 15th and H Streets, before it moved to Constitution Avenue, he and Winfield Riefler shared an office, were friendly, but had an amiable disagreement about fresh air and drafts. Riefler's guests were sometimes startled, I have been told, to look across the room to Gardner's desk and see his feet encased in brown paper bags, tied at the top with string. He wanted air, but disliked a draft on his ankles. Later in 1942 when an economist of my age group expressed an interest in transferring to OSS, Emile Despres said, "No: he needs another year in Gardner University."

The Federal Reserve was not only a source of supply of economists; it provided a refuge for one or two. In Gardner's division was a heroic German statistician from Jena, Paul Hermberg, an Aryan who had won the highest German decoration given to non-professional soldiers in the First World War (the highest are of course reserved for the professionals). He had refused to join the Nazi party when he was urged to do so by the rector of the university, writing him an insulting letter to say that he had had opportunities over many years to join the party and was not a recent convert like the rector. He was forced to resign, stayed as long as he could living on his army pension, but finally gave up and emigrated. At school his wife had sought to protect her very blond children by careful visits to their teachers to warn that the children had an anti-Nazi upbringing at home and the teacher should protect them from other children. A friend of the great economist Gerhard Colm, who started his career in the Institute for World Economics in Germany, came

Federal Reserve System

to the United States in the 1930s, and ended up after the war on the staff of the first Council of Economic Advisers, he had been helped by Colm to get the job at the Board.

A short time after working in the International Division with Gardner, Morse, and J. Burke Knapp, later a vice-president of the World Bank, I was asked to serve as American secretary of the Joint Economic Committee of Canada and the United States. The chairman was Alvin H. Hansen, a Harvard professor originally from Minnesota and before that Denmark, a much-beloved Keynesian economist, simple, direct, intuitive as an economist rather than a man of high-powered mathematical technique. The other American members of the Committee were Jacob Viner, the Chicago professor (at that time) and consultant to the Treasury, born and raised in Montreal, Harry D. White, William Batt from the War Production Board, and J. Dana Durand from the Tariff Commission. The Canadian chairman, William Mackintosh, was from Queens University in Kingston, Ontario, and had played a leading role in the writing of the Rowell–Sirois report of 1939 on Dominion Provincial Fiscal Relations. My opposite number, the Canadian secretary, was Alexander ("Sandy") Skelton, of the Bank of Canada, son of the former permanent secretary of the Canadian Foreign Office, a man on the verge of a career as an alcoholic who drank two double Scotches with lunch and 140-proof Demerera rum in the evening. We saw a great deal of one another, and I once went to his farm outside Ottawa. There at one time he had kept pregnant mares, bought wild in the prairies, and kept for their urine from which, in the days before synthesis, female hormones were produced. The urine, he said, was more valuable than milk, to the astonishment of his farmer neighbors. The foals were destroyed, and the unbroken mares after foaling sold off to unsuspecting farmer-buyers "as is."

The names of the other Canadian members are lost to me except for John J. Deutsch, who went on to a brilliant career in the Canadian government and then as the principal of Queens University. He started as an aide to Skelton. He was the oldest of twelve children of an immigrant German couple in Alberta or Manitoba, who had been away from home so long that he couldn't remember the names of his youngest brothers and sisters.

The task of the Joint Committee was to get on with wartime cooperation between Canada and the United States, and then to plan for the post-war world. On the first score the Committee ran itself out of a job very quickly; as soon as we had held a meeting of the production people on the two sides, or the price-control authorities, or the supply boards, we would be asked to step aside, not bother them, and let them get on with their work. Our role was largely one of effecting introductions. In planning for post-war economic cooperation between our countries, we produced reams of paper which the main members of the Committee were completely uninterested in – since there was a war on – and for which even the deputies they sent to meetings – among whom J. Douglass Brown of the War Production Board, whom I later joined at MIT – found it difficult to work up any warmth. I seriously doubt whether any official of either government ever consulted these papers later. Jacob Viner did not win my admiration or friendship. I was working on Canadian matters all day every day, and he would think about them only as he sat down at meetings. This limited current background did not prevent him from holding forth at length and authoritatively on Canadian–American issues, based on his birth and youth in Montreal. I must give him credit, however. In addition to writing a classic book, *Studies in the Theory of International Trade*, he once pointed out that New England attracts distinguished anticlimaxes, citing "the New York, New Haven, and Hartford railroad," and "for God, for country, and for Yale."

Meetings of the Joint Committees were held in Ottawa, Montreal, New York, and Washington, the two metropolitan cities occasionally chosen to simplify the long complex trainride from one capital to the other. In Ottawa I met Robert ("Bob") Bryce, the deputy and later the successor to the legendary William Clark, permanent secretary of the Canadian Ministry of Finance. Bryce had been at Cambridge with Salant, Cairncross, Villard *et al.* in the Keynes seminar, and later at

Harvard with Despres, the Sweezys, Tarshis, Samuelson, and so on. He was one of those brilliant civil servants whose names are largely unknown to the economics profession since they do not write for publication.

Years later when I served one year on the nominations committee of the American Economic Association (AEA), the chairman of the Committee mentioned in opening the meeting that the Association had never elected as president a woman, a Southerner, or a Canadian. I was a warm admirer of William Mackintosh, knew that he was a member of the AEA as I had seen him at annual meetings, and pushed hard for the election of a Canadian – in principle. So did Professor J. H. Elliott of the University of Toronto. When we won that point, I put forward the candidacy of Mackintosh, and Elliott urged on the Committee Harold Innis, the Toronto economic historian. As author of many books, Innis won the nomination, and since there is no alternative candidate, the election. He died before he had finished his duties as president-elect, and the preparation of the annual program devolved on vice-president Fritz Machlup.

Research on post-war problems produced one odd result. One day at the Board Alvin Hansen mentioned to me that *Foreign Affairs* had asked him to write an article on "The economic tasks of the post-war world," and wanted me to make a start on such a paper. I said I would. A week or so later, he asked whether I had made progress. I had not. A week or two still further along, same question, same answer. When I next saw him on the matter, he said he had written a draft of the article. I told him so had I. He took the two drafts, as he later told me, wove them together, one paragraph his, the following one mine, put my name on the title-page with his and gave me the whole fee of $50. A wonderful man.

I used to call on Alvin Hansen at his home in Belmont after he fully retired. The last time I did so was on a very hot day in the summer, perhaps in the mid-seventies. All the shades were down and the windows closed. I banged and banged on the door, since Mrs Hansen was deaf, and his hearing was not of the best. Finally Alvin came to the door wearing a shirt and tie, socks and shoes, his ever-present green eyeshade, underwear, but no trousers. We had our usual half-hour chat and he showed me out. I never learned whether or not he knew he had no trousers on.

At one stage, whether before or after the Canadian work I do not recall, I went along with Walter Gardner as part of an American team to discuss British finances in connection with lend-lease. These discussions were held in the Treasury and were dominated by the irrepressible Harry White. White was determined to make the British turn their pockets inside out, and this led to their being compelled to sell a prize investment in the United States, the American Viscose Company, owned by Courtaulds. There was a considerable current of resentment among the British, that I, Gardner, and any other Federal Reserve member could understand. My lowly task was to work on balance-of-payments estimates with the British working stiffs, of whom I remember mostly Roy Allen of the London School of Economics, and Edward Playfair. I was to see Playfair again in Moscow in 1947.

When Pearl Harbor came, I applied for a direct commission in the Navy, thinking that my experience in sailing meant that with some training I would be useful in small boats. The application process was time-consuming. In the spring my father had a heart attack, and I thought we might have to move back to New York to care for my mother and an unmarried sister with a record of nervous breakdowns. The Navy offered me a commission as a lieutenant, junior grade, and assigned me not to small-boat training but to a desk in the Washington Navy Yard. That was not my idea of winning the war, and between the trouble in Flushing and the offer in Washington, I lost my appetite for the life of a sailor. In due course, matters stabilized at home. First Emile Despres and then Chandler Morse moved over from the Federal Reserve to the newly established Office of Strategic Services. When they offered me a job in the summer of 1942, by which time I thought both that Canadian cooperation was on a back burner and that my obligation to the Board of Governors for bringing my furniture back from Europe had been amortized by two full years of work, I transferred.

12

Office of Strategic Services, Washington
1942–1943

The idea behind OSS, as I understood it, was that the Army, Navy, and Air Force would leave certain gaps in their military preparations, especially in intelligence, and William J. Donovan, a New York lawyer, First World War hero, and a hyperthyroid activist, would fill them. There were several divisions: Secret Intelligence – spy stuff; Secret Operations – sabotage; and Research and Analysis, or open intelligence based on scholarly sources, and employing social scientists – historians, geographers, economists. The history of the Research and Analysis branch has recently been published by Barrie Katz (*Foreign Intelligence*, Cambridge, MA, 1989), who is interested primarily in intellectual history and how the war experience affected historians. The book does have a chapter on the economists.

Research and Analysis was organized with a Board of Analysts, presided over by James Phinney Baxter, president of Williams College, and including such prominent historians as Sherman Kent of Yale, William Langer of Harvard, Geroid T. Robinson of Columbia, the geographer Richard Hartshorne of Wisconsin, and the economist Edward S. Mason of Harvard. I confidently believed that Emile Despres was a member of the Board of Analysts, but I am told that was not his position, which was somewhere between the Board and the Economics Division, headed by Chandler Morse. The economics division had five sections, dealing with manpower, agriculture, industry, military supplies, and one other I cannot recall, perhaps transport. Mason had a personal assistant in the person of Walt Whitman Rostow, who had recently completed his doctorate in economic history at Yale, and been teaching at Columbia. The division also had floating resources, such as Fritz Lieberman of Yale, a writer, and thus possessing a skill missing in many social scientists.

I was assigned to the Military Supplies section as its chief, and found it already staffed with Harold J. Barnett, who had started out as an economist in the Treasury after a master's degree from the University of California at Berkeley, and two Columbia BAs who had been members of a class taught by Rostow, Warren Baum, and Mark Kahn. Another man in the division, a geologist named Edward Mayer, was anxious to shift into my section from that on industry as he was an airplane enthusiast, interested in studying German aircraft production. Our task was to produce estimates of German capacities and output for planes, tanks, armored vehicles, warships, and the like.

As academic economists, we knew very little about factory production or the use of material. Barnett and I took a trip to Fort Knox to discuss the use and abuse of tanks. We learned that tanks were immortal so long as they did not burn up or fall off a cliff. Engine, gun, track, and the like would wear out and be replaced, so that a theory of spare parts was necessary. In due course we produced one. On my way back from Germany in June 1945, I shared a hotel billet in London for a night with a major who had spent the war in tank design, working on the suspensions. I asked him what sort of a war that was, and he said it was terrible. Every time his unit designed a suspension that was adequate for a particular tank, other designers would pile on a bigger gun, thicker armor, a heavier engine, etc., so that the shock absorbers and spring suspension once again proved inadequate.

OSS, Washington

At Fort Knox, Barney and I ran into Justice of the Supreme Court and former mayor of Detroit, Frank Murphy, a Tank Corps reservist with the rank of a brigadier-general. He seemed rather superficial. He thought that the Tank Corps needed special distinction to its uniforms, like the wings of aviators, the boots of paratroopers, or the berets of the Special Troops, to build morale. It did not seem a crucial matter to us. We may have been wrong.

At another point in the work in Washington, Mayer and I called on General Benny Meyer, the procurement officer for the Air Force, to discuss the process of building aircraft. While waiting, we saw a number of company brochures on the aircraft manufacturing process. We liberated them in the belief that our files provided a better allocation of resources than passing the time of day for people waiting to see the general.

In the fall of 1942 one Colonel Richard d'Oyly Hughes, the A-5 or planning officer of the United States Strategic Air Force (USSTAF), ran into Chandler Morse in London as Hughes was looking about for help in formulating the plans for the strategic bombing mission. He was aware that A-2 (Intelligence) in Washington did not have much in the way of target ideas or information. In the early stages he could rely on British sources, and indeed was obliged to for the production of maps and plots of targets to be used by planes. But there was a danger in relying too heavily on the British. They had concluded that daylight bombing was impossible. The US Air Force, with its Flying Fortresses and Norden bombsight, still believed in it. Hughes wanted an independent source of intelligence and planning. OSS, in fulfillment of Donovan's vision of creating an organization that could fill gaps, was ready to respond. It may be added that Hughes's quest was a continuation of his experience in civilian life.

Though born in the United States and an American citizen, Hughes had been at Sandhurst, the British equivalent of West Point, in the First World War, and served a year in France in 1918 as an infantry officer. After the war he stayed in the British Army and was stationed in India. There in fighting native uprisings in the Northwest he had the illuminating experience of attacking the enemy from an open cockpit airplane, and receiving hot machine-gun shell casings down the back of his neck. In 1930 he met an American woman on a round-the-world tour, fell in love, married her, retired from the Army and moved, with his life savings of perhaps $10,000, to St Louis, where she lived. He lost the nest-egg in an ill-timed investment in aircraft production, then took a position as head farmer to the wealthy widow of a shoe manufacturer who was losing $150,000 a year on her dairy farm, and wanted to reduce the number to a more manageable one such as $75,000. A competent military officer is a generalist who can solve all kinds of problems. Hughes went to work on the farm, increased productivity, marketed his super-rich milk at a premium over ordinary milk, and sought help from the agricultural research stations in the land-grant universities when he encountered a problem that did not yield readily to his uncommon degree of common sense. In due course he rendered the farm profitable. When he was ready for new challenges, he joined the US Air Force through friends from his aircraft days, and when Colonel Berliner, the original A-5, lost an arm in a flying accident, Hughes acceded to a position where his experience in organized research made him look for help.

In the fall of 1942 Chandler Morse went to London to head a small unit known as the Enemy Objectives Unit (EOU) of the Economic Warfare Division of the US Embassy. Its personnel came mostly from OSS but there was an admixture of bodies from the Board of Economic Warfare (BEW) which was the organizational counterpart of the British Ministry of Economic Warfare. With Morse were originally Walt Rostow and William A. Salant, younger brother of Walter S. Salant, a bachelor at the time, sent out of the country to protect him from the draft, though like so many of us he was ultimately commissioned. In due course Harold Barnett and Edward Mayer were added to the complement together with John C. deWilde of BEW. An office was set up at 40 Berkeley Square in the West End. The bureaucratic circumstances were ideal: one was housed by the

OSS, Washington

Embassy, paid by OSS, but worked for the Air Force. No one office could really push us around.

Meanwhile, in Washington the Military Supply Section was finding work to do. The Air Force called for a strategic bombing plan and found that its own files and personnel were inadequate. Secretary of War Patterson from a Wall Street law office called on the aging Elihu Root of Root, Clark, Buckner, and Ballantine to do some consulting, and Root enlisted Boston lawyer James B. Ames, Professor Barton Leach of the Harvard Law School, and Guido Peirera, a Boston trustee, to help out. It provided an interesting test of the wartime aptitudes of lawyers and economists. My father used to tell me, as I tell my journalist son about newswork, that lawyers don't know anything, but have to be quick learners in a case in a new field. Often, however, they are looking for adjustment, for compromise. Economists want to maximize return and minimize cost. In peacetime there are many arguments in the objective function, to use jargon: the task is to maximize output for a given cost, or minimize cost for a given output while balancing international payments, staying within an acceptable distribution of income, level of pollution, etc. The wartime problem is easy: win the war without unduly deranging the domestic economy. The wartime effort is optimized when there is no gain to be made from shifting people from the home to the war front or vice versa, or from one military service to another. An example of how not to do it is to be found in the British war effort, where the war ended with two million people in the Air Force, unable to bring power to bear against the Germans, and a mere handful of divisions fighting on the ground. Another is the position in Germany where the home front was long overmanned, so to speak, because of Hitler's beliefs that women should be concerned with the kitchen, the church, and children.

Our task in OSS was of course not nearly so grand as overall wartime allocation. It was to try to decide how best the enemy economy could be taken apart. Early bombing enthusiasts such as Douhet and Seversky talked in terms of battering the enemy economy to pieces – with 100 lb bombs. After the British found it impossible to attack specialized industries, they concentrated on bombing cities – partly in retribution for the Luftwaffe's terror bombing of London and major English cities, partly for lack of a better strategy. Air Chief Marshal Harris of Bomber Command thought the war could be won by bombing alone – all hammer and no anvil. It was not clear what the American Air Force thought, if anything concrete. It had a deep technical interest in the airplanes. Many of the leading Air Force generals had participated in such technical triumphs as the twenty-eight-day flight of the *I'm Alone* in California through refueling. Military and air attachés had gathered a certain amount of material in the files on potential targets. The effort was piecemeal and sporadic.

When the Joint Chiefs of Staff called for a plan of bombing attack, A-2 (Intelligence) of the US AF turned to OSS, and we tried to patch something together. It was amateurish, though not to the extent that a pure A-2 effort would have been.

And then in February 1943 I set sail for London to relieve Chandler Morse as the head of EOU. The original intention was that we would alternate, six months on, six months back in Washington. That failed to work out. I am unable to repress mention of that trip, in a six-knot convoy, twenty-two days from New York to Cardiff in February gales, with four locomotives aboard as deck cargo, threatening to break loose in the storms and sweep away the ship's superstructure and her fifteen passengers. For three weeks I sat at a table for four with the second mate, who wolfed his food noisily; a lady's maid from the British delegation in Washington, returning to England to join up; and a Polish medical army major, who had escaped Europe to Latin America, was joining a Polish unit in England, and spoke virtually no English. In one painful conversation I asked him, a neurologist, what army medicine was like compared to his peacetime practice: "Is not int'resting: no tumors." He was, however, an excellent bridge player, and he and I, plus two British accountants who had been in Canada setting up books for the Commonwealth Pilot Training Scheme, played incessantly. One of the youngest passengers was a French boy, Jacques Kaplan

OSS, Washington

of the furrier family in New York and Paris, signing up for his military duty.

I finally got to London, and moved into an apartment at 50 Great Cumberland Place with Barney, Eddie Mayer, Bill Salant, and for a day or two Chan Morse. Our landlady was the nice Mrs Burden who also did for us. We were entitled as civilians to full rations, but since we ate lunch and dinner near our work, first in restaurants and later in the army officers' mess, we ate our whole meat ration – bacon, sausage, chops, and steak – at breakfast. Outrageous.

13

Enemy Objectives Unit, London: strategic targets

Enemy Objectives Unit (EOU) was housed at 40 Berkeley Square in the West End of London, at an angle across the square from Lansdowne House, which was occupied by the British Ministry of Economic Warfare (MEW) and the target sections of Air Ministry Intelligence, with the uncommunicative designation of AI 3 (c) i. The head of MEW was Mark (later Sir Mark) Turner, and my opposite number was a serious economist who had earlier worked for the large department store Marks and Spencer – Oliver Lawrence, capable, hard-working, but curiously sunk without a trace as far as I have been concerned, after the war. We dealt to some extent with other branches of AI, located, at least some of them, in reinforced concrete underground structures behind Victoria Station. AI 3 (c) i was headed by Wing Commander (later Group Captain) Charles Verity, a workaholic who slept in his office and was said to have dined with his wife at home at most twice a year though they lived within commuting distance.

For a start, EOU had already begun to produce a theory of bombing before I arrived, had studied individual plants, mostly from AI 3 (c) i aerial photographs, and had begun to draw up separate industries into target "systems." The theory had a dual nature. In the short run, a modern industrial economy was a complex network of connected industries, with, for example, steel needed to produce coal, and coal needed to produce steel. After the war, this insight, which we reached intuitively and without producing tables, came to be known as "input–output theory," and gained a Nobel prize for Wassily Leontief, then of Harvard University. In the longer run, however, everything can be reduced to manpower. To have an impact on the fighting front, a bombing attack on an industrial target must take into account its "depth," that is, how near or far its output is from use in military operations, and whether the industry has reserves or inventories which can fill a gap while factories are being required, new factories built or substitutes found. Such inventories or capacity to compress depth we called a "cushion." It will use up manpower to damage an industry that lies deep behind the battle, but if manpower is available, from any source – the home front, prisoners-of-war, or labor drafted in occupied countries – it may not affect the enemy's fighting capacity. These sorts of considerations relate to branches of economics now known as capital theory.

All sorts of theories of bombing were floated. A number of people thought it would be worthwhile to attack the few plants in Germany making grinding wheels for polishing metal, mostly of carborundum. The idea was that grinding wheels necessary to make machinery are fragile and would shatter under attack, and they would also be difficult to transport over distances. Another theory expressed after the war by the US Strategic Bombing Survey, headed by George W. Ball and J. Kenneth Galbraith, was that the US Air Force should have attacked the electric-generating industry. But grinding wheels lay deep behind the fighting front, and most of the important armament plants had auxiliary electricity-generating stations that could serve as a cushion if the generating plants or switching stations could be knocked out from the air, which was doubtful. I was once reminded by James Schlesinger that I had told him early after the war that most industrialists recommended for attack in Germany their own industry, not from the selfish point of view that they wanted to eliminate post-war competition, but because self-esteem requires each of us to believe that our industry is of prime importance.

Our group was skeptical about the military value of area bombing achieved by crushing enemy morale. It proved true that bombing the home front was depressing to soldiers at the fighting front, unhappy about the involvement of their families in the hostilities, but the notion that a government could sue for peace to halt casualties among the civilian population seemed unlikely in the light of the British reaction to the blitz. Area bombing of German cities did cheer up the British, to be sure, a positive effect at home rather than a negative one abroad. I vividly recall the Lancasters and Wellingtons streaking over the evening London sky on May 31, 1943, in the first 1,000-plane raid against Cologne. The clever attack on the Dorpe and Möhne dams in the Ruhr used a spherical bomb made to spin forward at speed while still in the bomb bay so that on release it would bounce along on top of the water and leap across defending nets. Again it was a British morale-booster though it had little or no effect on the German economic war effort, as far as one could learn.

In the end, we recommended ball-bearings and aircraft. These proved to be right for the wrong reasons, as so often happens in life. German aircraft production never actually declined, despite repeated attack, and actually kept rising, but the Germans used their fighter aircraft to defend against the attack on this system, and used up their scarcer resource, pilots, to such an extent that they were unable to mount a serious air defense when the invasion took place in June 1944. Ball-bearings proved to be too deep and to have too much cushion. The Germans redesigned a number of items of equipment – aircraft, tanks, and trucks – to eliminate the need for ball-bearings and accept more wear on engines. Instead of maintaining the normal inventory of ball-bearings on assembly lines, they used salesmen, unneeded in wartime, to hand-carry bearings from plants such as those in Berlin and Schweinfurt to points where they were used and assemble them into equipment at the latest possible moment rather than at the most efficient moment from an assembly-line viewpoint. Moreover depth had to be measured against the time needed for the strategic bombers to recover from a punishing raid on such targets as Berlin or Schweinfurt in order to mount another attack on the same industry.

First, however, we had to win our spurs. This was done when we found out British air intelligence in a mistake. The British at this time were relying heavily on Ultra, from which our small civilian group was excluded. Ultra was the code word for the intelligence produced by breaking German ciphers for radio traffic, a feat made possible by the capture by Polish intelligence of an encoding machine, plus the brilliant work of British mathematicians. It was necessary to keep access to this intelligence limited in the extreme, and even to refuse to take defensive action in response to known German planned attacks, so as not to reveal the secret to the enemy. With this superb source, British officers sometimes tended to become lazy. Without it, our group had to use every possible source of information, including digging through the mountains of photostats produced by Polish intelligence (with workers spread throughout the German economy), aerial photography, prisoner-of-war interrogation, etc. Instead of passively examining the flow that came across our desks, we pushed. Polish intelligence suggested that the Focke–Wulf plant in Bremen, an accessible target of no deep penetration, had been transferred to Marienburg in East Prussia, several hundred miles further from the center of USSTAAF airbases in Mildenhall, Cambridgeshire. We asked prisoner-of-war interrogators to winnow through the thousands of prisoners arriving in Scotland from Rommel's army in North Africa, to find men who had worked in the factory in Bremen. There were a number such, but the prisoner-of-war unit involved made the mistake of bringing them down to London together, enabling them to determine why they had been selected out and to resolve to clam up. We called on Flight Officer Constance Babington-Smith of the British Women's Auxiliary Air Force (WAAF), who worked on the German aircraft industry for the Central (Photographic) Interpretation Unit at Medmenham, outside London, to analyze Focke–Wulf, Bremen, comparatively, over a period of years.

EOU, London: strategic targets

The Air Ministry, as she recalls in her book *Air Spy* (New York, 1957), had estimated that Bremen was producing eighty FW-190s a month when the US Air Force attacked it in April 1943, with a loss of ten B-17s and one hundred crew members. But comparative cover undertaken in May showed not nearly enough activity to support that estimate, and some planes photographed on the tarmac outside hangers had not even been moved in recent pictures. New reconnaissance was undertaken by the high-flying British Mosquito of Posen, Cottbus, Sorau, and Marienburg, and showed Marienburg, former Luftwaffe base, to have been adapted for fighter assembly. To clinch the matter, I went to check with Squadron Leader D. Allom in AI (2), as I recall the designation, who tried to persuade me that the FW-190s were still being made at Bremen. From shot-down German planes, Air Intelligence gathered name-plates of components and other material of interest, and collected the smaller items in a bag for each plane. From one FW-190 there was a compass-correction card, printed with spaces to fill in the deviation for each of the perhaps thirty degrees of the azimuth. Across the top were printed the words "Focke–Wulf Bremen." Allom handed me the card, and I happened to turn it over: there, written by hand, was "Focke-Wulf, Marienburg." The Air Ministry conceded. It was worked out that to protect EOU from flagrant error for lack of Ultra (which we, not knowing the name, but conscious of the existence of some source from which we were excluded, called "hokey-pokey"), Rostow would be seconded to Air Ministry intelligence in Victoria, initiated into the sacred mysteries, and would keep in touch with us evenings and weekends.

The detritus from shot-down German aircraft was used in another way and at another place, when EOU organized parties of our group on weekends at an RAF depot, to wash German ball-bearings in gasoline to get the oil off, and take down the information on them of company, date, serial number, and the like, in an effort to estimate ball-bearing production by different plants. Not every ball-bearing contained all the possible information, but it may be said as a matter of general policy that such information is often needed for efficient production despite the risk that it may be useful in some fashion to the enemy.

A similar story in the opposite direction turned up when I was in Twelfth Army Group. A counter-intelligence officer on the staff was shocked to learn that a laundry-service unit had been broadcasting in the clear to its operating companies where to pick up laundry by unit designation, thus providing the American order of battle to anyone who chose to listen, including the Wehrmacht. But the units had to know where to go for the dirty linen.

The concept was initiated, I believe, by Walt Rostow, but we recruited, for pushing it further, a young Russian who had grown up in Berlin and was then working as a clerk in the US consular offices or embassy, Oleg Hoeffding. In due course the so-called "numbers game" grew into a large-scale intelligence operation, with special equipment, for example, built for photographing numbers inside stalled German tanks. Among the OSS economists who brought the technique to its flowering were two later Yale economics professors, Richard Ruggles and William N. Parker. These economists are unaccountably not mentioned in Yale professor Robin Winks's book about Yale's role in OSS, *Cloak and Gown* (New York, 1987), a book calculated to irritate Harvard alumni by exaggerating the Yale role.

It was still necessary to plow through mountains of Polish and French intelligence, prisoner-of-war interrogations, and aerial photograph interpretation reports, and the task kept us going nights and weekends. There was an occasional rich haul: late one evening, anxious to get home through the blackout to 50 Great Cumberland Place and bed, I had glanced at a Polish photostat of a German plant report and tossed it aside, only to have my subconscious prod me and say, try that again. It was a discussion of the production and delivery schedule of a component called a *Steuerknupfel*, the steering coupling for the joystick of a Focke–Wulf 190. From the schedule of deliveries to specified assembly plants, one could tell the scale of planned production of complete Focke–Wulf 190 aircraft at those plants – minus whatever small proportion of deliveries was for repair work. If one processes enough hay, one can find a few needles.

Another triumph was that of the workers at a French aircraft plant, perhaps at Villacoublay outside Paris, who sent the intelligence community, including EOU, a schedule of completion of the Dornier 200 flying boats on which they were working for the Germans. The vertical axis showed the percentage of boats completed, the horizontal showed the number of days to completion. Four or five boats had been started in the five or so months, but none had yet been completed. The graph would go up for a few weeks, and then sideways, occasionally down a bit, but never hit 100 percent. It was photostated in 8 × 11 sheets that were pieced together horizontally and in all measured some 20 feet. One could share the pride that led French intelligence at some risk of life and limb to smuggle out of occupied Paris this testimony to the workers' ca'canny.

In the fall of 1943 I was called to Washington, for consultation, but only for a week (with another week of blessed leave), commissioned a captain, and returned to London, this time in the bomb bay of a British B-24, unheated except for a small stream of hot air that sped along the overhead and landed in the tail where the old-timers had lodged themselves. Our quarters at 40 Berkeley Square had been enlarged in my absence by breaking a stairway in to the apartment above. Upon arrival there was a large sign, "Welcome to Captain's Folly."

My memory of the rest of 1943 is a little clouded. EOU had branched into bomb-damage assessment, establishing in Princes Risborough economists, notably Charles Hitch, later president of the University of California and subsequently president of Resources for the Future, Inc., the natural-resources think-tank in Washington; and architects, notably Marc Peter of the Office of Scientific Research and Development. I recall interviewing a fire expert, who had come to help with the assessment of fire damage to German cities, one Horatio Bond, an MIT engineer and head fire expert of the National Board of Underwriters. He came in looking rather haggard, and said he had not slept well in the hotel because it was a firetrap. Looking about at the combustible material, he was virtually panic-stricken until after

EOU, London: strategic targets

several sleepless hours he finally realized that he had failed to allow for the high level of natural humidity in London. After that he relaxed and got some sleep.

Hitch had a few of us to his Rhodes scholarship college, Queens, in Oxford for Christmas. It is a rare Rhodes scholar who is asked to stay on as a don, and he was one. When the United States got into the war, he returned to the United States, met and married his Nancy in OSS, and after the war started to take up his old fellowship. But being an unmarried don at Oxford differs greatly from being a married one, with the pull of coming home for dinner rather than dining in Hall. Hitch tried to sell his electric blankets in Britain, rather than cart them home, but his friends were uninterested, *The Times* skeptical about his advertisement, and the British public unwilling to take steps to combat wet sheets.

One day in my office at 40 Berkeley Square I was discussing targets in Southern Europe with a young lieutenant who had finished his missions with the Fifteenth Air Force bombers, and had been transferred to target intelligence. A newly acquired young colleague, James Tyson, put his head around the door and recognized my visitor. "Moose," he said. "Fish," said Derek Banning, the visitor. I said, "You both must have gone to Kent." Such proved to have been the case, in the class of 1935, though I had not known of the affiliation in either instance. The school had a distinguished capacity for nicknames. Rat Moore was a member of the class of ca. 1925 and his younger brother, Mouse, of 1927, while Pig Appleton was a classmate of mine.

As the prospect of an invasion of the Continent drew nearer, EOU became more and more interested in the target system of oil. We were skeptical of the show-boat sort of raid, as that on Ploesti, where the loss could be readily absorbed in the civilian economy or even within the military. But oil as a system had all the attributes needed to support an invading army – a short distance behind the fighting front, that is, limited depth, limited inventories, and inefficient substitution through horses or gasogene trucks. The targets were deep inside Germany, but the development of the fighter-escort plane helped with that problem.

EOU, London: strategic targets

By a sort of serendipity, the two fighter aircraft developed by the US each proved wonderfully successful at the task assigned to the other. The P-47, with its radial air-cooled engine, was designed for high-altitude work but proved ideally suited to low-level fighting, able to sustain the loss of a cylinder or two in ground fire and keep on flying. The P-38, on the other hand, although designed for low-level fighting, was vulnerable to ground fire with its liquid-cooled engine, as it lost coolant and seized up, but a beautiful instrument for high-altitude bomber accompaniment after the development of the discardable wing-tanks.

By this time, Carl Kaysen had been added to our unit. He had been a civilian in the Industry Section of Research and Analysis Economics, and about to be drafted. Colonel Hughes had told us that if there were any bright economists being drafted that we wanted, we were to let him know and he would arrange a commission and a transfer. It proved impossible for him to arrange for Kaysen to finesse basic training in the Air Force, and he went through that trial in Atlantic city hotels. But Hughes did arrange for him then to be shipped to London – on the *Queen Mary*, three bunks from deck to overhead and three men to each bunk, sleeping in shifts, 18,000 men (if memory serves) as a whole. Kaysen chose not to use his bunk, and arrived in London somewhat bedraggled, scheduled to appear before a commissioning board before getting his second-lieutenant's bar. We had his uniform cleaned, rehearsed him in how to throw a snappy salute, gave a party (to which Rostow brought Dennis Brogan, who drank up almost all our one bottle of Scotch himself), and prayed that he would be ready for an officers' board on Monday. He was, and was commissioned.

In the winter of 1944, we began to think about tactical bombing, and how, in particular, to use the Air Force to help the ground forces effect a lodgment on the far shore.

14

Enemy Objectives Unit, London: tactical bombing

In the winter of 1983–4, Colonel Hughes dropped by 40 Berkeley Square one day and idly wondered aloud how the strategic bombers could best be used to assist the invasion. We agreed to think about it. First, we had to be cleared for a higher category of security than Top Secret, Bigot, which allowed us to know where the landing would be made. There was a still higher clearance to which we had no need to be admitted, that knew the date. Without that, one could still discuss timing in terms of D-day, ranging from D minus to D plus a number of days.

A week or so later, Hughes returned and said he had a plan. So did we. The two plans turned out to be broadly the same: to destroy the bridges along the Seine from Rouen to Paris, and others elsewhere so as not to disclose the landing area, and later along the Loire as far up from Nantes as the river was sizeable. Between the last Seine bridge with a long span outside Paris itself and the equivalent bridge upstream on the Loire, one would have to find other railroad structures that lent themselves to long-lasting destruction. Spans shorter than about 110 feet on a railroad or road bridge could be made passable with so-called Bailey bridges; longer ones took three weeks to repair. In the absence of bridges over wide rivers, one could interrupt rail traffic by destroying viaducts over a valley, and perhaps tunnels. Simple line cuts from a crater in the track whether from bombs or from *plastique* from the Resistance were not much good in isolation, as they could be repaired in about four hours. A series of craters was slightly better, because they had to be repaired seriatim, but not much. The real debate between the American and the British forces ultimately turned on the choice between attacking bridges to build a line of "interdiction" that would force German troops to detrain at railheads far from the battle, and to approach by road, exposed to fighter-bomber attack, or railway centers, called by the British marshalling yards, with their volume of standing railway cars, repair shops, roundhouses, watering stacks, coal stocks – in short, vital capital equipment, but many sets of tracks through the center which troop trains could be forced through. The British plan was developed especially by Solly (later Lord) Zuckerman, scientific adviser to Air Marshal Tedder, deputy commander of the Combined Allied Forces under General Dwight D. Eisenhower.

Zuckerman was originally a biologist who had worked with apes, and the first volume of his autobiography is entitled *From Apes to Warlord* (New York, 1978), the last being the code name for the invasion of France. He started in wartime in the Ministry of Home Security, working on defense against German bombing, and discovered by experimental research of various kinds that bombing did not kill human beings by blast, so much as by flying fragments. This result made it possible to build shelters for personnel in factories with two courses of light brick around chicken wire, to shield against fragments, instead of heavy concrete structures that would withstand blast. It was a notable accomplishment. In due course, as with so many other developments, what had been learned in defending Britain was turned around for use in attack. He went to North Africa with troops, and worked his way by stages to the post of scientific adviser to Tedder. One particular achievement was to calculate the weight of bombs necessary to force the surrender of the Italian island of Pantelleria. It happened that he was right for the wrong reason: the Italians surrendered after several thousand tons of bombs had been applied to their island, not because they were stunned into submission, but because one lucky hit cut their water supply and they were thirsty.

In the attack on Italy, Zuckerman found the evidence for his theory of the value of attacks on enemy marshalling yards. The experience did not strike us as capable of being generalized. The railroad yards at the port in question – Palermo – were at the end of a line, not a facility on a through-running line. Italian repairmen were not enthusiastic in repairing the yard for their German colleagues. And we later understood that Zuckerman disregarded some evidence of the success of destroying bridges when the fighting had moved to the Italian mainland and the Germans had to supply their troops on north–south lines. By this time EOU had supplied Bill Salant to the Fifteenth Air Force to help apply in the Italian theatre the lessons learned in England. We stayed in communication with him and checked through him on some of the Zuckerman claims. Zuckerman insisted that bridges were hard to hit, and that hitting them was not worthwhile.

I vividly remember one meeting on the subject, presided over by Air Chief Marshal Sir Trafford Leigh-Mallory, later commander of the Combined Tactical Air Forces in the invasion, with a formidable array of brass on the dais. Leigh-Mallory is another data point in one of my generalizations: that the airforce generals who began the Second World War were, with few exceptions, wonderful athletes who survived the heroic days of flying by instinctive kinesthetic responses to danger, but who would, if they had tried to think their way out of trouble, have augured in, as the expression went. As far as my observations went, Spaatz, Eaker, Vandenberg, but not Doolittle or Fred Anderson, were remarkable not for their thought processes so much as for their early flying ability. Fred Anderson, a two-star general, was on the row with four-star Leigh-Mallory and a galaxy of others. I was a mere captain, and had with me Second Lieutenant Kaysen. I told Kaysen that I was going to take my life in my hands and make the case for bridges, but if he tried to chime in informally I would kill him. As a civilian, Zuckerman had me at a total disadvantage. He had invited for the briefing a series of British railroad executives and engineers.

As so often happens in trial by combat, the outcome of the conflict is uncertain. I returned to the episode in an article in the British magazine *Encounter* (November 1978), taking exception to the things that Zuckerman had said about EOU in the first volume of his autobiography, called to my attention by William ("Bill") Casey who wrote a book on OSS. He replied in the issue of June 1979. We disagree. As I recall it, he asked the railroad men how they would like to have 2,000 tons of bombs dropped on their railroad yard, and they said they would hate it. Then I asked how long it would take them to get twenty troop trains through the yard after such an attack. They said, "Oh, a couple of hours." On that showing bombing marshalling yards is a great way to damage a railroad, but not especially effective in stopping railroad traffic for weeks at a time.

A similar failure to resolve the issue beyond doubt occurred later in the war in 1945. In the rapidly expanding net of German prisoners-of-war, there popped up in one report a mention of Colonel Höffner, who had been General des Transportswesen West, under Field-Marshal von Runstedt at the time of the invasion. I suggested to the head of the Ninth Air Force Prisoner-of-War Interrogation Unit, Colonel Eric Warburg – the Twelfth Army Group and the Ninth Air Force went around together so contact was easy – that we get hold of Höffner and ask *him* to resolve the question of whether bridge or railyard bombardment was the more effective in pushing the railheads far from the front. I vividly recall trying to frame the questions for Warburg to put to Höffner in as neutral a way as possible, so as not to "lead the witness." I may have failed. In the US interrogation as written up by Warburg and a captain journalist on his staff, interdiction of bridges gave them the more trouble. Later the British Air Ministry worked the poor man over again, and came out with a different answer: the marshalling yard attacks were more devastating.

Incidentally this sort of kibitzing after the game gives great pleasure. I asked Höffner why he had not relaid twelve miles of track in the gap between upstream Seine and upstream Loire, to provide another link from Germany and eastern France to Normandy. We had known that the track had been picked up on this little-used line, as other French double-tracks had been reduced to single-track status, to obtain scrap steel. Rather than repair a bridge, it would have made sense to relay the track as the structures were all intact. My unit had asked reconnaissance pilots to take low-oblique photographs of the line to try to detect whether new track had been laid, at some risk to the life and limb of the pilots. Höffner's answer was disarming: "That's a good idea; I never thought of it."

The debate over marshalling yards versus bridges went on through the early spring of 1944. It became partly entangled in the strategic issue of bombing oil plants, as the US Air Force partly argued that if it could restrict its operations to bridges, it would have substantial forces available for attacks on oil. I have observed, however, enough to formulate Kindleberger's Law of Alternatives, that when a sharp debate between alternative strategies is carried on for long, one often ends up doing both.

Two other examples are the debate in Britain in 1931 as to whether to devalue sterling or apply import tariffs; and in 1944–5 the question of whether financial reconstruction was better advanced by rebuilding the world monetary system all at once through the International Monetary Fund, or, following John Williams's key-currency advice, by reconstructing one currency at a time, using the British loan. In both cases, both strategies were pursued. For a time, the US Air Force had orders not to attack bridges. On May 8, 1944, a fighter-bomber squadron under a buck general whose name I have sadly forgotten, perhaps Smith, violated that order. Fourteen P-47s took off from southern England. Six aborted, but eight attacked the railroad bridge over the Seine at Vernon, and dropped it in the river. This demonstrable proof that it was possible to destroy a bridge may not have been the most scientific imaginable. It happened that this line from west to east across the Seine came to a dead end fairly rapidly, and could not have served east–west

EOU, London: tactical bombing

transport across the Seine for more than a few miles to the east. On that account it may not have been seriously defended. It was none the less a signal event.

This is not a scholarly account of an economist's life. For details on the period, I can refer the reader to W.W. Rostow's volume 1 in his series on Ideas and Action – mostly his ideas and the actions inspired by them – *Pre-Invasion Bombing Strategy: General Eisenhower's Decision of March 25, 1944* (Austin, TX, 1981) and to the chapter on EOU in Barrie Katz's *Foreign Intelligence* (Cambridge, MA, 1989). The latter goes into detail about the temporary break-up of EOU in the spring of 1944 to work underground on the bombing issue. Rostow was already assigned to the Air Ministry, and Kaysen was formally attached to the Ninth Air Force under General Hoyt Vandenberg, where he could come and go and give advice. Barnett managed to get himself transferred on temporary assignment to G-2, Supreme Headquarters, Allied Expeditionary Force (SHAEF), where his knowledge of matters strategic and tactical made him a key figure, if merely a first lieutenant. I went on detached service to the Tactical Air Command under Air Chief Marshal Sir Trafford Leigh-Mallory, working with a Canadian railroad-engineer major on the intelligence needed for the railroad and road attacks. We called it "Operation Octopus." It was striking how the various headquarters after a time were sounding the same notes. Barnett returned to EOU some time in the summer by means of an effective tactic. He had asked General Strong, the SHAEF G-2, if he could be released and was told he could not be, as he was too valuable. Thereafter for ten days or so, he refused to answer requests for information, even though he had it, telling the questioner rather who in the headquarters was responsible for the subject. At the end of the period when G-2 SHAEF had in effect been rewired and his telephone stopped ringing, he went back to the general and said he had done no business for three days, and hence was making no contribution. He was then released. In my own case, the headquarters was about to move to the far shore. The invasion was fairly solidly lodged by June 16. I wrote up an account of German troop

EOU, London: tactical bombing

movements to the battle by rail and road – published, as it happens, as Appendix F in Rostow's *Pre-Invasion Bombing Strategy* – and returned from Strathmore in the suburbs to London. At this time I had moved into a house taken by Chandler Morse, then in charge of Research and Analysis, London, along with OSS political colleagues Paul Sweezy, Arthur Schlesinger Jr, and Just Lunning. I did not stay long. An opportunity came to move with the field army to France. It was cowardly perhaps to leave London under siege of V-1 rockets and V-2 flying bombs. I none the less left.

15

G-2, Twelfth Army Group

Like Hughes, Colonel William Jackson, peacetime lawyer, member of G-2, Twelfth Army Group, Omar N. Bradley, commanding, was uneasy if he felt that there were things he did not know about that others did. He went to OSS (I guess), heard about our work in connection with the invasion, and asked me to transfer to the G-2 section where he was second in command under General Edwin Sibert, a West Point graduate. Jackson had been a member of the New York firm of Carter, Ledyard, and Milburn, and had temporarily filled in as president of the New York Stock Exchange in a time of turmoil. After the war he teamed up with General Donovan in intelligence and the early CIA. He was a bright, engaging man, a college athlete though small. I failed to maintain contact with him after the war, but have gathered that he had troubles of various kinds that cut off what I would have anticipated to be a brilliant career.

Others in the section were Alexander Standish, a financial Bostonian, William Weaver, later president of a metals company, Lyman Kirkpatrick, high up in the CIA after the war until he contracted polio, the young Gordon Gray, later secretary of defense and president of the University of North Carolina, and Constantine Fitzgibbon, the Irish novelist and critic. In due course when I needed help, OSS provided me with Robert V.

Twelfth Army Group

Roosa, later undersecretary of the Treasury before going to Brown Brothers Harriman.

My charge was intelligence on enemy supply and transport, and specifically to make recommendations to the Ninth Air Force, the tactical unit with medium bombers assigned to Twelfth Army Group, as to how that air force could assist the ground troops.

We spent a couple of days under canvas near Southampton where I almost lost my mind as a result of the group in the next tent playing a record by the Mills Brothers, "Paper Doll," twenty-five to fifty times a day. It's a good piece, which I have recently heard performed by the depleted quartet in Boston Pops, but in 1944 diminishing returns set in early and turned negative. On a day in early July we embarked for the far shore in a passenger vessel, later going over the side in nets to landing craft, and finally walking on the beach through the waves. Without enemy fire it was like play-acting. When we were five miles off, Lieutenant-Colonel Saussy, a Georgia country fellow in order-of-battle intelligence, said, "So that's France, eh? I don't like it."

The headquarters moved down the west coast of the Cotentin peninsula. It was realized that I should be included among the few members of the section who were cleared for Ultra, and General Sibert initiated me into its mysteries. Soon Twelfth Army Group divided in two, a tactical headquarters ("Eagle Tac"), and the main headquarters. Since I could not be in two places at once, I was told to get another economist officer from OSS London. There seemed to be no one but an excellent sergeant, I was told. I said it would not do, I needed an officer. They could not oblige so they sent me the sergeant, Robert V. Roosa, a Harvard economics PhD and student of John Williams. I briefed him at main headquarters for a day, went forward, and returned in several days, curious as to how he made out. As I arrived I came upon two colonels talking, Colonel Masson of air reconnaissance being the only one I remember. One was saying, "I don't know the answer to that question, and you don't know it, but that is what Kindleberger's sergeant says, so it must be right." Rank did not matter, though we finally managed to get Roosa a commission.

Teaching the tricks of the trade to other economists was easy. Another of our pupils was Peter L. Bernstein, today the owner of a financial consulting service and editor of the *Journal of Portfolio Management*, then another Harvard PhD (1940). He worked with us for a week or two at some point and then was shipped to General Dever's Sixth Army Group advancing northward through France from the Mediterranean. In lateral communication it helped that we understood one another.

Then came Patton's breakthrough, following the success of the cover plan that led the Germans to think Patton's army was scheduled to invade on the Pas de Calais, on the eastern side of the Seine. (It may be noticed that the interdiction of the Seine bridges, designed to impede the lateral movement of the German ground forces, fitted brilliantly into the cover plan, of which at the time, EOU had no knowledge.) Air power had only a limited role as Hitler insisted on his armies counterattacking against the neck of the allied penetration between Avranches and the Brittany peninsula. Patton wheeled east, as the dug-in infantry held the counterattack, and went on to the Argentan–Falaise gap to bag the German armies. But Montgomery had trouble advancing first to, and then from, Falaise, and the majority of troops escaped.

Two episodes from this time stand out in my memory, although I cannot date them exactly. On one occasion, there was a small briefing of staff cleared for Ultra, Bradley, perhaps his chief of staff, General Allen, Sibert, Jackson, perhaps Weaver and me, attended by General Eisenhower. Each of the specialists briefed the two top generals, and then General Bradley summarized his view of the battle. Exactly what he said I cannot reproduce, but it was brilliant. And I was struck that every comment made by General Eisenhower seemed rather banal, the sort of thing that I could easily have said to keep the conversation going. It was easy to see that Eisenhower was the diplomat, Bradley the soldier.

Another indication at about this time – I don't recall that it

Twelfth Army Group

was on the same occasion – related to the German retreat. In another restricted briefing, I stated that the Germans were still supplying their retreating armies, not by road, not by rail, but by barge. I urged that troops reach the Seine and cut off this supply line. The idea appealed to General Bradley, he said he would order it, and then added a remark which showed his tactical genius. "And I'll ask — to put a regimental combat team across the river as a feint, to make the Germans think we are crossing there, north of Paris." A small landing was made on the east side of the Seine and drew an immediate agitated response from the Wehrmacht.

Twelfth Army Group was not always in full accord with decisions at the SHAEF level. One such time came later in the Ardennes when Eisenhower turned over some of the First Army's troops from Bradley to Montgomery. Another came in August 1944 when Eisenhower divided the scarce gasoline between Montgomery and Bradley (read Patton whose army was circling Paris to the south) instead of giving it all to one or the other. This is what my fellow economists thought of as a lawyer-like decision, instead of the more effective economic solution.

About this time at the end of August I had to go to London to get the broad picture for G-2. The armies were stuck. Our headquarters were, or were about to be, in a field west of Chartres, with the spire of the cathedral on the horizon, but the stained glass removed and the porches encased in sandbags. While in London, I saw Hughes. He asked what the air forces could do now. We agreed that the greatest contribution they could make to the war was not to bomb bridges or marshalling yards which the Allies might need shortly, but to carry gasoline. Hughes and I saw General Fred Anderson, who agreed. They went to see Spaatz. Spaatz did not like the notion of the air forces serving as handmaidens to the ground forces, but reluctantly agreed, adding however, that he wanted a request direct from General Bradley to himself, not some routine request from a Twelfth Army Group G-4 (for supplies) to the USSTAF A-3 (for operations). When I relayed this message to Generals Sibert and Bradley the next day, Bradley was irritated that Spaatz made such a big thing of formal channels. In the event, I understood that the B-17s and B-24s did not carry much gasoline because the B-17 bomb bays could not accommodate many jerry cans, and the B-24 needed long runways not available on the forward airfields.

Returning to France from London, I asked Rosalene Honerkamp, the superb EOU secretary whom I had inherited from Ed Mason and Chan Morse, to get me a plane to Chartres. I ended up with one to Cherbourg. There I tried to get in touch with Eagle Tac, but could not get through on the field-wire telephone. So at 5:45 on a beautiful evening I started to hitchhike. In my city uniform, carrying a valet pack, I had rides in jeeps, weapons carriers, ammunition trucks, scout cars, reconnaissance cars, a car patrolling the oil pipeline (actually a canvas firehose) to prevent the French peasants from stabbing it with ice picks and collecting a pot full of fuel, and finally the Red Ball Express, a one-way major road for supplies for the front, made up of 6 × 6 trucks, with a lieutenant in a jeep as their sheep-dog. The problem in the dark with narrow slits for headlights, was that a local army truck might work its way into the line at some village, then turn off, and bring a lot of the convoy away with it before the lieutenant in the jeep could catch up. I got aboard a truck in one convoy at a major rendezvous about 9:45, rode until 5:45 a.m. to a town near Chartres, and got two more rides to make it to headquarters – all in all about 150 miles in thirteen hours.

As an officer, I was required to censor enlisted men's mail. One day General Sibert turned his L-5 (Piper Cub) airplane over to his sergeant for a visit to Paris after its capture. The rest of the headquarters had all been there. The non-commissioned pilot on the way back told Sergeant Cohen that his father had been in the Lafayette Esquadrille in the First World War and had flown a plane under the legs of the Eiffel Tower. Cohen said, "Very interesting." And the pilot then said, "And that's what I am going to do now." "No time, no time, I have to get back to help General Sibert." "Tough luck, old buddy." And they did fly under the Eiffel Tower, or so Sergeant Cohen tried to tell his family before

Twelfth Army Group

I crossed it all out as revealing the location of the unit.

Flying in these L-5 taxis at 2,000 feet or so around France was a delight. In the first place, one could do a little aerial archaeology, particularly tracing the scars of trenches from the First World War, not visible on the surface but clearly outlined from the air because of the discoloration of the soil. Second, one could see in the farms, geese or ducks parading in barnyards that were hidden from a jeep on the road. The young taxi-driver pilots enjoyed their gallivanting about. I recall an occasion when I wanted to go from Verdun to Rheims, and gave it something of a French pronunciation. The pilot thought I was headed for Rennes, halfway across France and was downcast when I finally got through to him that it was only a short hop.

From Chartres we moved to a place in the Marne, where my major impression was how different French peasants are from Americans in planting a crop of trees for harvesting by their grandchildren as they harvest trees planted by their own grandfathers. Then to Verdun, notable for an issue of Noilly Prat and real gin, and finally for 1944 to Luxembourg. The war had slowed down. It was cold and wet. The American armies were getting trench feet because of an inadequate supply of L.L. Bean-type rubber-footed boots called shoe-paks. The Allies were preparing for an attack just south of Cologne, where, it was thought, the Germans were assembling troops to defend.

One saw a lot of General Patton at Bradley's headquarters in those days, and I, for one, was put off. He would put his arm over Bradley's shoulders as they sat at a briefing, and Bradley would back away. Once General Sibert showed him a model of the Ardennes in relief that Lieutenant-Colonel Ingersoll (not Ralph Ingersoll, who was also in the headquarters in some secret-operations capacity, but Harold Ingersoll, a Department of the Interior engineer) had built. Patton threw it an imperious glance and said arrogantly, "Pay no attention to three-dimensional models of terrain. War has always been fought on roads. Except for a short time between 1485 and 1520 [dates arbitrarily from me], armies have always proceeded along roads.

All you need is a road map." And he turned away abruptly in a manner insulting to both Ingersoll, who was there, and General Sibert.

I may perhaps recall a briefing gaffe of my own at Ninth Air Force Headquarters, though this I judge was later in the spring of 1945 after the armies had broken loose again and Hitler was calling on old and young Germans to organize into the *Volksturm* to resist Allied armies. We had returned to Luxembourg for a time after retreating in the December Ardennes offensive to Namur in Belgium. I suggested that a good target for the medium-bombers of the Ninth Air Force were the factories in the Schwartzwald (Black Forest) producing rifles and machine guns, because the enemy had a long way to go to equip the *Volksturm*. I was trying to say that there was a small-arms shortage, but the ghost of Spooner, of Spoonerism fame, got to me, and it came out "short-arm smallage." It brought the house down.

In November or early December 1944 I got a call to go to Paris to be interviewed by Charles Murphy, a writer for *Fortune* magazine, who was doing a piece on the air war which was to include a passage on EOU. *En route* back to Luxembourg, I was asked to take a letter from General Eisenhower to General Bradley. We flew at night in fog and rain, and in overshooting the battle lines, were shot at by flak, my only experience with enemy fire. The pilot took evasive action. The several officers who were not wearing seatbelts bounced around the cabin, off one wall and on to another. It occurred to me that it was my duty to eat the letter before getting shot down in enemy territory, and I even went so far, I think, as to put one corner in my mouth. But my mouth was too dry. And presently, we had gotten back over our side of the line and all was serene. When the article came out, all mention of EOU had been deleted except for one dangling reference to Irwin Nat Pincus of BEW, who had taken over from me.

The Ardennes offensive of December 16 caught G-2, Twelfth Army Group, completely by surprise. We fell for the German cover plan, the Germans taking a page out of the book of the previous May–June, when the Allies feigned an attack by

Twelfth Army Group

Patton on the Pas de Calais. Looking back on it in the days after the attack, I could recall one or two, perhaps two or three messages on Ultra that should have alerted us to the attack. This traffic was limited, however, as the Germans were back in their own territory and used land-lines for the most part instead of radio that Ultra could intercept and decode. One message called for a German night reconnaissance over the Ardennes, but that could have been and probably was interpreted as looking for evidence of an Allied attack. We were not the only ones fooled. Bill Williams, the cocky young intelligence brigadier on Montgomery's staff, came out at the time with a statement that the enemy's power of attack had evaporated. The G-2 of the First Army, on Bradley's left flank, claimed that he had called the turn, but this was pointing to a possibility evidently judged to be remote. Army Intelligence School made a big point of training intelligence officers to think about capabilities instead of intentions. A great number of intelligence estimates thus were filled out with statements such as: "The enemy has the capability of retreating/surrendering/attacking/digging in." To point after the attack to the third item and claim to have predicted the attack was too much.

Bill Williams, a historian, and later the editor of the British *Dictionary of National Biography* as well as warden of Rhodes House in Oxford, which administered the Rhodes scholarships, was Montgomery's GSI (general staff chief of intelligence) in the desert at the age of twenty-one, and very bright indeed. But the successes of the Eighth Army against Rommel in North Africa have given Field-Marshal Montgomery and his staff too much credit. With Ultra, they were looking over Rommel's shoulder the whole time, reading his dispatches. A biography of the Field-Marshal written before the existence of Ultra had been made public would be very different from one written with the Ultra records on hand. The Eighth Army staff officers sent to London for Overlord aroused a great deal of irritation, with their disdain for those from the United States who had not been tested in battle. But the "Sandy boys," as they were known, never revealed – as of course they could not – that they won all their finesses by peeking.

Twelfth Army Group

It was hard to devise a suitable air defense against the Ardennes attack in midwinter, with long hours of darkness, bad weather, and few constrictions in the road network. We piled thousands of tons of bombs on a tiny town, Houfalize, at the bottom of a ravine with roads leading down one side and up another. But the enemy lack of gasoline was beginning to bite, the result of the strategic attack on oil. Trucks were driven into battle with gasogene, and horses pulled some light artillery pieces. For the success of their offensive the Germans counted on capturing allied POL dumps (petroleum, oil, and lubricants). I recall having estimated that the offensive had run out of gas, literally and figuratively, by December 26, ten days after it started. I fear I could not convince my colleagues, especially General Sibert and Colonel Standish, and they were still preparing estimates warning of the sting of German attack two or three weeks later in the middle of January.

The days from the 16th to Christmas were stirring ones in Luxembourg as the Third Army, which had been deployed well to the south, made its way through town to the north. One had to be careful crossing the main street as tanks and trucks would roll through at forty to fifty miles an hour on their way to the battle to the north. These were the days of McCauliffe, called on by the Germans at Bastogne to surrender, replying "Nuts." I have given some thought to what might have been a better reply as judged by a rhetorician, but have gotten nowhere. I assume that General McCauliffe considered and rejected some less cultivated one- or two-word responses. I suspect that "Nuts" will not survive along with "Don't give up the ship;" "Don't cheer men, can't you see the poor lads are dying;" or "Kiss me, Hardy."

General Eisenhower infuriated Twelfth Army Group by detaching the First Army from Bradley's command, giving it to Field-Marshal Montgomery, and moving Twelfth Army Group headquarters from the forward position eight miles from the battle back to Namur in Belgium. We rode to Namur in jeeps and had a chance to see the countryside in winter. As an economist, I was especially interested in sugar-beet culture: the vegetables, which looked like oversize turnips, were stored in wide, shallow trenches under black plastic sheets held down with old automobile tires: occasionally a wagon-load was dug up and driven to the extraction plant, where the farmer waited with his wagon and brought back a load of whitish pulp as cattle feed. Unfortunately I made the mistake of writing about all this to my wife. She did not share my interest and would have welcomed a more personal level of discourse. For over forty-four years now she has referred disdainfully to any letter containing an economic description as a "sugar-beet letter." In sorting out the letters home written during the war, I could not find the one that described sugar beets and their culture, and can only conclude that she tore it up in a fit of pique.

One insight about work was gained from an inspiration: to ask our prisoner-of-war interrogators to prepare a memorandum on how the German armies got to the Ardennes battle by rail – where the various divisions entrained, and the routes by which they moved to the detraining sites. The interrogators loved a creative task like that. They were used to asking questions according to a manual they had ingested in training school, and to break away from it was money for jam. They still had to get order-of-battle information; they would do this typically by asking the prisoners to fall in by unit, which they generally did despite their instructions to give out nothing but their name, rank and serial number. With many prisoners one had to eliminate those unlikely to have any information, as well as the genuine Nazis. The first task was accomplished by calling for all farmers, peasants, farm workers, etc., to go over to one side. These, it was said, did not know anything much – unlike North American farmers who were wonderfully skilled at working machinery – and could be repenned. The acid test for Nazis was to have the remaining troops come one by one at a distance from the rest, and ask them whether the Germans were going to win the war. Most ordinary soldiers shrugged their shoulders, looked sheepish, and were graded non-Nazi. Anyone that bristled, snarled, bared a fang, was directed to a holding stockade for Nazis. It was good to get the railroad information at the time. What remains to this day is the memory of the creative pleasure the young German-speaker Americans took in being given a task that was new, and in which they knew the information would be useful, rather than filed away in a pro forma manner.

The Ardennes was the Germans' last gasp, and the war wound down. Twelfth Army Group returned to Luxembourg, and then moved, after Patton had jumped the Rhine, to Wiesbaden. While we were still in Luxembourg, we got a request from London to check on a factory outside Frankfurt making parts for the V-1 or the V-2. Captain Milton Schloss of the Ninth Air Force and I drove down in a jeep with driver, helped a squad capture the plant and interrogated the management. I have published a letter describing the incident in a collection primarily about post-war reconstruction of Germany and Austria (*The German Economy, 1945–1947: Charles P. Kindleberger's Letters from the Field*, Westport, CT, 1989) and need not repeat it here, except to say perhaps that it was the only time I took my pistol out of its holster until I turned it in after the war, and I felt somewhat foolish in uniform with a pistol in my right hand and a briefcase in the left.

On one occasion, a school friend, Maitland Edey, who had worked for *Life* magazine and was then working on the air-force equivalent, stopped by in Luxembourg. He told me he had been impressed at seeing American airmen, who had been interned in Switzerland after parachuting there from crippled planes that had been hit over Germany, being transferred from Swiss to army trains in Geneva. Many were on stretchers, their legs splinted and bandaged. He asked whether they had broken their limbs as they landed in the mountains. The answer was no, they broke them skiing at Davos. The Swiss had lots of idle hotel space in Davos. As a neutral country they limited the number of airmen they allowed to "escape" each month. They reported, however, that at the height of the skiing season in February and March, those on the roster for escaping at the time could not always be found when required.

Colonel Hughes, with an understandable urge to get nearer to the action, transferred from USSTAF to the Ninth Air Force. In the middle of April 1945 he suggested that we explore a bit, perhaps capture and liberate a lot of gold, silver, and platinum said to be used in a German chemical plant in the Harz mountains, and visit a concentration camp. We visited the chemical plant, emerged empty-handed, and went on to see the concentration camp at Nordhausen and the underground factory associated with it at Ohrdruf. The sight was moving and appalling. There is a letter to my wife describing the trip in *The German Economy* so I will not reproduce the description here.

In Wiesbaden, my upbringing as the son of a lawyer gave me a twinge as I saw the Ninth Air Force move into the town hall, and throw room after room of deeds out into the courtyard to be burned to give the airmen clerks a little more room. The prospect was of endless litigation over land titles and a bonanza for lawyers. One morning, coming into the officers' mess at breakfast, I saw Colonel Eric Warburg seated at a table with a young French lieutenant. I joined them, and learned that the young man was named Rothschild, and that he had just been released from a German prison camp after five years, having been captured in 1940. Rather aggressively because of curiosity, I asked him how he liked Germans. He thought for a second and said, "Not at all, they follow orders too literally. They may be good fathers, music-lovers and have other admirable attributes, but if they are ordered to shoot a prisoner who comes within a meter of the barbed-wire perimeter of the Stalag, they do so even at 99 centimeters."

In Wiesbaden I picked up another story of a prisoner-of-war that was more uplifting. The USSTAF A-2 for intelligence was a general whose name I have forgotten. He had been an air attaché in Berlin before the war and was therefore known to the high command of the Luftwaffe. Like all officers who had been admitted to Ultra security he was forbidden to fly over Germany. Nevertheless, on one occasion he did. The B-17 Flying Fortress was hit and caught fire. The pilot ordered preparation for bailing out. The general bailed out, unnecessarily as it happened, because the fire was brought under control and the plane made it back to its base in East Anglia. Very embarrassing for a general caught disobeying orders. The general redeemed himself in my eyes, however, if the story be true, by one remark. As the senior officer in a *Luftlag* (prisoner-of-war camp for airmen), the general led the march of the camp when it was moved west by the Germans ahead of advancing Russian troops. At some point, the parade passed a German unit from which an officer emerged and asked, "General, would you like a cup of coffee?" The reply was: "If you have 20,000 cups of coffee, I would love one."

After some weeks at Wiesbaden, the Twelfth Army Group advanced headquarters moved up the valley to Kassel. I prepared to return home, have a long vacation, and in due course go to work in the Department of State to backstop the German Reparations Commission scheduled to go to Moscow and the economic side of the American delegation to Potsdam.

Touching down in Dusseldorf *en route* from Frankfurt airbase to London whence to Prestwick and New York, I saw a young aviator get into the bucket-seat C-47 with an elongated bed-roll. Someone he knew asked, "What the hell have you got there?" The answer was the telescope from the pocket battleship, the *Admiral Hipper*. The young flier had completed his missions, was on some kind of service in Germany, and had spent two days in Bremen, Kiel, or some other naval yard, filing through the brass fitting to liberate the six-foot telescope.

I spent two days waiting at Prestwick for a flight home. It gave me a chance to visit Robbie Burns's birthplace in Ayr and to inspect a lot of Ayrshire cattle, items of interest that had not been high on my list of priorities. I got back to Washington on June 12, having left Wiesbaden on the 5th.

Emile Despres said I could have a week off, but that it was then vital that I come to the State Department to prepare to backstop the economists on the American delegation going to Potsdam to work on the German question after the surrender. I protested with some heat but to no avail. While there wasn't a war on (in Europe that is), there was an emergency.

16

Office of Finance and Development, Department of State
Summer and early fall 1945

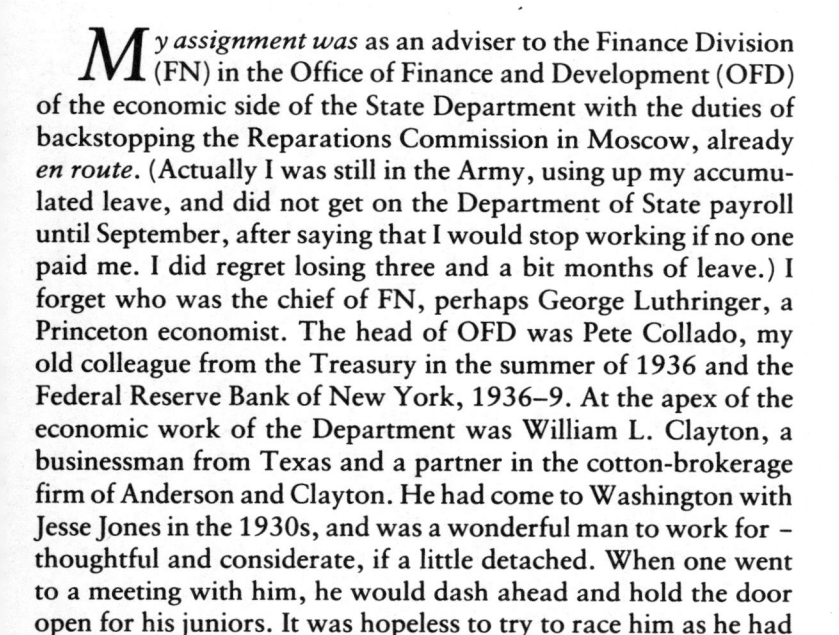

My assignment was as an adviser to the Finance Division (FN) in the Office of Finance and Development (OFD) of the economic side of the State Department with the duties of backstopping the Reparations Commission in Moscow, already *en route*. (Actually I was still in the Army, using up my accumulated leave, and did not get on the Department of State payroll until September, after saying that I would stop working if no one paid me. I did regret losing three and a bit months of leave.) I forget who was the chief of FN, perhaps George Luthringer, a Princeton economist. The head of OFD was Pete Collado, my old colleague from the Treasury in the summer of 1936 and the Federal Reserve Bank of New York, 1936–9. At the apex of the economic work of the Department was William L. Clayton, a businessman from Texas and a partner in the cotton-brokerage firm of Anderson and Clayton. He had come to Washington with Jesse Jones in the 1930s, and was a wonderful man to work for – thoughtful and considerate, if a little detached. When one went to a meeting with him, he would dash ahead and hold the door open for his juniors. It was hopeless to try to race him as he had long legs. I once complained about this a year or two later to

OFD, Department of State

Covey T. Oliver, with whom I worked on German and Austrian affairs, another Texan. I explained that Clayton was sixty, and I was thirty-six, he had $60 million and I had $60, and he was undersecretary of state and I was a mere division chief. Oliver replied: "No Texan ever sits with his back to a window or goes through a door first."

Under Clayton was first Edward S. Mason of OSS before he returned to Harvard, and then Willard L. Thorp, who had worked for the National Bureau of Economic Research in the 1920s, for the Electric Bond and Share Company in the 1930s, and was an all-round economist with a good feel for numbers. He is not to be confused with another Willard Thorp, a Princeton professor of English.

My memories of the summer of 1945 are limited. I was supposed to respond to requests for information from the American delegation to the Reparations Commission in Moscow, appointed under the terms of the Yalta agreement. This delegation was headed by Edwin Pauley, appointed by Truman over Isidor Lubin, who had been given the job by Roosevelt. Pauley did not endear himself to American GIs by bringing his wife with him to Russia and Berlin when every other American in the field was separated from his wife or sweetheart. I cannot recall the names of the staff below Lubin, except for Moses Abramovitz, Abram Bergson, and Sol Oser. But the Commission quickly became bogged down, and the negotiation was moved to Potsdam where the Big Three, Truman, Churchill, and Stalin, would take over. On the economic staff there were Clayton, Collado, and Despres. Again I cannot recall what requests were directed to me for information or how effectively I fulfilled them. I knew mainly that I was thoroughly fed up with German work, and when the delegation returned from Potsdam, I asked to be transferred to work on British finances. This I did for a short time. I recall especially accompanying Mr Clayton to Secretary of the Treasury Vinson's office to negotiate between the two departments on the British loan and I even think I can recall seeing the sheet of paper, over Mr Clayton's shoulder, that appears in Richard Gardner's book *Sterling–Dollar Diplomacy*

(2nd edn; New York, 1980). This shows the two initial positions on the desirable amount of the loan: $5 billions from Clayton, $3 billions from Vinson, then $4 billions, $3.5 billions, ending up at the actual figure reached of $3,750 millions. But it may be only that I have seen the illustration a number of times in Gardner, and merely imagine having laid eyes on it at first hand.

In about November 1945 my betters in the Department, probably Mason but perhaps Thorp, if Mason had returned to his teaching post at Harvard, called on me to go back to the German economic work which was piling up. A new office on the economic side of the Department was proposed, an Office of Economic Security (OES) under which would be three divisions, one for German and Austrian economic affairs (GA), another for Japanese and Korean economic affairs (JK), and a third on Economic Security Policy (ESP), to handle the so-called Safehaven program dealing with enemy assets in neutral countries, largely legal problems. But before I get to the substance of the German work on which I spent the next year and a half until the Marshall Plan, I want to digress long enough to discuss Seminary Hill and the car pool. This involves going back to 1940, and our return from Switzerland.

17

Seminary Hill and the car pool

In 1940, *on* returning from Basle and Château d'Oex in Switzerland, my wife and I stayed for a number of weeks in Baltimore with our new child while I commuted, and then looked for a place to live near Washington. Chandler Morse, a colleague in the international section of Research and Analysis in the Federal Reserve Board, knew of a house for rent on Seminary Hill, Alexandria, about three miles west of the city of Alexandria. It was called Seminary Hill because of the presence there of the Episcopal Seminary of Virginia, located on a large property of woods and open fields next to the Episcopal High School of Virginia, not a public high school as it happened, but a private boarding school with a substantial fraction of day scholars. A well-known pattern of education for Episcopalian clerics from Virginia was to attend *The* High School, *The* University (in Charlottesville), and *The* Seminary. The Seminary had been a Union hospital in the Civil War, and traces of defensive breastworks could be seen in the landscape about it. The small wooden house we rented was in an elbow of High School land, with large open fields to the north and west. Behind us were two more substantial houses, one colonial brick structure belonging to William Schuyler Livingston, a lawyer in the Defense Plant Corporation, and a stone house rented by Thomas

Seminary Hill and the car pool

H. Eliot, a congressman from Cambridge, Massachusetts, who had earlier been general counsel of the Social Security System, much later chancellor of Washington University in St Louis. At the time these were the only three houses on a lane leading in from Seminary Road at the end of the Seminary property.

Across Seminary Road the land was somewhat more heavily settled, though it was still country. One large summer house had been "The Nunnery," occupied during the New Deal by women college graduates who worked in government, among whom were Eileen O'Daniel, later Mrs George Eddy, and her Smith classmate, Lois Jamison, later Mrs Thomas Eliot. That house was occupied during the war by Chandler and Sarah Robbins, he working seven days a week in Pentagon procurement of textiles, having come from cotton mills in Lewiston and Auburn in Maine, she learning to cut his hair as he never had time to get to the barber. (They sublet us the house for a month or two in 1945, until we got an opportunity to rent the stone house previously occupied by the Eliots. It was then taken over by Leonard Miall, the BBC Washington correspondent, and his wife Lorna.) Next south to the Robbins were Clifford J. and Virginia Durr, originally from Alabama. He had been a Rhodes scholar, became a lawyer, worked first in the Reconstruction Finance Corporation and then as general counsel of the Defense Plant Corporation before being appointed to the Federal Communications Commission. Mrs Durr attended Wellesley, developed a social conscience, and worked as a volunteer for the Southern Conference for Human Welfare, devoted primarily to the repeal of the poll tax in the South. Still further along to the south was Charles Siepmann, of English origin, a First World War winner of the Military Cross in the British Army at the age of eighteen, later director of BBC Talks, and at this time an American citizen working for the Office of War Information (OWI). He had married Jane Tyler, sister of Mrs Zabriskie, whose husband was the dean of the Seminary.

Seminary Hill was an idyllic spot. Football games at the high school were far enough away not to bother us, when we chose not to attend, near enough to walk to when we felt otherwise.

Seminary Hill and the car pool

The seminarians had a small problem since each one believed that he had come to the Seminary with a clear call to go out to the trenches as a chaplain and comfort distressed dog-faces, but admissions had built up to such an extent that the world thought, and they were aware of it, that the study of theology was a means of escaping the draft. They were thus somewhat socially uneasy. But they made wonderful baby-sitters, as their high standards of ethics meant that they did not drink one's liquor, make long-distance calls on the telephone, or eat too much out of the refrigerator. One evening, being taken back to the Seminary dormitory, one asked respectfully what I did. I replied that I was an economist. "That, sir, is a branch of theology I have not studied." Touché.

The year 1941 or early 1942 also marked a saddle-point in the history of the United States, a fact which was brought home to us forcefully. When we first arrived at Seminary Hill with a baby, we managed to hire a pleasant young black woman as a nurse and mother's helper, at $18 a week, if I remember the figure, not living in, but walking to the house across the field from the collection of houses or shacks where she lived. One day she announced that she was stopping. She had gotten a job in the torpedo plant in Alexandria at a much higher wage. That was the last of weekly as opposed to hourly help.

I do want to record an episode in the early married life of the Durrs. It was a Sunday evening in Montgomery, Alabama. The maid was off. Virginia made the supper, and Cliff helped her bring it into the living-room. They had settled down, when Virginia looked up and said, "Cliff, brother needs a fork." Cliff's rising irritation at his brother-in-law's relaxed composure during the early preparations boiled over, and he shouted, "Let brother get his own goddamn fork!" It became a byword in the extended Kindleberger family. One might add that Virginia Foster's sister married Hugo Black, who became successively senator from Alabama and justice of the Supreme Court.

Durr, Livingston, Eliot, Siepmann, and I were members of a car pool that flourished for many years, at least from 1940 to 1948 (with time out for OSS and the Army overseas). After the

Seminary Hill and the car pool

war, Tom Eliot went back to Cambridge and the law firm of Foley, Hoag, and Eliot, before switching from law into teaching and academic administration. His place was taken by Leonard Miall. The car pool played a large part in the lives of its members and their families, including guests. The Durrs, for example, took in Decca Romilly when her husband enrolled in the Royal Air Force and was later missing in action. She is better known as Jessica Mitford, author of *Hons and Rebels*, a record of her life in Britain with her father, Lord Redesdale, and famous sisters, Nancy and Unity. Her husband, Romilly, was a nephew of Winston Churchill, who as first lord of the Admiralty had sent a destroyer after them when they eloped to join the Spanish loyalists. For a time she went to secretarial school and rode in the pool, often finding it necessary to borrow a dollar from Cliff Durr for lunch: "Cliff: give me a dollar." Other guests would be brought home for dinner, among them those of the Siepmanns, of whom I remember Owen Lattimore, who had known Jane Siepmann in China before the war, and Ivy Litvinov, the English wife of the Soviet foreign minister.

The wives of the car-pool members were personalities to conjure with. Mary Walton Livingston belonged to an old Virginia family, was a woman of great integrity and forthrightness, who later, as a widow, worked in National Archives and single-handedly spoiled President Nixon's attempt to obtain a large tax deduction for giving his papers to Archives by backdating the deed of gift to a date before a change of legislation. She knew the exact date of the gift, could prove it, and would not countenance any attempt to alter it. She is the godparent of one of our children, Cliff Durr that of another, Chan Morse that of a third.

Virginia Durr was and is a character. Her autobiography is published (*Outside the Magic Circle*, Tuscaloosa, AL, 1985) and her name has appeared in various accounts of the post-war United States, for example in *Black Ballots*, a *New Yorker* disquisition, a piece by Studs Terkel, and elsewhere. After an abortive attempt by a different writer Clifford Durr's biography was written by an Australian historian, John A. Salmond (*The Conscience of a Lawyer: Clifford J. Durr and American Civil*

Seminary Hill and the car pool

Liberties, 1899–1975, Tuscaloosa, AL, 1990). Cliff was enormously loyal to and protective of Virginia, but on occasion it seemed to me that her liberal grandstanding – such as a trip to Poland in 1946 or 1947 – was not particularly calculated to help him. His antipathy to the loyalty oath led him to decline Truman's offer of reappointment to the Federal Communications Commission, on which he had been a strong advocate of the public interest instead of a protector of the radio and television industry. He then got a job as house counsel for a union in Denver, but when adverse publicity appeared in print against both Durrs, was fired and returned to Montgomery, Alabama. There, supported by a retainer from his brother's successful chemical business, he undertook an enormous amount of *pro bono* work, at little or no recompense, including the early maneuverings in support of Rosa Parks and the Montgomery bus boycott, before it became necessary that her evident supporters should all be black. Rosa Parks came to his memorial service in Washington Cathedral, along with a host of admirers such as Ben Cohen, Thurman Arnold, Paul Porter, Abe Fortas, and Izzy Stone. His goddaughter, my daughter Randall, was more moved by shaking the hand of Rosa Parks than by meeting the galaxy of Washington celebrities.

The car pool has been written up in connection with the Marshall Plan. I vividly recall, as we were circling the Lincoln Memorial *en route* home, and approaching the Arlington bridge, being asked by Leonard Miall about the press release he had just obtained. I was not privy to the writing of the June 5, 1947, speech for Harvard commencement, but asked to see it. By the time we had crossed the bridge, I told Miall that he had better discard the broadcast he had already transmitted, and start again. This was real and big. He did. The British embassy mailed the speech – "just another Commencement address" – and John Miller of *The Times* gave it no play. Only Muggeridge of the *Telegraph* and Miall of the BBC recognized its epoch-making character, as the first announcement of the Marshall Plan.

The car pool has stayed together over the subsequent five decades. Reunions are mostly held in the Boston area, when

Seminary Hill and the car pool

Mary Walton Livingston stops by on her way to Nantucket, or Virginia Durr goes to Martha's Vineyard for a visit to her daughter and son-in-law, Dr and Mrs Sheldon Hackney. An honorary member is J. Kenneth Galbraith, who used to come out to Seminary Hill in summer. Unhappily as the years go on, too many reunions are for memorial services of ancient members. One highly valued association is with Leonard Miall, who moved back to London, had a turn in charge of BBC-TV talks, the BBC New York office, then Eurovision for the European network; in retirement he helped Asa Briggs to write the history of the BBC. He remarried after having been widowered, and stayed with us at our home in Lincoln on his honeymoon with Sally, on a grand tour of the east coast seeing Joe Harsch, Scotty Reston, Joe Barnes, Eric Severeid, and such characters.

18

Division of German and Austrian Economic Affairs, Department of State
1945–1947

The Division of German and Austrian Economic Affairs (GA) was staffed initially by EOU personnel. Having helped take Germany apart, it was time to help put it back together. There was a deputy chief, John C. deWilde, who had been second-in-charge of EOU as a BEW representative until succeeded by Nat Pincus. Below deWilde and me were five sections, dealing with reparations, industry, finance, trade, and property. Harold Barnett started in reparations until he decided to take the GI bill and go to Harvard for a PhD. Walt Rostow headed the industry section until he, in turn, went to Geneva to work under Gunnar Myrdal in the Economic Commission for Europe, which had been largely his idea. As set forth in his *The Division of Europe after World War II – 1946* (Austin, TX, 1981) he mainly, with some limited help from me, suggested that various organizations established by the Allies after the war – the European Coal Organization, the European Commission for Inland Transport Organization, and the Emergency Economic Committee for Europe – should be pulled together in a European Commission for Europe, open to the Eastern bloc, and the German occupied zones, in an effort to increase the speed and efficiency of economic recovery and avoid a political split of the

GA, Department of State

Continent. Bill Salant was our finance man, with a major contribution from deWilde: between the two of them they set in motion the Colm–Dodge–Goldsmith report in West Germany that ultimately produced German monetary reform in June 1948 – and the Soviet air blockade of West Berlin. For trade and property we recruited others, Henry Koch and Munroe Karasik, the former a businessman coming out of the Navy, Karasik a New York lawyer who had worked on the Safehaven program with Walter Surrey and Seymour Rubin, then going into the Economic Security Policy (ESP).

GA's task was to make economic policy for the Office of Military Government, US (OMGUS) in the economic field. The War Department administered OMGUS from Washington, but of course the field commander, General Lucius D. Clay, was responsible for day-to-day operations. Clay was an imperious personality, who had the normal desire to receive instructions only from Secretary of State Byrnes with whom he had worked in General Sommervell's office on supply during the war, or Undersecretary Clayton, but not from "little people" like Rubin, Rostow, and me. GA was paralleled on the political side by the Division of Central Europe (CE) under Jimmy Riddleberger, in the office of European Affairs (EUR) under H. Freeman ("Doc") Matthews. On one occasion I got a telephone call from Justice Frankfurter about a visa case, and had to wait minutes before I could get a wedge into the stream of talk to persuade him that Kindleberger was not Riddleberger. (It reminded me that in college I had once been introduced to a Dunkelberger by an Eichelberger.)

The first task of the newly created division was to make some sense of the Potsdam agreement and the reparations plan, which called for the removal of a certain amount of capital equipment from Germany for distribution to the Allies, based on a Level of Industry agreement that would guarantee the Germans a standard of living at the level of the neighboring countries, with balanced trade and the four zones treated as a single economic unit. This meant especially the first-charge principle, that exports from any one zone would have as a first charge against them, imports into any of the four zones. The Soviet Union would have to pay for exports from Germany so long as other zones had to import food and raw materials.

The problems of GA are dealt with by me elsewhere (see *Marshall Plan Days*, London, 1987, and *The German Economy, 1945–1947: Charles P. Kindleberger's Letters from the Field*, Westport, CT, 1989). I would, however, make a couple of points about German policy, and spend a moment on the problems I suffered in the McCarthy era from having worked for three months ten years earlier under Harry White.

First was the task of trying to make the Potsdam agreement workable. This we sought to do by reinterpreting it. With the help of Colonel Ernest Gross, a New York lawyer who later served as the US representative to the United Nations and who worked at this time for General Hilldring, the War Department's backstop of OMGUS, we wrote a Statement of the Department and one by Secretary Byrnes, suggesting that the capital removals for reparations under the Level of Industry agreement were meant to be a quick, clean solution to the reparations and disarmament problem, after which the Germans could work out their own salvation themselves, apart from military equipment. The Level of Industry was a floor and not a ceiling. The statements were issued on December 12, 1945, about a month after the division had gotten underway and were studiously ignored by General Clay, who was off on his own negotiation over the Level of Industry, and especially steel, in a manner that Cairncross in *The Price of War* (Oxford, 1986) and *A Country to Play With* (Gerrards Cross, 1986), described as chaotic. Alexander (later Sir Alec) Cairncross was a British economist at the working level and thought the Statements helpful, as did Clay's staff. Most of the same points were taken up by Byrnes again in his Stuttgart speech of September 1946, written by Kenneth Galbraith and approved by Clay. The Stuttgart speech is generally taken to be the turning-point in American policy, but one could make the case that the turn had been taken nine months earlier.

Second, there was a problem about investments in Germany

before the dust had settled, and especially before monetary reform, which would make money valuable again. Monetary reform was hung up on a false issue: where to print the new notes issued to replace those withdrawn. The *Reichsdruckerei*, or government printing office, was in the Soviet zone, and a simple-minded view held that the Russians could not be trusted not to print a great deal of extra money – despite controls – and use it for their own ends. The issue was especially confused because Harry White had given the Russians plates for printing the occupation currency, and the United States had lost several hundred million dollars converting worthless Reichsmarks and occupation currency into dollars. The two events were not connected. The United States would not have lost any money if they had refused to convert marks into dollars, and they would have lost a great deal if they had converted even if the Russians had printed none, because of the vast amount of German marks in circulation and those printed by the Western Allies. Economists in GA could never figure out whether the military paymasters had permitted conversion of marks into dollars because they were unable to see the result, or whether they understood but were willing to lose $300 or $400,000,000 to raise troop morale.

Meanwhile money was worthless, and it was undesirable for the occupation forces to let Allied countrymen buy up German property, as many wanted to. To support democracy in Germany it was important not to have all German assets, or a major share of them, in foreign ownership. Restitution of assets taken from Jews who had fled abroad would render a significant volume of property foreign. Taking German ahead of Allied capital equipment under reparations removals would go further in the same direction. But the more general argument, formulated after the war more rigorously as the theory of the second-best, is that when markets don't work, one should not use them. We did not, in fact, express the matter this way, but managed to find an effective formula. Secretary Byrnes came from South Carolina, Undersecretary Clayton from Texas, and General Clay from Georgia. The virtue of a moratorium on the Allied acquisition of German assets until the German economy had been stabilized and monetary order restored was communicated to them with one word: carpetbagging. The South well knew the misery caused in the Confederacy by northern carpetbaggers who bought up valuable property for a song after the Civil War. (The same mistake, it might be added, was made in Cuba in 1898 after the defeat of Spain.)

The property cases were difficult. Mr Clayton was adroit in refusing all invitations on the part of businessmen, instead inviting them to join him in his private dining-room at the Metropolitan Club where he took lunch. He would often bring staff, and their presence inhibited the more outrageous proposals that Mr Clayton might not have seen through. I recall one lunch with Sosthenes Behn of ITT present. I cannot remember the issue but I do recall remarking that ITT did not deserve special consideration because of its property troubles in Europe as it had already made deals to sell properties in Roumania to Hitlerian Germany, and owned a sizeable block of stock in the Focke–Wulf Company. Its original purpose had been to work with the airplane company on perfecting blind-landing equipment, but presumably there were other companies with which that could have been done.

While Mr Clayton was responsive to our hammering away at carpetbagging, he reacted as well to other catchphrases. A Mr Lightner of or representing the Singer Sewing Machine Company approached him to request permission to buy the Pfaff Sewing Machine Company in Germany. Singer's plant lay in the Russian zone of occupation on the east bank of the Elbe, and had been seized by the Soviets as war booty because it was making machine guns. Legally, I understand, war booty in international law is limited to items actually owned by the defeated armies, not private property, but the Russians did not seem to be overly nice in these distinctions. As a result of losing its plant, which used to supply half of the sewing machines sold in Germany, Singer had lost its "trading position," a matter that could be remedied if it were allowed to buy up its largest competitor. As a commodity man, Mr Clayton was impressed by "trading positions," and overruled his staff. Luckily for the sanctity of the moratorium, Pfaff and a second company found lots of reasons not to sell to Singer.

The troubles with the FBI over my ten-years-back, three-month association with White, Coe *et al.* came to a head as a result of two columns written by George P. Sokolsky, a right-wing columnist for the *Washington Times–Herald*, one on June 5, 1947, and another on July 23, 1947. The first said that I had been installed in the State Department to carry out the Morgenthau Plan, the second that I had conspired in the Department to get rid of General Mark W. Clark, the US High Commissioner to the Allied Commission in Austria, and hinting that in so doing, and in fighting to keep the Morgenthau Plan alive I was not carrying out the policies of the president and the secretary of state. This was the height of the McCarthy era, and I asked a lawyer to threaten to sue Sokolsky for slander (or is it libel?). It was hard to make the case that my reputation had been damaged since no one I knew read the *Times–Herald* or the columns of Sokolsky; the columns had appeared in the *New York Sun* and were brought to my attention through some reader telling my father. Sokolsky's lawyer wrote back for him that he knew that what he said was true, but that because he could not reveal the source, he apologized and withdrew any slanderous or libellous implications – under duress. That did not help much, but Harold Leventhal, later a judge, who represented me without charge, thought that that was as far as we could go, and that it was far enough. It was much further than my State Department colleagues wanted me to go – they suggested forgetting the whole business, but I thought a point of principle involved.

Months later, thinking about the Mark Clark story, I realized what had happened. In the seven weeks at Moscow on the staff of the American delegation to the Council of Foreign Ministers, meeting in March and April, I had had nothing to do with Mark Clark. I was working on German problems, and a different group dealt with Austrian issues. But before going to Moscow, Francis Williamson on the Austrian desk of CE, had called me on the telephone to ask me to attend a meeting to discuss the behavior of Clark, who, it seems, had been acting up. I went, though it was not an issue that concerned me. I then concluded that the FBI had been tapping my telephone in an effort to follow up on all the associates of Harry White. And because they could find nothing in my conversation that was actionable in any way, they fed gossip to the columnists they kept on a string.

On another occasion, Felix Belair called me on the telephone to ask what I thought of President Truman appointing Herbert Hoover to investigate the food situation in Germany. I said I did not like it, not because of any animosity against Mr Hoover, though that would not be difficult to work up, but because the problem of feeding Germany was difficult enough between the War Department, the State Department, the Combined Boards, and so on, and another player would merely complicate the problem more. The story made the front page of the *New York Times* the next day, and by that afternoon I was told the whole town knew that I had expressed that opinion, even though the news account did not identify the source. Again, I suspect that the FBI had broadcast its wire-tapped information.

In March 1947, I went to Moscow as a member of the American delegation to the Council of Foreign Ministers. Secretary of State Marshall was of course the head of the delegation, supported by General Bedell Smith, the ambassador to Moscow, Chip Bohlen, his interpreter and adviser, Ben Cohen, the Department counsellor, John Foster Dulles, the former Republican senator, an adviser, and a handful of staff from CE and GA on the one hand, and from OMGUS on the other. Edward S. Mason was brought along as a consultant to lead the economic side of the Department. General Clay came and went back to Berlin; other OMGUS personnel were Henry Parkman and Edward Litchfield on the political side, and General Draper and Don D. Humphreys for economics. I thought Marshall and Cohen were wonderful, though I was troubled by Marshall's need to see a movie every night to rest his mental faculties. Clay and especially Dulles did not appeal. This was, however, very much a worm's eye view, as I was four levels down from the secretary. A picture of the meeting published in the *New York Times* shows the top of my head far in the back of what I learned to call the *Americanski delegatsi.*

At one stage in a discussion of technical information taken from Germany by the United States, Molotov attacked US behavior. I happened to have a letter I had brought along from a man in the Department of Commerce, asking whether we could arrange for the Soviets to be more forthcoming about the information that they had taken from Germany. We had made all our material public; they had not. I passed this to Matthews who pushed it to Cohen, who handed it to the secretary, who read it, making quite a stir. As he withdrew after the meeting, the secretary thanked me for the timely find. My witty and not very respectful brother-in-law, Francis Miles, reading about how Kindleberger dived into his briefcase (in *Time Magazine*) thought there ought to be a competition for bureaucrats, the briefcase dive, with required variations – from a sitting position, from standing, and perhaps a few voluntary figures, with the briefcase, for example, across the room.

Moscow was hard work. For one thing the service in the Hotel Moscova was appallingly slow, as untrained waiters learned their way around the kitchen and dining-room. Sometimes a meal would take as long as two and a half hours. Second, we prepared for the meetings at the American residence, Spasso House, where a large group of the lower brass were packed into the ballroom. George Jacobs of GA and I worked on a small vanity table about three feet by two. One would work in the morning, get lunch, go to the meetings at four, meet until eight or nine, try to get dinner, and then often go back to prepare more memoranda before bedtime. Arthur Marget, the well-known monetary economist, who had come from Vienna with General Clark as a member of the delegation for Austrian financial questions, never worked at night. He was a balletomane and opera buff, and found it necessary, to the irritation of all the rest of us, to attend the Bolshoi for every performance.

The meeting was a failure. Having looted East Germany of a great deal of capital equipment – even pulling electrical equipment out of the wall, and ripping plumbing fixtures from bathrooms – the Russians found they could not use most of it. Intelligence reports indicated that much of it was left on railroad cars for months and finally scrapped. They then wanted reparations out of current production. The first-charge agreement at Potsdam meant that exports from Germany should be reserved for the payment of imports until the trade accounts were balanced, as in the western zones they were not. It seemed clear that the Soviet Union would not in practice work to treat Germany as a single economic unit, and in late April the delegation returned to Washington.

19

The Marshall Plan, Department of State
1947–1948

The winter of 1946–7 was a severe one in Europe. There were floods that washed seed out of the ground, and frosts which tied up the transport of coal at the same time that they increased the demand for it. The regular system of distribution of farm produce to the city broke down, and thousands of city dwellers made their way to the countryside to trade their household possessions – clothes, lamps, crockery, and the like – for eggs and potatoes. Undersecretary of State Clayton, returning from the first meeting of the Economic Commission for Europe, was struck by what he thought was the collapse of the economic division of labor. Others were concerned. In March 1947 Walter Lippmann had written a series of articles on the need for American assistance to European recovery. The Council of Foreign Relations had had a series of meetings in New York on Europe and the economic role of Germany within it. I spoke at one such meeting before sailing for Moscow, and at another on returning.

The regular economic side of the Department of State had also not been idle. Harold van Buren ("Van") Cleveland and Ben Moore had written a memorandum on European recovery. On my return, they asked me to contribute a passage on the German question. The whole Cleveland–Moore–Kindleberger memorandum, as it came to be called, was duplicated on June 12, 1947. Meanwhile, however, Charles Bohlen had woven two memoranda, one by George Kennan on the politics of European recovery, and one by Will Clayton on the economics, into the speech that the secretary gave at Harvard on June 5, calling on the Europeans to produce a cooperative program for recovery to which the United States might furnish concrete assistance. It was time to end the piecemeal *ad hoc* series of programs for meeting crises and work out a more orderly process.

Starting some time in May, the economic staff of the Department under Willard Thorp had been holding weekly luncheon meetings on European recovery. With the speech at Harvard, I was drawn into the work, being transferred from GA to become an adviser in, I think, the assistant secretary's office. I became the secretary to the economics group, and in due course the chairman of a small coordinating committee that stood between an elaborate system of commodity committees on the one hand, and country committees on the other. These were drawn not only from the Department but from the government as a whole. This structure of committees at the working level operated under the top level, consisting of Robert Lovett, as undersecretary of state, and an intermediate level of policy people among whom were Tic Bonesteel, Paul Nitze, Lincoln Gordon, and perhaps others. Bonesteel had been a colonel in Twelfth Army Group in G-3 (plans), usually two plans behind as General Bradley produced his plans and put them into effect without the elaborate standard operating procedures of the manuals. He was later a major-general or lieutenant-general of the American forces in Korea. Nitze had been an investment banker in New York who later made an outstanding career as an arms-control negotiator. Lincoln Gordon had been professor of politics at the Harvard Business School, the boy wonder of the Office of Production Management during the war, and later ambassador to Brazil, and president of Johns Hopkins University. On the commodity committees were such stalwarts as Walter Levy, the OSS oil expert, who singlehandedly worked to ensure in the Marshall

The Marshall Plan

Plan that the oil companies did *not* charge Gulf-of-Mexico-plus for oil delivered from the Middle East to Europe, but established a new basing-point in the Eastern Mediterranean. Gulf-of-Mexico-plus would have been an artificial price including "phantom freight" for oil actually delivered from a nearer source. The country committees contained among others Albert Hirschman, later professor of social sciences at the Institute for Advanced Studies at Princeton. With me at the coordinating committee were William Phillips, later of the School of Advanced International Studies of Johns Hopkins University, the School being in Washington, and Robert W. Tufts, later of Oberlin, William Bray, and others.

It was grinding work, which expanded to fill nights and weekends. We had rented a cottage for a month's leave at Nag's Head, North Carolina, but I had to give up. My wife did not relish taking it on alone, as she did, with three small children.

One of the difficulties of working for a political constituency, the Congress, is that one cannot come completely clean and confess to slips and errors, or adjust for changes and new information. We early settled on a figure of $5.2 billions for the first fifteen months, from April 1 to June 30, 1948, and for the fiscal year that followed and thereafter were unable to change it, no matter what new data became available or corrections were made. It was one of the first uses of computers known to me, those in the basement of the Pentagon, and we joked that for years thereafter whenever these machines were asked a question the answer always came out $5.2 billions. One worker fell asleep after working all night at the Pentagon and wrecked his car. We took up a collection to pay the $50 deductible not covered by insurance, and the then undersecretary, Dean Acheson, if I have the occasion right, contributed one-fifth of the amount. It was also necessary to keep chauffeurs on hand to take the secretaries home late at night or early in the morning. I overheard a conversation in an Old State washroom between two black chauffeurs. One said to the other, "Man, you look terrible." The other said, "I have been up all night working on the Marshall Plan." Enthusiasm for the effort was widely shared.

The Marshall Plan

One canard I must deny, although it may be a mistake to bring it up again since the people who shared it have departed or been scattered and the calumny has lost circulation. The country people had to estimate not only production and consumption but also exports and imports, these by twenty-six commodity groups and all other, and broken down into the categories United States, Europe, colonies, and all other. In adding up what the European countries expected to export to one another, and to import from one another, I found that exports exceeded imports by a wide margin. Within bureaucratic circles this was called "the Kindleberger surplus," as if I did not know that the exports of the group to the group must equal the imports of the group from the group; I was, however, merely the person who put his finger on the anomaly.

There were long days of testifying before Congressional committee, mostly by commodity and country experts, though I had the dubious task of trying to defend the "residual" for Belgium. It happened that Belgium was rich after the war: it had been overrun by the Germans so quickly that undertaking a large war effort was completely beyond it; it had recovered its gold from France when the Germans took it from the French; it had sold uranium from the Congo to the United States; and had earned a lot of dollars on reverse lend-lease, for renting accommodations to the US forces during the long period in which US armies were stalled in Belgium. The Belgians had spent a lot of money in 1946 on luxury goods, silk stockings, Coca-Cola, even Cadillacs and small airplanes, so that after subtracting all the prime imports in the twenty-six commodity categories, the country estimator thought it necessary to add a substantial fudge factor to avoid a sharp decline in 1947 and 1948 imports from the 1946 levels. Luckily, John Taber of the House appropriations committee never lighted on this gap in our armor. All members of the various committees on foreign affairs and appropriations – for the act had to go through the Congress twice, once for the authorization and a second time for the appropriation – were seduced by Walter Levy's testimony because he so readily moved back and forth in discussing petroleum between barrels per day and tons per year. The answer was simple: a million barrels a day is the equivalent of 50 million tons a year. Walter Levy designed and had manufactured a circular slide rule for all sorts of conversions, not only avoirdupois and distance to metric, Fahrenheit to Celsius and the like, but others similar to the barrels per day and tons per year. I kept the one he gave me for years until the plastic finally buckled and broke.

When the legislation cleared the committees, the Department of State was asked to delegate someone to sit in the back of the Senate during the debate as a resource that could be called upon by the Foreign Relations Committee in case it needed more precise information. The assignment fell to me, and I sat in the Senate, as inconspicuously as possible, for two weeks, listening to the debate. It was an education the like of which should be universalized. I learned, for example, that presence was more important than cogency. Senator Smith from New Jersey was among the most intelligent members of the Foreign Relations Committee, but he was not nearly as effective as Henry Cabot Lodge, whose voice was stentorian and manner assured. On one occasion Senator Joseph Ball of Minnesota, a recent convert to isolationism, suggested that the Marshall Plan was not needed and that all the European countries needed to do was to balance their budgets and adjust their exchange rates to the purchasing-power parity. I felt fairly certain that Senator Arthur Vandenberg, the chairman of the Committee, would not know how to respond to this, and hastily started to formulate arguments to counter the thrust, including explaining what the purchasing-power parity was. I looked over to see whether Francis Willcox, the clerk of the Committee, would start to amble in my direction. No movement. Then Senator Vandenberg rose to his feet: "The Honorable Senator from Minnesota says that the European countries should devalue their currencies to the purchasing-power parity. Purchasing-power parity is a concept developed by the English economist Keynes. We want no part of any such doctrine." I imagine that I was the only person in the chamber who knew that the doctrine had come from the Swedish economist Gustav Cassel. But error made no difference in the debate as long as the voice that spoke it was loud and confident.

There were other senators worth observing, especially Joseph McCarthy of Wisconsin and William Jenner of Indiana, isolationists and reactionaries who whispered together and opposed all aid. I was also struck by Robert Taft, whom President Kennedy later included among a group of six *Profiles in Courage* (New York, 1957). I was not impressed by Senator Taft's courage. He wanted to oppose foreign aid, but did not dare; instead he kept trying to cut the amount. Senator Vandenberg disposed of this tactic with the remark that it does no good to throw a fifteen-foot rope to a man drowning twenty feet away.

In the early spring of 1948 I developed a kidney stone which gave me a severe case of kidney colic. The stone was removed but I spent almost ten days in the hospital recovering from the fever. On release, we went to Florida for a week to recuperate. My weight had gone from 163 pounds to below 140, at which point I promised my wife I would leave the government. I was not, repeat not, discharged on loyalty grounds, but once on the outside I could not get cleared for consulting work with the government until finally under the Kennedy administration, the whole shameful business was given up.

I disliked intensely being refused clearance, and applied under the Freedom of Information Act for my file, received copies of all the applications for civil service status I had made – Form 57 if I remember – and accounts of interviews with unnamed friends, neighbors, and colleagues that produced no "derogatory" information. On appeal there was more of the same, but some sheets of paper with most of the writing crossed out, including one in which a blacked-out informant had called me a Russian spy. Interesting, sick, but a little scary. At one stage in the late 1950s, I decided that I had better clear the whole thing up, and asked Walter Surrey, then in private law practice in Washington, how to go about it. He suggested that I write as complete an account as I could of all the people I knew who had been mentioned or denounced by the various groups peddling McCarthyism, apply for a job as a consultant through a friend,

The Marshall Plan

and try to arrange for a hearing if I could not get cleared. Those already employed in government could get hearings to gain security clearance, those on the outside could not. George Shultz who had been on the staff of the MIT economics department and was then a member of the Council of Economic Advisers, was agreeable to my applying there, but Arthur F. Burns was not: it meant too much trouble. In any event, I wrote 100 pages at white heat in a week, complete with a collection of letters of recommendation, citations for military decorations, and the like. It makes an interesting document for private circulation in the family, but is a little too frank in stating opinions; not that it denounced anyone as disloyal, but it did suggest that some of my friends were less than circumspect in the way they responded to the witchhunt.

20

Goodbye Washington, hello Academia

The *decision to* leave Washington and look for an academic job was well timed. The market had picked up enormously since the 1930s with the GI bill and the flood of returned soldiers. Don Wallace was looking for someone to teach in the Woodrow Wilson School at Princeton and to edit the publications of the International Finance Section. He arranged an invitation for me to give a seminar at Princeton. Friedrich Lutz, who had written a paper arguing against the need for foreign aid, was in the chair. I tried to defend the Marshall Plan. The first remark – hardly a question – came from Frank D. Graham, who said, "I cannot recall a time when I have heard so much nonsense in such a short space of time in my whole life." I thought that fairly drastic, but defended myself as best I could. Then my old *bête noire*, Jacob Viner, chimed in with the conservative Chicago view that disequilibrium can cure itself. Lutz was much friendlier in manner, but clearly on the side of those that believed that any structural disequilibrium could be cured by leaving it to the market, a view expressed today by the economic historian, Alan Milward, and by Van Cleveland. This last had been instrumental in writing the early papers in the State Department urging massive foreign aid in 1947 but later became converted to monetarism and the Chicago view.

Goodbye Washington, hello Academia

I have since wondered whether Professor Graham was in the incipient stages of a breakdown. Thomson ("Tom") Whitin, who later taught at MIT for a time before moving on to Wesleyan, had been a student of Graham and was examined by him on his general examination. Graham asked a question and Whitin furnished an answer. Graham said, "No." Whitin offered another answer. Graham said, "No." Whitin tried a third time, and Graham again said, "No." At that point Whitin said, "I am afraid I do not know what sort of an answer you want, Professor Graham. I suggest you fail me on that question and we move to another topic." Graham said, "No." It required the intervention of the other professors to haul Professor Graham off the back of poor Whitin. It happened that Graham later committed suicide by jumping off the upper deck of Palmer Stadium in Princeton.

Following my disastrous afternoon, Wallace said that he had withdrawn my name from consideration. Unlike – or like – Zuleika Dobson, who, after devastating Oxford, went on to Cambridge, I had a try at Yale. Viner happened to be visiting. I gave the same seminar which he, unnecessarily to my mind, attended, and he remained negative if polite. This did not work out. Finally, however, Richard Bissell with whom I had worked on the Marshall Plan – he in fact wrote most of the Harriman Report, which worked up public sympathy for the venture – asked me whether I would like to go to MIT. I said I would. I visited Cambridge, had lunch with Jim Killian, then a vice-president, Ralph Freeman, the head of the department, and W. Rupert Maclaurin, the energetic son of a former president, member of the department, and impresario who more than Freeman was the entrepreneur concerned to build the economics department. After an interview with a dean, I was offered a job and took it – an associate professor with a promise of full professor in three years. It was an act of faith on MIT's part, based on twelve years of government and army work, a published thesis, and three or four articles. (In later years, as an adviser to graduate students, I used to tell those headed for non-academic jobs to try to get two articles published before leaving graduate school as a foot in the door into academic work if they decided in due course to go into that field.)

It may be of mild interest that one of the early articles on "International monetary stabilization" written for a symposium edited by Seymour Harris, said more or less casually that it was possible for an increase in exports to lead to an import surplus. In Washington during the post-war years, it was a frequent occurrence to meet an economist on the street and have him tell me that he had had a graduate student who had proved that my result was impossible. It was only later, after moving to MIT and reading the demonstration of this case in a textbook by Enke and Salera, based on a proof of Arthur Bloomfield, that I worked out that my intuition had been fine. The case against it was based on the standard assumption about savings, used in the foreign-trade multiplier analysis, that the marginal propensity to save is positive, that is, each increase in income from the spending of the income from exports will go partly into imports but partly into savings. But there is another possible outcome: that the increase in income kicks off an increase in investment, as with an accelerator model, and in this instance, an increase in exports can lead to a rise in imports greater than that in exports. I wrote an answer to Bloomfield for the *American Economic Review* as one of my first tasks at MIT.

This time, I chose not to give up accumulated leave. The Economic Cooperation Act passed the Congress and was signed by President Truman early in April. I had work to do in cleaning up my files, but I chose not to leave the Department of State until July 31. About the end of June I was a thorough lame duck and amused myself during July writing an account of "The origin of the Marshall Plan." This was only semi-serious, recounting rumor, jokes, and myth along with a thread of reality. Among jokes, for example, it recounted a meeting with Philander P. Claxton who worked with General Hilldring on German matters, who said he had not seen me lately. I said I was working on the European Recovery Program:

CLAXTON: Is that based on the speech the secretary gave at Princeton?

Goodbye Washington, hello Academia

CPK: Phil, where did you go to college?
CLAXTON: Princeton.
CPK: That's what I thought.

The memorandum was written for the files. Years later when young historians would interview me about the origins of the Marshall Plan, I would drag the memorandum out of a file called "Archives," and show it to them. One day when I did so, the young person said, "I know, I know." I asked how he happened to know. He said it was published in *Foreign Relations of the United States, 1947*, volume III: *The British Commonwealth, Europe* (Washington, DC, 1972). State Department papers selected for publication see the light of day twenty-five years after the events they relate to, and the files had turned up this light-hearted document, as Rostow later referred to it. It is the longest time lag I have had between writing and publication, but I have had others running thirteen and nine years.

In June 1948 my wife and I drove to Cambridge, and bought the house we lived in for forty-one years, having found out about it from classified ads in the *Boston Herald*; this had been sent to us for a month by Harold Barnett of EOU and GA friendship, then working on a PhD at Harvard.

En route to Cambridge in August we stopped off, among other places, in Keene Valley, in the Adirondacks, and hiked on Mount Marcy. At one rest it started to rain, and my brother-in-law, Frank Miles, asked me how I planned to begin my first lecture. Without hesitating I said, "All economics consists in making little ones out of big ones or big ones out of little ones." It was a good line that was useful in starting needed conversation, but of course it is untrue. Some economics processes have no shape at all, and others retain their size. A friend of mine, the Reverend Rollin J. Fairbanks, was fond of enunciating, "What doesn't kill, strengthens." But that is not true either. Something that might not kill you might nevertheless leave you crippled.

21

MIT and Lincoln
The forties and fifties

When I took the MIT job, I asked Dick Bissell where I should live. He replied, "If you want to live in the city, live in Cambridge; if in the suburbs, in Belmont; if you want to live in the country, Lincoln." We had lived in the country on Seminary Hill and liked it. The ad for the house we bought in Lincoln called it a farmhouse on a hill. We did not have much money, especially as moving from government to academic life caused a drop in salary from $9,000 to $7,500. But with the help of my mother-in-law, who gave us the mortgage, we bought the farmhouse, undertook certain improvements to make it more suitable for a married couple and three children, increased a year later to four, and never looked back. We had stumbled on to a good location – if one believes the real-estate bromide that the three important things about residential property are location, location, location – a good town in which to raise children, take a modest role in town affairs, saw wood, shovel snow, mow lawns, and garden.

We had but one car for a number of years, and, living far from shops, it was necessary once again to car pool. Members of the car pool changed over the years, sometimes they were MIT folk, sometimes neighbors who led other sorts of lives.

I soon observed that there was a different sociology between

MIT and Lincoln

Harvard and MIT. Harvard academic staff lived as near as possible to the Yard in Cambridge, or if they could not afford the houses on Brattle Street, huge arks built by sea captains and merchants, they concentrated in Belmont. MIT people lived everywhere – North Shore, South Shore, Cambridge, and Belmont to be sure, but also Wellesley, and other western suburbs such as Lincoln. When I mentioned this observation to a neighbor, he pointed out that Lincoln had as residents a number of professors from the Harvard Business School. That proved, I suggested, that the Business School was not the real Harvard. Another proof: the restless Seymour Harris tried living in Concord and in Acton. In the end he gave up and moved back to Cambridge.

I am not clear whether the observation that Harvard and MIT staff were like iron filings, with the Harvard magnet giving off a positive charge, the MIT magnet a negative one, is macro-sociology or micro-sociology. I am convinced, however, that micro-sociology plays an enormous role in vocational lives. Adam Smith says both in *Moral Sentiments* and in the *Wealth of Nations* that emulation is the most pervasive force in peoples' lives. If I had gotten my first academic job in some backwater college or university where no member of my department put out much effort, I would have followed suit. If I had gone to Williams, or Swarthmore, or Oberlin, all my energy would have gone into teaching. At MIT teaching was a valued activity – we all taught both undergraduate and graduate courses – but research was vital. People worked their heads off, some like Paul Samuelson with the most relaxed air in the world, others practically running from place to place. But the department was wonderfully supportive: no bickering, no feuds, not too much in-group socializing, but enough, the staff ready to read each others' papers and criticize, but constructively. I could not have been more blessed to land there.

My first bit of research was to defend myself against the Grahams, Lutzes, and Viners of the world who thought that international economic equilibrium could easily be achieved under any and all circumstances, including a devastating five-year war. The book I wrote was called *The Dollar Shortage* (New York, 1950), a term on the lips of many journalists and economists. I used the exercise to teach myself a lot of the international trade and financial theory that had been produced during the war when I was largely cut off from reading the journals and books. After the shortage turned to a glut in the late 1950s, I was the object of a considerable bit of teasing, especially by chairmen of seminars I was addressing. I realized later that I should have given the monograph a less sexy title such as "Persistent disequilibrium in balances of payments," emphasizing what seems obvious to all but the most hard-bitten neoclassical economists, that the international economy is more like a see-saw than a neatly balanced set of scales. My copy has a pink MIT memorandum slip that reads: "Bertil Ohlin visited Cambridge in December 1959 and said that he had lately reread *The Dollar Shortage* and found that it was carefully guarded, except perhaps for some remarks about stagnation in the United States." It happened that Professor Ohlin, later a Nobel laureate, was enormously generous in encouraging younger men (I was forty-nine, to be sure, but younger than he and younger than I am now). None the less, it was a boost. I also have the feeling that the Appendix on political equilibrium and equilibrium in the balance of payments was slightly prescient of the work in the 1970s of Fred Hirsch, Mancur Olson *et al.*, and contemporaneous work on structural inflation by Henry Aujac, David Felix, and Albert Hirschman. It rated no iota of attention, but that's the way the intellectual market sometimes works.

Some time thereafter I started to write a textbook on international economics. This was finished in March 1953 and published within five months. Richard D. Irwin, the economics and business publisher, had an attractive salesman, who later left the company, and the appealing come-on for authors of getting their books out fast. This was accomplished by rushing the book into print with virtually no copy-editing. The first printing was full of errors, mostly mine perhaps, but editing helps on the ground that two heads are better than one. One reader generously thought that I had deliberately strewn the book with errors as a pedagogical device to keep students on their toes. Not so. I have always been rather sloppy – a temperamental condition which is far from admirable, but better for the world, in my judgment, than the opposite condition – a perfectionist block. (There is, to be sure, a golden mean.)

The operation was undertaken to make a little money for the family. I originally called it "Operation 5 Cs," indicating that I hoped to reap $500 a year for some years from it. In fact it did better than that, paid off college bills for children, and built up a tax-exempt (Keogh-bill) nest-egg. It was no Samuelson whopper, to be sure. I remember being told that for every 100 elementary textbooks in economics that are sold, a publisher will sell only 20 textbooks in money and banking, and about 10 in international economics. But the latter do spread the word far and wide. Even though I wrote my last edition in 1973, I met people in 1989 in Greece, Denmark, and Korea who were brought up on the book.

The introduction to the first edition – it went through five at my hands before I turned it over lock, stock, and barrel to a collaborator, Peter Lindert – mentioned that there were already institutional and historical textbooks in international trade but that mine would be theoretical. This has a curious sound for me today, since I have never been much of a theorist and have more and more moved into history. I judge that the institutional book I had in mind was that by Stephen Enke and Virgil Salera, which started out as two books and was telescoped by a publisher. They killed it eventually by trying to broaden its appeal to political scientists, adding chapters, for example, on the State Department and how "economic foreign policy is made." It was lucky that I chose the theoretical approach, and a higher level of instruction – somewhere between first-year graduate school and high-level seniors – and kept adding more technical appendices, slowly raising the rigor of the book. In due course still more rigorous textbooks would eat into its market – those of Richard Caves and Ronald Jones, for example, and to some degree Miltiades Chacholiades. Jones and Chacholiades were MIT graduates whose PhD theses I supervised. But that is the

MIT and Lincoln

way academic life works: one climbs on the shoulders of the older generation and occasionally steps on a face.

I stopped at five editions – on a five-year cycle – not because it was no longer financially rewarding, but because I was sick of taking a summer off every fifth year and wallowing in my own words. The second edition was a big improvement on the first, and the fourth may have been the best that I did. The fifth involved chopping out a lot of material to reverse the process of fattening that had gone on – from 550 pages to 636 to 686, and then 610 in the fourth and 526 in the fifth. Some of these changes are spurious, to be sure, as the publisher can vary the size of a book by choice of type and leading. But I became so fed-up that I turned the book over entirely to Lindert, refusing to criticize his changes or edit his words. Since there was a substantial rent in the first five editions, our arrangement was that he got one-third of the royalty on the sixth edition, with my name first on the spine, two-thirds for the seventh, with his name first, and it was all his for the eighth. With a change from a five-year to a four-year cycle, this was slightly modified, but it gives the essential idea. In addition, I wrote an introduction for Lindert, *International Economics*, posing the philosophical question as to whether this was Kindleberger, 8th edn, or Lindert, 1st.

The textbook was moderately successful financially, and it spread one's name about the country and even the world. Textbook writers, I believe, do better in contested elections for American Economic Association posts because they are better known – at least this was the case before these last years when it seems to pay to belong to a minority group. But it was not intellectually satisfying. One is writing for students, not one's peers, and collating the advances in the field rather than making them. Paul Samuelson, whom I seem to be quoting a lot, advises textbook writers to leave out the "personal piffle." I did one more textbook in the fifties – on *Economic Development*. Seymour Harris wanted someone to teach the subject in Harvard Summer School, and offered me a job and a contract to write for his McGraw-Hill Handbook series on the subject. The book came out in 1958 and in a second edition in 1965 before I turned that over on the same terms as *International Economics*, to Bruce Herrick.

Before the rewards from this textbook activity began to be reaped, I began a small amount of moonlighting. Columbia University was loaded with students under the GI Bill, many of whom had been in the army in Europe, and wanted a course on "The Economy of Europe," to run one day a week for two hours, both terms. I was happy to accept. I would take the *Owl* to the Grand Central Station on Tuesday night, teach a class from ten to twelve on Wednesday, and return either on the *Yankee Clipper*, leaving New York at 1 p.m., or on the *Merchants' Limited* at five, both crack trains that made the distance in four hours. Whether I stayed or not depended on whether there was anything I wanted to do in New York or not. My classes at MIT were mostly on Tuesday and Thursday, with an occasional third hour on Monday. On Friday I worked at home on writing. The train returning to Boston was wonderful for reading, unless to one's dismay one met a friend who wanted to chat.

Work on the German and Austrian economies, and on the Marshall Plan provided all the material I needed for the second term. For the first, however, I needed a running start, this in nineteenth-century and inter-war European economic history. I had the use of the Columbia Library, far richer in historical material than the economics library at MIT. In the course of preparation for the first semester – two weeks to a month ahead of the students – I observed the different reactions of Britain, France, Italy, Germany, and Denmark to the fall in the price of wheat from 1870 to the end of the century, as railroads brought wheat from the plains to ports in the Ukraine, Australia, Argentina, and the United States, and the iron-clad, propeller-driven, compound steam-engine ship cheapened ocean transport from the ports to Europe. France and Germany put on tariffs, England did not and allowed the industry to be liquidated. Italy put up its tariffs belatedly, and experienced massive emigration from the wheat-growing areas in the South. Denmark did not impose tariffs, liquidated the industry, but unlike Britain converted its export trade in grain to the export of dairy products, eggs, and bacon, whilst importing grain as feed – a dynamic rather than a static solution, and done without policy decision-making. The exercise in comparative economic history appeared in the *Journal of Political Economy* in February 1951, my first foray into economic history, and an early step on the path to growing disenchantment with international trade theory. I have a shameful confession to make in this connection. I needed a page of statistics on wheat-growing or wheat-trade from the *Retrospectif* volume of the French *Annuaire Statistique*. It was in the days before photocopiers, and there was far too much to copy out by hand in the time available. I therefore brought a razor blade to the library one day, cut out the page, returned the following week with some Scotch tape and restored it, mutilated, to almost the *status quo ante*. Had the Xerox invention appeared slightly earlier, it would have lightened the load of guilt I have carried for close to forty years.

While I am confessing scholarly crimes, I note another that I hope is less heinous. When I arrived at MIT in the fall of 1948 to teach international economics, I hoped to refer students to my dissertation. Unfortunately the Dewey (economics) Library at MIT had neglected to buy a copy, and the edition was out of print. For a couple of years we went without. Then a student who was paying his way by teaching elementary economics at Babson Institute, told me that it had a copy, which had never been taken out in twelve or so years. We offered to buy the Babson copy. They refused, saying that to sell was "contrary to policy." The student (in Babson's eyes, instructor) took out the book, "lost it," paid for it ($3), and later "found" it. It was sold to MIT for $3. Some economists would fault the exercise for having failed to reap the rent available. Others would celebrate the efficiency gain in asset relocation. A minimally nagging conscience still poses the question of whether the end justified the means.

From this start in economic history, focused on the 1880s and 1890s, I have wended my way slowly back in time, occasionally a century at a clip. *Economic Growth in France and Britain* (Cambridge, MA, 1964) covers 1851–1950, an even century,

MIT and Lincoln

and a gentle implicit rebuke to the many authors who think that a century should run from 1850 to 1950. In the celebration of the bicentennial of Adam Smith's *The Wealth of Nations*, I did some work on the industrial revolution in Britain in the years around 1776. For *Manias, Panics, and Crashes* (New York, 1978) I started with the South Sea and Mississippi bubbles of 1720. Most recently I have been doing research on another inflationary expansion and collapse, the so-called *Kipper- und Wipperzeit* (period of currency debasement in the Holy Roman Empire) which peaked in 1619–23. A slightly earlier paper on the distribution of the silver produced in Spanish America runs from 1550 to 1750 (two centuries plus a year), but 1550 is as far back as I choose to go.

Other moonlighting occurred at the Fletcher School of Law and Diplomacy, located in Medford, a twenty-minute drive from MIT. This I did for a number of years, on Tuesday and Thursday afternoons, keeping Mondays and Wednesdays – except for one year at Columbia when I did not teach at Fletcher – free for students at MIT. I taught at Fletcher only what I did not teach at MIT, no international economics, but economic development, the economy of France, the economy of Britain, etc. It was broadening as to subject matter. The students were bright young people mostly headed for the foreign service or multinational corporations. One particularly successful course was on economic development, taught with Don D. Humphrey, my old OMGUS opposite number and friend, who had actually been in an underdeveloped country or two as I had not. We did not always agree, and the arguments between us were both edifying and enjoyable to the members of the class, who called it the "Don and Charlie Show," after the briefings by Everett Dirksen and Charles Halleck of the Senate and House of Representatives called the "Ev and Charlie Show." I later taught a course with Rudiger Dornbusch at MIT. Joint teaching is expensive, but it has great pedagogical advantages in keeping the instructors alert, developing the intricacies of the subject, and stimulating study.

In September 1961 I attended a meeting of the International

MIT and Lincoln

Economic Association – one of at least four I have been to over the years – at Brissago, Italy. The intellectual fare was modest. What was memorable was a climb of a small mountain behind the hotel on Lake Maggiore by a large part of the assembled company of economists. Some years before I had read *The White Tower* by James Ramsay Ullman, in which an Englishman, a Frenchman, a German, who happened to be a Nazi, and an American climbed a mountain together, each one demonstrating his national characteristics in a dramatic way. Our climb on the free Wednesday afternoon could have been said – with considerable exaggeration, verging on caricature – similarly to exhibit signs of national character. The Burmese, Hla Myint, got blisters early and turned back. The Britons, Donald MacDougall and Roy Harrod, the latter with only half a stomach after operations for ulcers, were dressed almost for the city, with inadequate shoes, but carried on doggedly if slowly up the slopes, and finally made it. The Germans and the Americans – Egon Sohmen is the only one I remember in the first category, and Raymond Mikesell and me in the second – raced to get to the peak first. Gottfried Haberler, resplendent in his native Austrian hiking outfit and boots, and with his German shepherd dog, both great hikers in Cambridge, Massachusetts, finally turned back, but whether because he or the dog was tired I do not recall. There were Frenchmen and Italians along who doubtless performed characteristically though I have lost the details. I do sadly recall that the half-blind Maurice Byé cut his head open at a swimming session, diving into the lake without his glasses and hitting a rock.

Round about this time I was asked by Jerrold Zacharias and Jerome Wiesner if I could come with them on a consulting mission to the Kerr–McGee oil company in Oklahoma City. They needed an economist, and others in the department, asked first, had not been available. They had a relationship with Dean McGee rather than Senator Kerr, and consulted regularly with the company. They had even arranged a mode of cooperation between Oklahoma City University, which was a pet project of Mr McGee, and MIT.

MIT and Lincoln

As we got in the plane, I excused myself from sitting with them as I had a book that I had agreed to review. They said that this was fine. When they went on a trip they usually spent the time inventing something.

In New York we picked up Isador Rabi, the Columbia physicist and Nobel laureate, and Lloyd Berkner, the head of the Brookhaven atomic laboratory. James Webb joined the group at some stage. I was way over my head in science.

In Oklahoma City, we held a sort of seminar with Kerr-McGee executives, in the course of which I enraged Lloyd Berkner by saying that to be worth anything resources had to be accessible. "Take, for instance, coal at the South Pole. It has no value because it would cost too much to bring it to a market." I had not realized that Berkner had been to the South Pole with Admiral Byrd, and was a South Pole chauvinist, unwilling to listen to anything said against it.

At one stage Mr McGee interrupted the proceedings, saying, "Now we are due at the university." This was news to me. We piled into limousines, rode a mile or two, and emerged on a stage facing a thousand or more students for a convocation to give Dr Rabi an honorary degree. Rabi then gave a talk in the course of which he said, "And so I may say how glad I am to be at Monmouth College," apparently the *situs* of his most recent degree. Facing the throng of youthful faces, it was hard not to smile.

There followed an Oklahoma City University lunch at which Rabi, Berkner, Zacharias, and Wiesner all made short, pithy speeches extolling science. Their names were on the program. Mine was not. But the president of the college, anxious to be polite to his additional-starter guest, finally called on me. Luckily no mention had been made of the humanities or social sciences, and I had room to maneuver in suggesting that science and technology did not exhaust the realm of learning.

The crowning touch to this edifying occasion was a check for $3,000, at the Rabi, Berkner, Zacharias, and Wiesner rate of $1,000 a day. It reminded me of nothing so much as my achieving an A in Homer as a freshman at Penn, along with graduate students Harris and Seifert, and senior Cataldo. It is pleasant when people refuse to make invidious distinctions in circumstances where they may be indicated.

Some years later I heard an echo of the Rabi gaffe about Monmouth College. It was at a meeting of the Japanese Ministry of Trade and Industry (MITI) in Tokyo. Roy Harrod had the word, as the French put it, and said, "Next week I shall be in Japan." He was in Japan. But the talk had been presumably written for an earlier occasion in another country, presumably England.

MIT had no sabbatical policy in those days – it developed one later – but it allowed staff leave if an individual could finance his own research. The Merrill Foundation was run by Bert Fox, first at Williams College and then at the Harvard Business School, and by Kermit Gordon of Williams. I applied for a grant to prepare a monograph on the terms of trade, especially to test empirically the Raul Prebisch thesis that the industrial countries had turned the terms of trade against less-developed countries engaged in the production of primary products. The Prebisch thesis had been enunciated in publications of the Economic Commission for Latin America, and rested, I was told much later by Rosemary Thorp of the Oxford Institute of Statistics, on some idea Prebisch picked up from a youthful indiscretion of mine, a note in the *Quarterly Journal of Economics* on "The urgency of demand," in which I discuss demand conditions in international trade but fail to distinguish adequately between income elasticity and price elasticity. As I understand it, a remark or two in that paper, accepted for publication by Professor Frank W. Taussig, who wrote to me on penny postcards mailed from his summer home in Cotuit, Massachusetts, caused Prebisch to believe that industrial demand for raw materials was price-inelastic, whereas less-developed countries' demand for manufactures was income-elastic – or something of that order – resulting in the terms of trade, that is, the price at which exports exchange for imports, running continuously against the less-developed countries.

I proposed to study the question factually using trade

statistics, and calculating the terms of trade of large areas of the world such as industrial Europe, other Europe, the United States, areas of recent settlement (Argentina, Australia, Canada, New Zealand, etc.), and all other (meaning the less-developed world) for selected dates. In those days before computers, I needed staff to turn the cranks of calculating machines to divide value (PQ) by quantity (Q) to get price (P), or more accurately unit value. To bring assistants from the United States to Europe would have been too costly so I asked James Meade to recommend one of his European students from the London School of Economics, Hal Lary, who was in charge of research at the Economic Commission for Europe, to produce a local, and planned to acquire a secretary in Geneva where the Economic Commission for Europe promised to house me in the Library of the Palais des Nations. Herman van der Tak from Holland came from the London School of Economics and later went on to work at the World Bank; Lary produced a stateless statistician from Czechoslovakia whom the Economic Commission for Europe could hire for no more than a year, Jaroslav Vanek, later a professor of economics at Cornell. Jean Bradley from New York did the typing as she helped put her husband through the University of Fribourg medical school. I cannot recall how large the budget was, about $30,000, if I have the order of magnitude correct. Kermit Gordon was amazed, he later told me, that we finished the book, *The Terms of Trade: A European Case Study* (Cambridge, MA, 1956), in the academic year and parts of two summers, and managed additionally to turn back several thousand dollars not spent. Each event, he said, is unlikely in the history of foundation grants; the two together a rarity.

Since the League of Nations had been founded only in 1919, its library lacked the volumes of trade statistics I wanted for 1872 and 1900, although it had initially acquired those for 1913, and in due course later volumes for 1928, 1938, and 1952. From national libraries it borrowed those for 1872 and 1900. We could not go further back because such a country as Germany did not exist until 1871, and even its 1872 figures of trade by commodity and country were primitive, recording commodities by the border they crossed, north, west, east or south, rather than by country of destination. There were hundreds of makeshifts, such as calculating the unit value of radio parts by dividing value by pounds of parts. In the end, however, we reached the conclusion that seems to me still to stand up, that the terms of trade were not the problem. Rather, the capacity of a country to reallocate its resources from unprofitable to profitable uses was critical. With such capacity, the terms of trade could be ignored. Without this "capacity to transform," the terms of trade would shift against such countries, not because of the nature of the demand for given products, but because others would enter its profitable fields, and it would fail to exit from the unprofitable ones.

One line in the introduction evoked a sympathetic response from reviewers. I wrote that this would be the last empirical study I would undertake, as the most fascinating local results uncovered during the work turned out on deeper examination to have been the result of calculating errors. Some years later, accompanying a group of Sloan Fellows on the first of their annual trips between examinations and commencement, I visited a Saint Gobain plant that made plate glass. Conveyor belts carried ingredients up to a boiling cauldron which spilled its contents on to a conveyor belt that rolled and squeezed and pressed the continuous sheet. At the end we saw six men smashing the glass as it reached the end of the quarter-mile belt. I was highly amused: shades of "A Nous la Liberté," the movie, or Charlie Chaplin in "City Lights." The Sloan Fellows empathized, however. "That's always the way," one said. "When there is a plant visit, something always goes wrong." The troubles of professionals amuse outsiders; they are not funny to the club.

22

Geneva
1953–1954

I should perhaps not digress from an account of my life as an economist to say how pleasant it was living in Geneva those fifteen months, more or less. When we arrived, we arranged to rent a villa down the Rhône by the Pont Butin, high above the gorge through which the river tumbled. It was owned by a Swiss woman who lived in Paris, and like all tenants of Swiss property we had to sign the *inventaire* so as to be prepared to make good any damages at the end of our stay. It had a glorious view of Mount Salève, an adjoining farm with wine presses, barns, chickens, and cows that returned from the mountains at the end of the summer. We were at the end of one bus line, and the three children of school age would take a bus down to the center of the city, change to another and go via the route des Chênes straight through to the International School. I rode a bicycle to the Palais des Nations, often taking the three-year-old on the back and dropping her off at the Home d'Enfants. Her French vocabulary diverged from mine, as she pointed out when she learned that I did not know the words for witch or ghost in French (I do now: *sorcière* and *phantôme*). The gardener at the Home, she said, was an Eskimo. We were incredulous. Her defense: one of her siblings had told her that Eskimos kiss by rubbing noses. The gardener had rubbed his nose against hers.

Geneva

Today, I suppose, we would call that child-molesting.

We got into the house only in August. In July we tried to get a chalet in Champéry only to find that the last one had gone the day before to another economist, Ragnar Nurkse. We ended up in primitive accommodations in the next village, Val d'Illiez, met the Nurkses, and had a fine time with them in walks, teas, and the like. When I say the chalet was primitive, I am not overstating the case. The crystal ware consisted of jelly jars, and the facilities of an inside-outhouse, if I make myself clear. The latter had a picture of the Dents du Midi in color against a wall. Similar pictures are available in books, magazines, and picture-frames all over the world. I cannot see them without my bowels loosening; my wife without hers tightening.

In Geneva we had a *chauffeur* – not a man to drive the car, but a furnace man, who gets up the heat to *chauffer* the house. As maid we had Thérèse, who had failed her examinations as a hairdresser, and did this as second-best. There were three weeks at Verbier skiing at Christmas, thirteen weekends thereafter of skiing at resorts in the Jura and the foothills of the Alps. In April, my son Charlie and I took the Haute Route with a guide, he at fourteen just old enough – poor Dick at twelve was not up to it – I at forty-four hoping to be just young enough. Jack Downie of the Economic Commission for Europe came along. He was not in condition, as we more or less were, and got altitude sickness as we crossed from Verbier to Zermatt over ranges up to 12,000 feet. Jack left the party at Arolla, a favorite summer climbing spot of the economist Albert Kervyn de Lettenhove of Louvain-la-Neuve in Belgium, and next to Les Haudères, where John Hicks used to summer. Some time later, when I became seventy, I gave myself a birthday present of a trip back to the Valais to go walking with my two sons, this time they taking care of me, rather than as in 1953–4, my looking out for them. We had a week in June, coming down from the Grand Saint Bernard to Champéry and Martigny, by way of Champex. The real present to me, of course, was the week off their wives gave them for my sake.

Gunnar Myrdal was the executive director of the Economic

Commission for Europe, and we got to know him and his expansive personality to some extent. On one occasion he had a paper to write for a bicentennial celebration at Columbia. The topic was economic integration. He asked Hal Lary for a memorandum on the subject to get him started, and Lary, up to his ears in the annual report or a quarterly bulletin, turned to me. I dashed off a memorandum in an afternoon, drawing on the international-trade theory I had been teaching. The factor-price-equalization theorem suggested that the prices of factors can be equalized by factor movements – migration and capital flows – but in their absence and under certain rigid conditions, including free trade, by trade in goods. I suggested that the ultimate test of economic integration between countries was equality of wages, interest rates, and to a lesser degree the rent of land, but that instead of trade leading to factor-price equalization it was more likely that factor-price equalization led to free trade. Myrdal took the idea and ran with it, writing a long article for the Columbia symposium, and then expanding that into a book, *The International Economy* (London, 1956), adding the pregnant notion that free trade between countries that were very different might widen wage and interest-rate differentials in a backwash effect. As a test of the original idea, it should be noted that the legislation for the Kennedy round of tariff reductions under the General Agreement on Tariffs and Trade (GATT) called for 50 percent tariff reductions in general, but allowed for reductions of 100 percent among countries where 80 percent, if I remember the figure, of a commodity was produced by a few countries; in other words, wider reductions for countries that were similar in resource allocation and levels of wages.

In the summer of 1954 I taught a short course at the Institut des Hautes Etudes Internationales in Geneva, the so-called Rappard Institute run by William Rappard. He was something of a tartar and decapitated his speakers either in his introduction or in his polished words of thanks at the end. I recall that at the close of a lecture by Hans Morgenthau, the Chicago political scientist in international relations, who had complained in his lecture that President Eisenhower was not showing enough

Geneva

leadership, Rappard declared this to be a strange notion coming from a refugee from a country that had suffered from an excess of the *Führerprinzip*. In my case he said after the inaugural lecture that he had enjoyed it a great deal, but wondered whether it had not been over the heads of the students.

One interesting character in Geneva that year was Michael Hoffman, the *New York Times* correspondent for economics in Europe as a whole, a former graduate student from Chicago who had worked under Jacob Viner, and later worked for the World Bank and for a Belgian banking firm, Lambert Freres.

Jaroslav Vanek wanted to go to graduate school in economics in the United States. I suggested that having served on the MIT graduate admissions committee I knew how to write a persuasive application and he should let me help him apply for Yale, which had lots of money. I wrote what I thought was a powerful document, but he got turned down. We then admitted him to MIT. His departure was delayed in the fall of 1954 and he arrived in Cambridge one day in the following January, just as I was going to lunch. I brought him along, introduced him to my colleagues at our regular economics faculty club table, that handled eight but could be stretched to ten or eleven by pushing chairs further back. After lunch I introduced him to Professor Karl W. Deutsch, a political scientist, born in Czechoslovakia, who later taught at Yale, then Harvard, then the Free University of Berlin. Deutsch is a large man, owlish and portly. Vanek whispered to me afterwards: "That is what I think of as a professor. The members of your department are, what shall I say, so *sportif*." French was his second language after Czech, and English a good third. It is a story treasured, however, by Samuelson, Solow, Brown, *et al*.

Plate 1 CPK as deck-boy, on freighter SS *Bird City*, bound for Copenhagen, Danzig, Helsingfors, Leningrad, Kotka, Raumo, and Kemi, Copenhagen again, and Portland, Maine, August 1930.

Plate 2 With Sarah in Davos, Switzerland, winter 1940.

Plate 3 Rear Admiral Charles P. Kindleberger USN Medical Corps, retired, Charles P. Kindleberger 3rd, and Charles P. Kindleberger 2nd, Seminary Hill, Alexandria, Virginia, about September 1941.

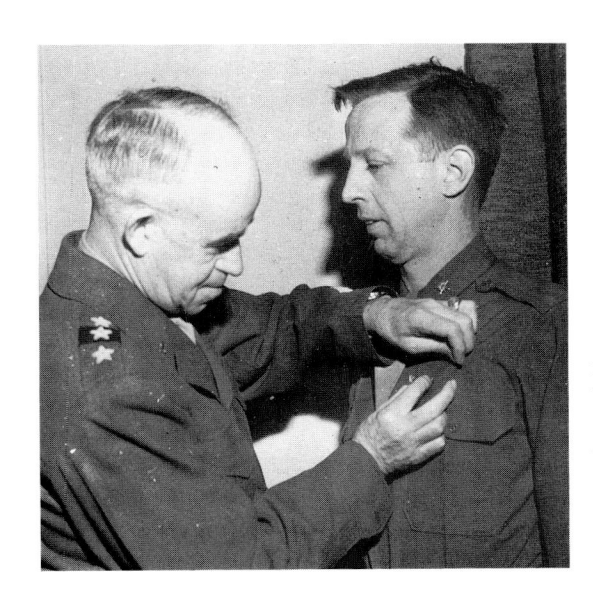

Plate 4 Award of Bronze Star by General Omar N. Bradley, Commanding General, Twelfth Army Group, US Army, at Luxembourg Headquarters, November 1944.

Plate 5 Emile Despres and Werner Knoke, staff economist and vice-president for foreign operations, respectively, Federal Reserve Bank of New York, *en route* to Europe on a banking visit, June 1938.

Plate 6 Ragnar Nurkse lunching at Morzine, a French ski resort near Geneva, Switzerland, March 1954.

Plate 7 Jean van der Tak, Gottfried Haberler, student chairman, and CPK at a dinner in Professor Haberler's honor at the Institut des Hautes Etudes Internationales, Geneva, Switzerland, July 1954.

Plate 8 Department of Economics and Social Science, MIT, spring 1950. From left to right: *front row* – Robert Bishop, Ithiel Pool (Political Science), Max Millikan, Donald Tucker, Paul Samuelson, CPK, Elspeth Rostow; *second row* – Romney Robinson, Abraham Siegel, George ("Jim") Baldwin, Joseph Licklider (Psychology), James Boyce (Political Science), Jack Coleman, Robert Solow, Cary Brown, Everett Hagen, Benjamin Higgins; *missing* – Ralph Freeman (department head), Harold Freeman, Rupert Maclaurin, Paul N. Rosenstein-Rodan, George Shultz, Wilfrid Malenbaum. Walt Rostow was in the history department but taught in economics.

Plate 9 The Kindleberger family in Lincoln, Massachusetts, in the late 1960s. From left to right: Dick, Randall, Sarah, Sally, CPK, Charlie.

Plate 10 Celebration of the retirement of Professor Albert Kervyn de Lettenhove from the economics department of the Catholic University of Louvain-la-Neuve, Belgium, May 1986. From left to right: Robert Solow, Lord Kaldor, Francis Bator, Albert Kervyn, CPK, Daniel Weisserbs, Alfred Steinherr.

Plate 11 Robert Solow, Jagdish Bhagwati, CPK, Ronald Findlay, and Ronald Jones at Haselby Conference Center, outside Stockholm, at a symposium in honor of Bertil Ohlin, June 1976. Bhagwati, Findlay, and Jones are among MIT's many distinguished PhD graduates.

Plate 12 With Lord Franks, former chairman of the Organization for European Economic Cooperation, at the 30th anniversary, held in Paris, June 1977, of the speech by Secretary George C. Marshall on June 7, 1947, which launched the idea of the Marshall Plan.

Plate 13 Department of Economics, MIT, 1976. From left to right: *front row* – Evsey Domar, Paul Samuelson, CPK, Cary Brown (department head), Franco Modigliani, Sidney Alexander, Robert Bishop; *second row* – Edwin Kuh, Morris Adelman, Abraham Siegel, Richard Eckaus, Martin Weizman; *third row* – Stanley Fischer, Jagdish Bhagwati, Rudiger Dornbusch, Ann Friedlander, Robert Solow, Robert Hall; *fourth row* – Paul Joskow, Harold Freeman, Hal Varian, Jerome Rothenberg, Peter Diamond, Jerry Hausman, visiting scholar; *missing* – Michael Piore, Peter Temin, Franklin Fisher, Lester Thurow, Lance Taylor.

Plate 14 In the doorway of the garden toolhouse, Lincoln, Massachusetts, about 1970.

23

MIT *again in the fifties*

As indicated earlier, I taught economic development in the summer school at Harvard in 1955, and also ran the William Yandell Elliott international seminar section on economics. A question asked early on in the class by a young Japanese immediately alerted me to the fact that here was an economist of power. His name was Ryutaro Komiya. He had come to Harvard to work on input–output analysis with Wassily Leontief, and on arriving early took a few classes. We became good friends. He later spent a year at MIT. I have seen him both in Cambridge and Tokyo. He was president of the Japanese Economic Association as I held a comparable position in the United States, and has now given up his professorship at the University of Tokyo to be the head of the Research Institute of the Ministry of Trade and Industry in the Japanese government (MITI).

Another Japanese connection was forged in that class: that with a Jesuit priest, Father Hirschmeyer, later president of the University of Nagoya. One summer when I was in Japan he invited me to Nagoya for a visit to the Mikimoto pearl fisheries, and dinner. Afterward I asked a knowledgeable acquaintance what I could do in return. I was told to make a contribution covering the cost of the day. Father Hirschmeyer was a deep

MIT *again*

student of Schumpeter's work, having written his thesis on the man, and was interested in applying Schumpeter's ideas on entrepreneurship to Japanese history.

There was one Korean undergraduate in the class, Pyung Chun Hahn; he had finished a degree at Northwestern University, and was filling in time before he attended the Harvard Law School. I found him excellent and tried to persuade him to give up the law and come into economics, with a fellowship to MIT, but to no avail. We became friendly. I have pictures of him with his wife and two boys accoutered in colonial tricorn hats at a 4th of July parade in Lincoln. He went back to Seoul to a post in the law school but had a difficult time adjusting. Soon I got anguished letters from him offering to return to the United States and even study economics, if he had to. I published one anonymously in an essay on "Study abroad and emigration," in a symposium on *The Brain Drain* (New York, 1968), edited by Walter Adams. In due course his laments ceased. He got a postgraduate fellowship to study more law at Yale. He returned to Seoul, and went into government as a personal assistant to President Rhee. He was among the five or six Korean cabinet ministers who were killed by an explosion under the platform where they were sitting at a ceremony in Burma.

One further episode troubles me from that summer. An American student did not do well, and I suggested to him that he might consider giving up economics, for the study of which it did not seem that he was particularly suited, and try something else. He took it hard. A number of years later I saw him again, and he said somewhat defiantly that he was an economist, working in an AID mission somewhere. I remain doubtful that he was a good economist, but I regret having been so blunt and unsparing of feelings.

It was in the summer of 1956, I think, that I was invited to spend six weeks at the Merrill Center in Southampton on Long Island. This was an 18-acre estate given by Charles Merrill of Merrill, Lynch, etc., to his old college, Amherst, with the stipulation that they could not sell it for ten years. Willard Thorp, then at Amherst, sought to use it in summer as a research center,

MIT *again*

gathering economists, some for the summer, some for two-week periods, to wrestle with a problem. This particular summer the problem was international trade. I was invited for six weeks but could stay only four. Thorp or his bright wife Clarice had worked out a scheme to pay members nothing for the first two weeks if they were invited for more, but a great deal for each week thereafter. Our group had Harry Johnson of Chicago for the summer along with Erik Hoffmeyer, later governor of the National Bank of Denmark, today the central banker with the longest tenure of office in Europe (twenty-five years), Brian Reddaway of Cambridge University Division of Applied Research, and Just Faaland of the Bergen School of Business in Norway. Wives were expressly not invited. In previous years some had brought wives and found places for them to stay in town, going out in the evenings to visit the wife, like a boarding-school boy escaping into the village.

I suppose I got to know Harry Johnson this particular summer. He was one who never did anything by halves: writing, editing, eating, drinking, smoking, and after giving up smoking, whittling in conferences. He was a superb editor, often taking a rather muddy submitted paper and rewriting it to show the author what he really meant. He was frequently asked to summarize a conference and did so brilliantly. His gift was exposition, sometimes taking the idea of another and making it more accessible by, for example, turning a diagram on its side. On occasion, he would write book reviews that were mean-spirited, such as his review in the *Economic Journal* of Meade's *Balance of Payments*, that elsewhere of Linder's *Essay on Trade and Transformation*, or his consistent early rejection of Hymer's work on the multinational corporation. I have hypothesized that he was pursued by some sort of demon that made him act compulsively and to excess, that his attacks on these original ideas basically came from a chagrin that he had not had them himself. But I warn the reader against giving too much credence to my pop sociology or psychology.

Willard Thorp was an urbane chairman. He had been a cool and collected negotiator with the Russians, smoking an

MIT again

air-cooled pipe and physically being well padded in the rear so that the Russians failed in their attempts to outwait him, a tactic so successful at Potsdam witn Truman and Byrnes. Clarice Thorp was a wonderfully fiery personality, who did not take kindly to the disorganized life led by such people as Harry Johnson and Stephen Enke, a two-week visitor, who, in his dressing-gown, asked if she could get him a stenographer as he wanted to dictate.

I have continued to see Erik Hoffmeyer in Copenhagen over the years, once when I gave a seminar at the National Bank, and once dining with him on the occasion of a visit to the University of Copenhagen.

The 1950s produced *The Terms of Trade*, two editions of *International Economics*, and one of *Economic Development*. It also produced some wonderful students. It is perhaps invidious to mention any names when there were so many of distinction, but perhaps I can recite a list I have noted elsewhere: Jagdish Bhagwati, William Branson, Carlos Diaz Alejandro, Miltiades Chacholiades, Ronald Findlay, Ronald Jones, Stephen Hymer, Stephen Magee, Robert Mundell, Egon Sohmen, Jaroslav Vanek. Three of them – Diaz Alejandro, Hymer, and Sohmen – have since died, and in each case I have had the sad duty of writing something about them. Sohmen and I never agreed on fixed versus flexible exchange rates. He became more Chicago than Friedman on this issue, and we would argue in Cambridge, Saarbrucken, Heidelberg, and, at one International Economic Association meeting, at Algarve, Portugal. Hymer became radicalized in the late 1960s, partly I find it ironic to note, in the course of a fellowship granted by that most establishment of organizations, the Council of Foreign Relations, which I helped him get. Carlos Diaz Alejandro, born in Cuba, educated in the United States, and the leading American expert on Latin American economics at the time of his death in 1985, paid me the ultimate compliment of gradually moving from international-trade theory to economic and financial history, not that of Europe to be sure, but of Latin America. My paper for one of his two memorial symposia was entitled "From graduate

MIT *again*

student to professional peer," and traced out the rewarding if uneasy trajectory of the relationship between *Doktorvater* as the Germans call it, and student, as it shifts from vertical to horizontal.

In the last year of the decade, and the first of the next, I participated in a seminar at the Center for International Affairs (CFIA) at Harvard on contemporary France. The CFIA was headed by Robert R. Bowie, earlier a professor of law at Harvard who had gradually shifted his interests from law to international relations, especially those between the United States and Europe. His deputy was Henry Kissinger. Bowie had served with OMGUS under John J. McCloy, again as head of the Policy Planning Staff in the Department of State under John Foster Dulles, and was an old Baltimorean friend of my wife's family, a classmate of her brother, Frank, and a student at the Gilman School when her father, L. Wardlaw Miles, was the headmaster. It was partly because of these associations that I joined the interdisciplinary seminar, perhaps, but mainly because I was interested in France, and no economist on the Harvard faculty seemed to have an interest in it. The regular members of the seminar included Stanley Hoffmann in the department of government, Laurence Wylie in sociology, Joe W. Saxe, an economist, of the CFIA, who acted as secretary of the group. Also from outside Harvard were Jesse R. Pitts, a sociologist from Wayne State University, Nancy Roelker of Boston University, and visitors from France, notably Jean-Baptiste Duroselle, the historian. Seminar presentations would occasionally come from other scholars. The regular governmental fellows of the Center, who came for a year, would also attend meetings and participate in the discussion. It was for me an exhilarating exercise in interdisciplinary research, and wonderful preparation for my 1960–1 sabbatical year in Oxford and Paris, working on a comparison of economic growth in France and Britain. The seminar produced a book (Stanley Hoffmann *et al.*, *In Search of France*, Cambridge, MA, 1963), in which I had a paper on "The postwar resurgence of the French economy." The experience had another dimension that was briefly maddening and highly

MIT *again*

instructive over time: a close encounter with that superb editor, Max Hall, who grilled the authors as their papers were completed, to make sure they meant what they said and said what they meant. Over the years I have encountered many editors, some with a light and even close to no touch, others with a propensity to rewrite. I claim I write well enough to need only shallow editing, but my experience with Hall, which infuriated me during the several hours he was ripping my paragraphs and sentences apart, was most rewarding in showing how much a diligent and experienced editor can improve one's exposition.

As a footnote to *In Search of France*, I record that the CFIA tried to repeat the prescription with Germany, in an exercise led by Henry Kissinger. Instead of a two-year seminar, however, they held a single session over a weekend. Papers were commissioned and paid for from a group of experts around the country, and I imagine most of them were turned in. But Kissinger lost interest, failed to write his piece, perhaps the introduction, and the project aborted. In academic life, slow cooking works better than the microwave.

In the summers of 1959 and 1960, in intervals between spurts of research on France, I wrote a little book entitled *Foreign Trade and the National Economy* (New Haven, CT, 1962). This was undertaken for a project of an Inter-University Committee on Comparative Economics, headed by Lloyd Reynolds of Yale University, who raised the money from the Ford Foundation in which he had previously been working on economic projects while on leave from Yale. The idea was for a series of monographs on separate functions in various economies, rather than the usual comparative approach across the whole range of functions, through capitalism, socialism, communism, fascism, etc. Other authors were Henry Phelps Brown on labor, Eric Lundberg on business cycles, Raymond Goldsmith on financial institutions, Abram Bergson on planning, and so on, with a final synthesis by Reynolds. The first choice for the volume on trade, I understood, was Ragnar Nurkse, but he died in 1959. Arrangements were on a generous scale, with money to pay for graduate assistance on the one hand, and to hire a critic on the other, not to mention a whopping honorarium for the author. (Mine was used to build an addition on my house that I sometimes refer to as the Lloyd M. Reynolds Memorial Study.) I spent the money for the assistant on Charles ("Chuck") Cooper, a graduate student working on Soviet trade problems, at a time when he was particularly needy. As critic, I obtained Harry Johnson, who I knew would pull no punches. The book was written on the basis of accumulated knowledge rather than new research, at white heat, in perhaps only six weeks for the rough writing. None the less it has some interesting contributions, such as the impact of transport costs (from location theory), and of random factors – war, pestilence, variability of the harvest, strikes, and the like. There were chapters on the impact of growth on trade and of trade on growth. Tucked in my desk copy is a letter from Bertil Ohlin, replying to my letter of congratulations to him on his Nobel prize, which reads in part:

> I don't remember if I told you that a couple of years ago I reread your book about *Foreign Trade and the National Economy* of 1962 and found that it added a great deal to what one could obtain from the ordinary textbooks of international trade.

As noted earlier in connection with *The Dollar Shortage*, Professor Ohlin was extraordinarily generous and encouraging to younger economists.

For a time I tried to produce an aphorism a year and to remember them; all are now forgotten except two, which I can no longer place in time. The first of these related to the folk wisdom (?) of sailors in 1930. "Gonorrhea," they said – I shifted the subject to a McCarthy-type attack on one's loyalty – "is no worse than a bad cold, and you are not a man until you have had it." The second, *à propos* the lush funding of *Foreign Trade and the National Economy* (with apologies to Lord Acton): "Foundations corrupt, and the Ford Foundation corrupts absolutely."

Let me work into this treatment of the 1950s my several experiences in this and the succeeding decade with honors examinations at Swarthmore. Swarthmore had an honors program which was optional in the last two years, consisting of two seminars in each of the four terms, on all eight of which a student was examined at the end of his or her senior year, by an outsider. External examinations are a test of manhood (womanhood, personhood?) in a college, as the staff tests itself against outside instead of inside, sometimes overly charitable, standards. External examiners were invited to prepare questions for written examinations, based on the seminar curricula which were sent to them, grade the written work, and then to come to Swarthmore in a mass to give oral examinations to the candidates over Friday and Saturday. The orals were completed by noon on Saturday, following which the raft of external examiners would meet to award a single grade – highest honors (*Summa*), high honors (*Magna*), honors (*Cum Laude*) – or, if a failure, return to course to decide whether or not a degree should be awarded, based on the candidate's performance in all eight seminars. There were almost never more than three seminars in a single subject, such as economics, English literature, history, etc.

The interest came in the big meeting on Saturday afternoon, where several disciplines occasionally were unable to agree. Since no one could leave for home until all the students had been graded, holdouts – professors in one discipline who insisted on higher honors for students in their own subject, or lower honors for students in other subjects who had not done well on their examination (the usual bone of contention) – made the meetings occasionally tense. The Swarthmore faculty was not present – that was critical to the test of manhood – but the relevant faculty members in a given subject could be invited in and asked "yes" or "no" questions such as: "Has this student ever had a nervous breakdown?" or "Would it be a grave miscarriage of justice if this student were refused honors?"

I served as external examiner at Swarthmore three times, I believe, and it was most enjoyable. The students were very good indeed. One stayed with a professor, making it a sort of house-party (I stayed twice with Clair Wilcox, a widower, who had

MIT *again*

married Marcia Wallace, Don Wallace's widow; they were delightful people, and their remarriage led my wife to exclaim, "Good for them. I do love to use up leftovers.") The Saturday afternoon meeting had the same fascination that C.P. Snow's novels on Cambridge life have. Each year some departmental examiners played the role of villains, others of politically adroit problem-solvers. While it was pleasurable to go to Swarthmore for these occasions, one strong incentive was to continue to get the superb graduate students they produced.

Five quasi-academic stories wind up this chapter, mostly placeable in the 1950s.

Very early on in teaching my graduate classes in international economics, I would bring the entire class (then twenty or less) to Lincoln for a picnic. On the first occasion we bought some cheap ice-cream which gave a number in the class diarrhea. One student, Hy Gadon, had an accident on the Sunday after the outing on Saturday and was visited, still in bed, by an insurance adjuster on Monday. He was unaware of the condition of his classmates, ascribed the problem to the shake-up, and received a check for $250.

Some years later, I wanted to put back on a stone wall bordering our house a boulder that had been knocked off, one too big for me to handle alone. Armed with crowbars and lead-pipe, a few of the students accomplished the task in minutes. Two or three years later, I learned that John Fei, who had gone on from MIT to work on the Leontief project at Harvard, was circulating the story that Kindleberger used to bring students out from MIT to work on his place, and that this particular year the group on departing had left a sign: "This driveway is submitted in partial fulfillment of the requirements for the PhD in Economics at the Massachusetts Institute of Technology." While it lacked all truth, the story was well told.

On one occasion the Graduate Economics Club organized a debate over a point in international macro-economics between me and Franco Modigliani, the ebullient and effervescent Italian-born Nobel laureate (later), who spoke like a machine gun. My opener was: "I do not want equal time in this debate; I want

MIT *again*

equal words. Since Franco speaks twice as fast as I, I should have twice as long."

One of my neighbors in Lincoln was a banker named J. Warren Olmstead, whose family of wife and four children decided once to defuse Christmas materialism by having each member give only one present to one other member, drawn secretly by lot well in advance. One of the sons, Jay, was a senior at Earlham College, and preparing to go home for Christmas, visited a Miss Coppock whom he had been dating to say goodbye. While there he happened to mention that he still faced the task of buying the present for his father. Professor Joseph D. Coppock, who taught economics at Earlham and who had been a colleague of mine in the State Department during the Marshall Plan, offered a suggestion. He presented Jay with a copy of his new book on commodity agreements to pass along to Banker Olmstead. Thus my neighbor's present from his family for the year was J.D. Coppock's *International Economic Instability* (New York, 1962) – not a book to curl up with in front of the fire.

Some time in the late 1970s I was asked to attend a conference in Philadelphia to comment on a paper by Harry Johnson on "Networks of economists: their role in international monetary reforms," later published, lacking my comment, in William M. Evan, ed., *Knowledge and Power in a Global Society* (Beverly Hills, 1981). The conference had been organized by sociologists, and I knew no one there beyond Johnson. Our session was scheduled for early afternoon. I planned to arrive for lunch, only to learn that the group was not providing lunch. I suggested to Harry that we go together to a restaurant. He had had his stroke by that time, walked poorly, and said he had brought a brown-bag lunch which he was going to eat *in situ*. In occurred to me that I could get some lunch at my old fraternity, so I walked from Market Street to 3637 Locust, and invited myself. A young member on my left slowly recognized that I had written his textbook in international economics. I offered to pay for the lunch; this was refused. As I prepared to leave, the budding student of international economics asked me to inscribe his text. This I did

MIT *again*

as follows: "Economics teaches us that there is no free lunch. Thanks for the free lunch." A couple of weeks later, back in Lincoln, I received a circular from the Philadelphia chapter, saying that they hoped to send a fraternity crew to Henley, and were soliciting the alumni for contributions. As an erstwhile oarsman who had recently partaken of the group's largesse, I had to respond. Economics won again. The lunch cost me $25.

24

Oxford and Paris
1960–1961

Seven years from 1953–4 brings one to 1960–1, and it seemed to me time for another sabbatical. Escape from the academy is rewarding for the escaper, but hard on the students whose theses he is supervising. Universities that encourage a two-platoon system, with half the faculty on leave every year, seem to me derelict in their duty. One year off (with perhaps the extra summer) every seventh year does refresh the teacher–administrator – and I had served a great deal as graduate-student adviser – and gets some research done. As in the year in Geneva, I shaped the application for a Ford Faculty Fellowship to where we wanted to go, Oxford and Paris, to write *Economic Growth in France and Britain, 1851–1950* (Cambridge, MA, 1964). I started ahead in the summer of 1960 for Paris, alone. Our sons were in college, and my wife brought the girls over to England in September, after summer camps.

I found a pension in the sixth arrondissement, on the rue Saint-Romain lying between the rue de Sèvres and the rue du Cherche-Midi. It was a great success. We stayed there in January 1961, while looking for an apartment, and two of my MIT colleagues later used it as a base in Paris while working out longer-term arrangements. My name was unpronounceable to the maids, so I was known as Monsieur Cinq, after the number

Oxford and Paris

of my bedroom. I would walk weekdays down to the Seine and across to the Treasury part of the Louvre on the rue du Rivoli, take an elevator to the fourth floor, and then walk up the stairway into the large cupola atop the Treasury wing of the Louvre. This was the Ministry of Finance library. From the stairs one could look over the Tuileries to the Champs-Elysées and see in the distance the Arc de Triomphe. It was a magnificent place to work.

The library itself was fairly primitive. The handwritten catalogue told in which of the three rooms a book was, in which tier of shelves, and the number of the shelf. There were about fifty or sixty books per shelf and one had to sort over the lot to find the item one was looking for. But this system had superb externalities. In looking for book A, you found books B, C, D ... Y, and Z that you had not known existed. I brought a portable typewriter and typed my notes in Salle O unless there were two other readers there that I might disturb. One was not enough to make me desist. He could always go into another room to read in quiet. I sat across from an employee, or so I judged him, who came every day with his briefcase. As soon as he arrived he took from it a newspaper and read the comic strips, holding it up within inches of his eyes, because he was practically blind; at lunchtime he took out his sandwich and a bottle of wine. I went out to lunch in neighboring restaurants – cheap ones – staying with one until I got bored with it. Weekends were spent walking along the streets of Paris, the Seine banks, watching *boules*, and writing letters. It was a most productive summer, and my French loose-leaf notebooks are thicker than those of Britain, Germany, or *a fortiori*, Italy, Scandinavia, and the rest of Europe.

At the end of the summer, I bought a car and drove it to Southampton where I was reunited with the Kindleberger women. We spent a couple of nights at the Cadogan Hotel in Chelsea, of Oscar Wilde fame, and thence to Oxford. I had rented Lawrence Stone's house on Woodstock Road for the fall, had privileges at Nuffield College, and started on the English reading of French and British economic growth. The walk

Oxford and Paris

down the canal towpath to Nuffield was a delight, despite an occasional scare from a swan coming in for a landing behind me. Nuffield was the college of Max Hartwell in English economic history, which helped enormously; I attended his seminar. The G.D.H. Cole collection in the library was splendid, and I met Cole's son, and talked with him about his work on Bristol buses and locomotive replacements, topics that grew naturally out of my wartime interest in spare parts and standardization. Changes from one standard to an improved one are helped enormously if there is a secondhand market for getting rid of the older types. It happens too that British individuals collect locomotive numbers by type as young people, and some pursue the game into later life. I heard the story of a man who chased to Scotland and India to fill out his numbers on Bristol buses – the Scots liking secondhand equipment because they were thrifty, the Indians because of poverty. In selling off the old models, the Bristol company thoughtfully included a great many spare parts. Failing to understand the need for spare parts, the Indians assembled one set into a new bus. The philosophical question one collector put to himself was whether this was in fact a Bristol bus.

Lawrence Stone, my landlord, was spending a year in the history department at Princeton, a department he later joined permanently. One day there was a knock at our door, and Max Hartwell asked whether he could come in. Stone had written to him, asking him to go to his rooms in Wadham, get the key to his file cabinet in 234 Woodstock Road, and retrieve, to send to Princeton, a file marked "Ideas." It seems that Stone had left for a year's leave without his ideas.

Spending the Michaelmas term at Nuffield was very enjoyable. The college deals with graduate students only, like the later-established St Antony College. Fellows at the time included, in addition to Hartwell, the warden, Norman Chester, Donald MacDougall, Hugh Clegg, and Francis Seton. Peter Jay, later British ambassador to the United States under the Labor Government, was a student, and not very friendly. Another was the later United States trade expert consultant, Harold Malmgren. One daughter, Sally, was in a boarding school in Dorset, where the headmistress was familiarly known as "Caesar." Randall attended the Oxford High School for Girls, wearing a uniform of which she would slip the necktie over her head each day rather than make the knot anew, until it looked like an old rope. We spent many weekends in the southwest – Maiden Castle, Dorset, Stonehenge, Salisbury, Avebury. A success. I have the feeling that my habits rather undermined those of the college since I could be seen reading at my desk while the fellows and students went to the common room for coffee in the morning, and even, on occasion, when they went for tea in the afternoon. *Sitzfleisch* is something developed at MIT but rarely encountered in Oxbridge. We had Christmas with the Mialls from Seminary Hill days at their place in Taplow, and in early January set off for Paris, leaving Sally, however, in Shillingstone, Dorset.

After a few days in the Villa Saint-Romain, we rented an apartment at 8 place du Palais Bourbon, just behind the Chamber of Deputies. The square was a delight to behold, built in 1776, with classic architecture that I do not know how to describe, and while our apartment on the fourth floor was a little behind in maintenance – *delaboré*, was one word the French used, or *poussière* – it had great charm. It belonged to the American daughter of a 1920s expatriate, Charles Bird. Ernest Hemingway had played with our landlady, then a child, under the grand piano, and Ezra Pound had been a frequent guest. There was usually room to park the car in the square. *Vogue* had an office on one side of the square and a studio on the other, and models sometimes crossed from one to the other, delighting the eye. One resident of the square was Paul Reynaud, the pre-war prime minister, and in the apartment above us, under the roof, was a woman who was said to have been the mistress of President Doumer, assassinated in 1931. We once tried to start a fire in the fireplace and she came running down the stairs as the smoke poured into her apartment. The "run-down, walk-up" as I called it, had the tub behind a curtain in the bedroom; the coal was kept in a locker in the WC; but it was a great place to work. My desk overlooked the square and the Chamber of Deputies. In the spring of 1961 we were awakened at 3 a.m. one

Oxford and Paris

morning by a fire in the Chamber, set by a *plastiquer*, and spent an anxious hour watching the *pompiers* battle the flames. I happened to be in Belgium on a trip when the president asked the citizens of Paris to go to the porte d'Orléans and to block the parachutists who, he feared, were making an attack on Paris from their bases in North Africa.

In due course I finished *Economic Growth in France and Britain*, an exercise in comparative economic history which sought to test theories of why French growth was slow compared to British, rejecting most single-valued explanations: that the French lacked coal, or were unduly wedded to the family firm, or failed to get ahead sufficiently rapidly in agriculture, etc. The debate has gone on, of course, and the revisionists are even disputing the facts, much less the explanation. One day I was talking to my Harvard Press editor, who suggested that the ending should have more punch. I misguidedly provided it with the following rash words: "Economic history, like all history, is absorbing, beguiling, great fun. But, for scientific problems, can it be taken seriously?" This produced if not an angry, at least an extremely irritated, outburst. I have since retracted the insult with apologies. The trouble lies not with economic history but with simplistic monocausal theories.

In May 1961 I was invited to serve as the first faculty opponent of Staffan Burenstam Linder, whose major thesis (like the German *Habilitationschrift*, somewhat higher than the American PhD) was to be defended at the Stockholm School of Economics. Linder had spent a year as a visiting fellow at MIT, and written some of his dissertation there. The invitation was for a week. Professor Ohlin, the supervisor, was chairman of the jury. There was a second opponent selected from among Linder's peers, Bo Södersten, and a third opponent, whose task was to act as a jester, making jokes. (For example: "As George Bernard Shaw said about another work, 'It is a remarkable piece of writing and I shall lose no time in reading it.'") He was Jacob Palmstierna, now president of the Scandinaviska Enskilda Bank. The thesis was nailed to the door. The public can attend these occasions, and the audience often includes several generations, among them babes-in-arms. The candidate and his opponents used to appear at 10 a.m. in white tie and tails – a formality now, alas, abandoned. The usual practice with a Scandinavian examination is for the first opponent to make long speeches. The American custom is to ask a series of pointed questions, rather like a legal cross-examination. This I did, and Linder acquitted himself with distinction. The jury then invited me to sit with it briefly before it began its deliberations. Ohlin asked, "What grade do you think he should get?" I asked to be told what the grading system was.

The highest grade is 1, I was told, and it has been given only twice in Swedish academic history, once to Wicksell, and the second time to Myrdal. (I rather read between the lines that Ohlin was slightly aggrieved not to have received it.) He added: "I do not think this performance rated a 1."

"The lowest grade is 3. That is a failure. I would not have let Linder take the examination if I had thought that he would get a 3," Ohlin continued.

I suggested that he was making my problem easy. "No," said Ohlin, "there is room for maneuver within the grade of 2. A 2 plus means he qualifies for a teaching position at a major university; a 2 means he can teach at high school; and a 2 minus means that the candidate must seek a non-academic job."

The examination had gone on for two hours, adjourned for lunch, and was then resumed briefly after lunch. The candidate is not told his grade until the following week, but gives a dinner on the evening of the examination day at which the chairman of the jury, giving the main address, throws out hints of the result. The dinner, given at the apartment of Linder's grandmother-in-law, was a sumptuous feast. I do not recall the menu, but I do remember the number of wines – four, including a Château d'Yquem – and I recall that it was the best meal I had had in Europe that year, much of it spent at Oxford high tables and in Paris. Again white tie and tails were *de rigueur* – one hired the kit with two stiff shirts and two ties so as not to show in the evening the grime of the day's academic toil. I was asked for a few words and remember having offered an old Schumpeter story. Schumpeter said that when, perhaps at Bonn, they had an average candidate for the doctorate, they would ask, "When did Goethe go to Weimar?" When the candidate was quite good, they would ask, "When did Goethe go where?" and of a brilliant one, "When did who go where?" There was, of course, some link to the day's proceedings.

In the event, Linder got the 2 plus, a job teaching at the Stockholm School of Economics, of which he is now the president, after a career in politics with the Conservative party.

Our sons joined us in the summer. Charlie's twenty-first birthday party was celebrated in the restaurant of the Eiffel Tower, with music, champagne, and dessert in the form of baked Alaskas shaped like miniature Eiffel Towers. We drove *en famille* to Denmark, where we chartered a boat for two weeks, and also rented an apartment in a farmhouse with our friends, the Hardcastles. The two families were twelve in all, with boat and apartment each sleeping six. The two men were on the boat all the time, the two youngest children only on the weekend. Each mother with her three older children sailed for Monday through Friday, and on the middle weekend the two couples and the two younger children were together. It was a linear-programming problem, the solution of which was worked out without mathematics or computers. The sail in the Skagerrak, the Kattegat, the Isefjord, and along the Swedish coast was a delight. One of the younger children was heard by a mother to say to the other in the back of the car, "Which sight in Europe did you hate the most?" In driving from Paris to Copenhagen, we dropped son Charlie off in Hanover to make his way to Berlin. There in East Berlin, in August 1961, a month before the wall went up, he was getting back into a train for the western city when an old English couple dithered about whether to get on this train or not. The wife got on, the doors shut. Charlie shouted through the doors, "I'll push her off at the next stop." He did, but never learned whether the couple was ultimately reunited.

25

MIT *administration*

I have already noted two publications of the early 1960s that had their origin at the end of the fifties. Before going forward with the research of the next decade, perhaps a word on academic administrative duties is in order. The role of graduate-student adviser has been mentioned. I did this at length in the years to the mid-sixties. There was a spurt of activity at the beginning of each term as student programs were approved, and another at the end of term when "degrees and low grades" were dealt with. General examinations were a time of particular intensity, with the need to schedule written and oral examinations, and have them graded by the relevant instructors. Meanwhile there was the monthly meeting of the Committee on Graduate School Policy (CGSP), and of having to make oneself available to help a graduate student who had a problem. I used to keep my door open until a rearrangement of offices put three secretaries in the outer office and gave rise to a certain amount of chatter. But before closing the door I had it equipped with a window, so a student could see whether I was there, wave to attract my attention, and be waved in by me.

MIT thought it did better by its students than some other graduate schools. There were horror stories elsewhere of having to make an appointment to see a professor a month ahead, or of a professor saying that he could see a student the following Tuesday if the young person would ride with him in a taxi to the airport, and make his own way back. Size is important in these matters, another manifestation of micro-sociology. If a department is too small, there is insufficient stimulation from diversity. If too big, it tends to break up into groups that go their separate ways, and to interact mainly when formal meetings are held, usually with a sizeable fraction of the members of the department away on leave, consulting, giving seminars at other universities, or otherwise failing to mind the store.

The CGSP produced some of the dullest hours of my life. The heart of graduate education is in the departments, which mostly set their own standards. The dean of the Graduate School has certain housekeeping functions on degrees, grades, and dismissals, but primary responsibility there too lies in departments. The School has a limited amount of money for fellowships. With twenty-one or more departments one has to sit through interminable discussions of the trivial problems of others while waiting to make a small point of one's own.

With due modesty, I can say that I am not too bad at administrative work. In one of my early years at MIT I got a telephone call from President Killian to say that he wanted to come to my office to see me. I sensed trouble. He asked me whether I would run a conference MIT was planning for the Combined Program, a scheme in which young people could take three years at a liberal arts college, come to MIT for two more years, and receive a BA from the college, and a BS from MIT. The purpose, of course, was to attract bright young people who might otherwise not consider MIT at all. The danger, of course, the realization of which finally brought the program to an end, was that young people who might otherwise come to MIT would be diverted to start at Williams, Swarthmore, Haverford, and so on, and stay there for the last of the glorious college years. I said to Dr Killian that I would run the conference, that I thought I was good at such administration, but that I did not like or welcome it as a diversion from research. It was harsh to say so, but I think it paid off.

MIT administration

Two slight incidents may be worth noting from my early years at MIT. For a time I was chairman of the Faculty Club's luncheon meetings before the Club moved into its permanent quarters in the Sloan Building in 1954. The meetings were occasional and held in a basement dining-room in Ashdown House. Judge Charles Wyzanski of the First Circuit Court of Appeals agreed to come and talk on loyalty problems. He suggested that he bring his Webster tape recorder as he was fearful of being misquoted and would like to have a record of what he said. I pooh-poohed the idea, said that MIT would be glad to tape the talk for him, and asked the Acoustics Lab to undertake it. When the day came, the laboratory assistants came into the room halfway through the lunch with several huge cases of equipment which they set up. They were still working on the equipment when we had to start the talk because of one o'clock classes. I had to leave for my class before the question period was fully over. I was told that the lab technician wanted to charge Judge Wyzanski $5 for the tape. As it turned out, the tape was blank. I am afraid I was mildly amused, and wondered aloud to a friend whether they had forgotten to say "1, 2, 3, testing." This word got back to Jerry Wiesner, then of the Acoustics Laboratory, and he was irritated.

Later, when the Faculty Club was ensconced on the top floor of the Sloan Building, we had Senator John F. Kennedy come to give us a talk in the 1956 senatorial campaign. He was late, ate nothing during the remainder of the meal, produced minimal responses to my attempts, as president of the club and chairman, at small talk, and gave what I thought was a terrible speech. I recall only his impassioned plea for a tariff on fish imports. He must have thought he was in Gloucester.

The departmental admissions process was time-consuming. In later years these tasks were broken up, but at the start the graduate registration officer handled admissions too, a heavy weight of correspondence and then agonizing judgments. It was important for each member of the committee to keep his grades separate from the others because the opinions of others are infectious. But I recall one session when I read a letter and said

MIT administration

to Bob Solow: "This letter is hyperbolic." Without a moment's hesitation, he replied, "That's OK so long as it is not elliptical." I cannot withhold another example of the Solow wit. At one point in time, to use a Nixon expression, a distinguished middle-aged professor of accounting dropped dead of a heart attack. The Institute wondered whether the stress of life at MIT was too much, and offered the faculty, free, a medical examination, complete even to the inclusion of half an hour with a psychiatrist. My report contained a sentence from "my psychiatrist" (to whom I referred in these terms at cocktail parties for some weeks) that I found amusing. "You are high-strung, but adjusted to it." When I later recounted this to a faculty luncheon round table, Solow came back with "I guess that's better than being low-strung and unable to stand it." This is a mathematical sort of wit, taking a sentence and multiplying both parts of it by minus one.

Many academic departments have a system of rotating chairmanship. MIT did not. In my years there from 1948 to 1981 economics had only three: Ralph Freeman, Robert L. Bishop, who later got bumped up to dean of the School of Humanities and Social Science, and E. Cary Brown. It is a creative job, with great satisfactions, but it diverts time from research. A rotating chairmanship is fine to the extent that it limits the time of compulsive researchers diverted to administration, but it often results in assigning responsibilities to people with little administrative ability. It is hard to say which system is inherently superior, but in the MIT economics case it has worked out well to the satisfaction of all.

In 1965 I became chairman of the MIT faculty with responsibilities outside the department. The office is elective, but with only one candidate. Ascher Shapiro had been chosen in the spring of 1965, but in the fall he became head of the Department of Mechanical Engineering and could not go on in two positions. The Nominations Committee, acting with power, appointed me, and for two years I operated in the post, two quiet years, thank the Lord, before the turmoil of 1968. The chairman was also the chairman of the top faculty committee, the Committee on Educational Policy. He, or now she, presided at faculty meetings in the absence of the president of the Institute, and attended the weekly Tuesday meetings of the Academic Council, made up of the president, provost, deans and other top brass. The task was so time-consuming that one's teaching was cut back from two courses to one. I finally used it as an excuse to resign from President Lyndon B. Johnson's Presidential Committee on International Monetary Policy, about which more below. I had, to be sure, long given up moonlighting, as textbook royalties made that financially unnecessary.

One episode as chairman of the faculty amused me. I was home one Thursday evening when I received a telephone call from Dr Vannevar Bush, the eminent scientist who had been the head of the Office of Scientific Research and Development in the war, and was then chairman of the MIT Corporation. He said he would like to see me, and wondered whether he could call at my office on Friday. I demurred, saying Fridays I stayed home to do my writing, and could I come to see him Monday. No, he said, he would be happy to come to my house. I protested, offered to interrupt the writing and come see him the next day, but he insisted, saying he did not have that much to do.

The next morning I got a call from Jim Killian. Dr Bush had had a mild heart attack and could not come. Killian would come to see me. Heavens no, I protested. I would come to see him. Perhaps we could lunch together at the Faculty Club. No, he said, I should come to his office and we could have lunch there.

It fell out that Jay Stratton was retiring as president of MIT and there was a problem with choosing his successor. There were two main candidates, Charles Townes and Jerome Wiesner. The faculty had been consulted extensively, but divided, with half enthusiastic about one, the other half about the other. The Corporation had then hit on an entirely new choice, Howard W. Johnson, who had accepted. But the faculty had not been consulted. When Killian mentioned Johnson's name I said, "Great!" and recounted a conversation I had had a week or two before with Bob Bishop. Johnson had been the dean of the Sloan

School of Management but had just resigned to take a position with Federated Stores. His academic specialty was personnel, and department stores have overwhelming personnel problems in recruiting, training, and retaining good staff. Bishop had said that it was too bad that Johnson was leaving for Federated Stores in Cincinnati as he would have made a great MIT president. Killian was much relieved. The faculty – in my person – had now been consulted on the new appointment and had approved it. The announcement set for Monday could be made. Incidentally the lunch he provided consisted in a single sandwich, which we split. The following week I got one protest from a faculty member, a partisan of either Townes or Wiesner, I don't remember which, but I managed to persuade him that the Corporation had no choice given the faculty division. Charles Townes left MIT, and after Johnson eventually resigned, Wiesner was chosen as his successor. Johnson's tenure of the office through the stormy days of student and faculty unrest was superb.

A word or two about the President's Advisory Committee on International Monetary Policy before getting back to research. President Johnson, or perhaps only his secretary of the Treasury, Henry H. ("Joe") Fowler, needed help in the mid-sixties on the problems of the dollar. They appointed a committee to advise them consisting of bankers, David Rockefeller, Douglas Dillon, and André Meyer (of Lazard Freres), a quasi-banker, Robert V. Roosa of Brown Brothers Harriman and before that undersecretary of the Treasury, Edward Bernstein, an IMF official who had gone into writing a newsletter on central banking problems, and me. The experience revealed to me the persistence of the White House in hunting down its quarry. In the summer when my mother-in-law stayed with us for extended periods, my study became a guest room, and I was relegated to the outdoor study – an old chicken house in the backyard. It had no telephone. When the White House failed to get me at the office or at home, it learned somehow about the chicken house, located a neighbor and asked him to go to my place and ascertain whether I was in the chicken house. It created a small stir next door.

MIT administration

My time on the Committee was fun, but not very edifying. I had my own views on the problems of the dollar which I tried to sell and failed. They will appear below in the discussion of the Despres–Kindleberger–Salant article that appeared in *The Economist* of February 5, 1966. The discussion about Special Drawing Rights was interminable, with extended debate between my good friends, Eddie Bernstein and Bob Roosa, the content of which I have forgotten, although I well remember the tedium. As soon as I saw that the exercise was going nowhere, beyond accepting the Special Drawing Right, itself a dud, I used the excuse of my chairman-of-the-faculty duties at MIT to withdraw. Meanwhile, I amused myself by observing the ways of the wealthy.

The Rockefeller brothers kept a limousine and chauffeur full time in Washington for the use of any member of the family who might need it. Douglas Dillon and André Meyer would each hire a limousine for the day, to meet them at the airport, and at the end of the day take them back. When the meeting was over, there were three limousines waiting to go to the airport and a certain amount of competition for the business of the rest of us who were taxi-riders. David Rockefeller would tip his family's chauffeur $5, which was the cost of the taxi ride. With a limousine there was no need to lose one's dignity frantically trying to signal down a cab during the evening rush hour.

On one occasion, David Rockefeller was giving an evening talk at the Harvard Business School and gave me a ride to Boston in his Chase Manhattan jet. The reduction in stress is evident: instead of having to catch the plane, you let it catch you. I have a theory that dreams are to a remarkable extent about low-level anxiety problems: travel, taking exams, giving lectures, losing luggage, missing trains, and so on. With private planes and limos laid on, sleep should be dreamless.

For a time thereafter I collected limousine stories; I especially liked the story of the president of the Pennsylvania Railroad, who flew to Washington but had his company car drive there to take him from the airport to his meeting and back.

26

Research
The sixties

My study of the post-war recovery of France led naturally to that of the recovery of Europe as a whole, and the question of why France, Germany, and Italy had done well whereas Britain and Belgium had not. I fastened on a good idea: that the W. Arthur Lewis model of growth with unlimited supplies of labor might be said to apply to some countries, but not to others. Available extra labor holds down wages, relatively at least, and means that the benefits from an increase in demand or a reduction in costs go mainly to profits. If these are reinvested in further cost-reductions, the process becomes self-perpetuating, until the labor surplus is exhausted. I suggested to the CFIA at Harvard that it might finance a summer's trip to Europe to explore this notion. It acceded. In the summer of 1964, therefore, I had a trip around Belgium, the Netherlands, France, Switzerland, and Italy exploring the contribution to the labor supply of various groups: the unemployed left over from the war, and refugees, especially from the East; the cutting off of emigration to such colonies as those of the Netherlands; immigrant guest workers; and sideways shifts within countries from inefficient agriculture, retail distribution, or artisanry to modern modes.

My wife came to join me in the middle of the summer. The

Research

Rockefeller Foundation blessed my proposal that I be given a week to organize my notes at its superb conference center in Bellagio, on Lake Como, before returning to Cambridge. The center is mainly used for conferences, with only an occasional short-term scholar in residence. When we were there, there was a conference on the contribution made by banking to economic growth, with Rondo Cameron, Raymond Goldsmith, Maurice Lévy-Leboyer, Richard Tilly, and others in attendance. It was my first meeting with Cameron, whose *France and the Economic Development of Europe, 1800–1914* (Princeton, NJ, 1963) I had reviewed in a tone that he regarded as somewhat supercilious. When I left, he remarked that I was not as dreadful a person as he had thought. We have since remained good friends and friendly critics of each other's work in progress.

On another occasion at an international conference, I was sitting at breakfast next to James Meade when a French economist came down, and shook hands with everyone at the table. Meade said wryly: "The French shake hands every day; the British once a war."

My wife returned to the United States a few days before I could get away, to get the children ready for school (I guess). I was on my way to interviews in the Organization of Economic Cooperation and Development from the Villa Saint-Romain when, emerging from behind a double-parked car to cross the rue de Sèvres, I was clobbered by a Peugeot 203. It was one of those multiple-causation accidents – his fault for driving too fast, my fault for not looking more carefully around the second car, though I was "between the nails" (*entre les clous*) that the French have instead of the British zebras as sanctuary for pedestrians. An ambulance took me to the nearby Hôpital Lannec, a fifteenth-century monastery with nursing care of comparable vintage (though the medicine was excellent). The gendarmerie called off my appointment, and the man I was to see called my friend Joe Saxe, who had set it up. That evening it was clear that I was bleeding internally. The resident doctor thought it advisable to operate. My friends suggested they get the professor. He came, found the leak and plugged it. Sarah came back from

Boston to stand by. After a few uncomfortable days in Hôpital Lannec, I was taken to the American Hospital in Neuilly, a luxurious establishment that has sheltered the likes of Ernest Hemingway and doubtless F. Scott Fitzgerald. I got back to Cambridge late, took a few weeks to recover, then resumed teaching, and finished writing *Europe's Postwar Growth: The Role of the Labor Supply* (Cambridge, MA, 1967).

Europe's Postwar Growth was dedicated to the Reverend Rollin J. and Phyllis M. Fairbanks, dear friends of Lincoln, Cambridge, cruising in New England waters, and intertwined families. At this time, Fairbanks, who taught pastoral care at the Episcopal Theological Seminary in Cambridge and had moved from Lincoln to the Cambridge campus, had a Gordon setter called Mr Chips. I used to see Chips running along Garden Street from time to time and greet him, without much in the way of reciprocation. Mr Chips found the glue in the binding of *Europe's Postwar Growth* delicious and did an effective job of chewing it to a pulp. I replaced the desecrated object and sent it to the Harvard Press with a letter which ran something like this: "I cannot recall ever having seen such savage and biting criticism. The critic evidently could not stomach my treatment of recent European economic history, but he took it apart." At the time, the Press circulated a newsletter, *The Browser*, to friends. One issue printed a picture of the tattered volume, and an excerpt from the letter.

At about this time I was developing a different view of the dollar. In fact the basic idea occurred to me when I was on a TV panel of the Boston educational station, with Professor Milton Katz of the Harvard Law School in the chair, and a camera staring me in the face; I asserted that the dollar was not weak but strong, and that it should not be judged like other currencies, just as the strength of a bank should not be judged by the same standards as that of a corporation. Those, like Robert Triffin, who thought that the accumulated dollar balances of foreign countries represented a deficit, and that when it was corrected, as it would be, the world would be short of liquidity, were mistaken. Liquidity was provided instantly for foreign countries, which could borrow dollars long and hold them on deposit, in effect lending short. The United States was a bank for the world. As a bank, it had problems, to be sure, but they were not helped by all the moaning and groaning about the accumulation of dollars, which foreign countries wanted to hold for their liquidity. I wrote one paper on the subject for the *Princeton Essays in International Finance*. Then Emile Despres, Walter Salant, and I thought of writing up the idea for *The Economist*, which very occasionally took signed articles. The paper was called "The dollar and world liquidity: a minority view," was published in the February 5, 1966, issue of that magazine, and created quite a stir. It was reprinted in Despres's *International Monetary Reform* (Oxford, 1973) and in my *International Money* (London, 1981), as well as in a special report of the Brookings Institution, where Walter Salant worked. The analogy between the United States and a bank remains a good one, despite the troubles of the dollar in the years that followed, so long as it is remembered that banks grow happily with rising deposits, but need to have their reserves grow in parallel.

In the summer of 1966 (Northern Hemisphere) I was invited to go to the University of Canterbury in Christchurch, New Zealand, to teach in their (Southern Hemisphere) winter term. It occurred to me that it would be wise to prepare a series of lectures in advance, against the likelihood that I would be asked to provide a connected discourse rather than an assortment of lectures and seminars. To this end, I chose the subject of the multinational corporation that had been advanced intellectually by Stephen Hymer whose thesis I had supervised. I had been unable to get MIT to publish it in our series of outstanding dissertations. One member of the committee had objected, saying that the central idea of the thesis was obvious. I was unable to overcome this objection, try as I might, using the argument that a monograph that takes a muddy, confused subject and reduces it to order so that the central idea appears obvious has made an outstanding contribution. (The thesis was published in 1976 after Hymer's premature death in an automobile accident.) Meanwhile, however, the thesis had had an underground circulation as a consequence of my abandonment of old theories of direct investment for the Hymer treatment in the third edition of *International Economics* (Homewood, IL, 1963). Textbooks are read mostly by students, and not always by instructors in the course. To reach a wider range of economists, one needed another vehicle. I proposed to give a series of lectures in New Zealand on the theory and practice of direct investment and publish them later as a small book. No coherent series of lectures was wanted, as it happened, and I was unable to finish the six lectures that summer. I did take them with me to Atlanta in 1967–8 and polished them off there. They were published as *American Business Abroad: Six Lectures on Direct Investment* (New Haven, CT, 1969).

I said earlier that I have written two textbooks. That is true if one counts only books that were used as texts. I was sufficiently interested in the boundaries between international economics and international politics to try my hand in the summer of 1969, with the encouragement of Martin Kessler, editor at Basic Books, at a book to be used to supplement courses in international economics and international politics. It had a jazzy title: *Power and Money*, with the more descriptive subtitle: *The Politics of International Economics and the Economics of International Politics*. After a brief methodological introduction, there was a series of chapters on the economics of international politics, dealing with sovereignty, power, imperialism, war, and peacekeeping, followed by the politics of international economics on, successively, trade, aid, migration, capital movements corporations, payments, and money.

It was not a bad idea, but it didn't work. The book fell between two stools, and sank like a stone, unwanted in a departmentalized intellectual world by teachers both in international relations and in international economics. There is something to be said for this point of view. Interdisciplinary study is not for youth but for masters of a subject who late in their careers peer over its confines. To try to teach at the interdisciplinary level produces mostly a muddle. But the main title, *Power and Money*, was very useful for inscriptions in complimentary

Research

copies. To Bob Bowie, I wrote "More of Both to You."

In about the fall of 1969 Professor Wolfram Fischer, the distinguished economic historian of the Free University of Berlin, came to Cambridge and asked Alexander Gerschenkron to participate in a project of his. Historians package their subject in various ways: by centuries, countries, continents, subjects, debates. His handle for a series was to be decades in the twentieth century, including the *belle époque* to 1914, the First World War, the twenties, the thirties, the Second World War, and the post-war period. This was world history, not particularly limited to Europe. Fischer was in the early stages of the project and he offered Gerschenkron a choice of any of the six volumes. Gerschenkron had a full plate of research, and for some reason suggested that Fischer try me. I jumped at it and chose the 1930s. The depression was where I came in. I have a strong impression that economics is a countercyclical industry that attracts adherents when times are troubled. Some are drawn to the subject by the opportunity to do good, to save the world so to speak by curing depression. The stronger drive in my view is curiosity. How does the economy work, and what has gone wrong? In any event it was a great piece of luck to be offered a choice between the full range of options. And the 1930s proved to be an exciting topic not only in its own right, but because it led me deeper into other financial crises of the past, into financial history, and more or less provided the agenda for the next twenty years.

The Fischer series was undertaken for Deutsche Taschenbuch Verlag (German Pocketbook Press), which distributed its product widely throughout the western German-speaking world, and started out with an initial printing of 15,000, which would have been an enormous number for serious economics books in the United States and Britain. I finished the English original version of *The World in Depression, 1929–1939* (Berkeley, CA, 1973) in the spring of 1971, before, that is, the currency troubles of the dollar in August of that year, the closing down of the gold window, and the temporary Nixon price freeze. The book did not appear in English until two years later, however, as Allen Lane in England and the University of California Press, with the

English and American rights respectively, had to wait for translation and publication in German.

Unlike *Power and Money*, *The World in Depression* had a play in both economics and international relations. In economics, it attacked the simplistic monetary view of the depression, set out by Milton Friedman and Anna Schwartz in their magisterial *Monetary History of the United States, 1867–1960* (Princeton, NJ, 1963). This ruled out any effect of the 1929 stock-market crash, and roles of countries other than the United States in starting the depression, and ascribed the whole debâcle to mistakes of Federal Reserve policy. My contention was that the matter was far more complex, with the stock-market collapse causing US banks to seize up and cut off lending to commodity brokers on the one hand, and on automobile loans and house mortgages on the other, and with critical international repercussions from the United States to Europe and major commodity producers in the Antipodes and Latin America, and vice versa. For the political scientists, it argued that spreading financial collapse might be halted if there is a lender of last resort, as articulated by Walter Bagehot in *Lombard Street* (1873). National lenders of last resort were typically the central bank, treasury, or an informal group of banks. The role of an international lender of last resort typically fell in financial crises to a leading country: Britain up to 1914. In the 1920s and 1930s, however, Britain was no longer capable of serving in this leadership role of responsibility for world stability, and the United States was as yet unready to assume the mantle. For the world economy to be stable, there needed to be a stabilizer. I called for leadership and responsibility. Political scientists changed the terms to that of a hegemon, and the book set off a considerable literature in international relations over the question of whether the world needed to be organized hierarchically, with a hegemon in charge, or whether other systems of stability, for example pluralism, balance of power, or regional organization, would suffice. In a second edition of the book, which appeared in 1986, I developed the discussion of leadership, expanding the economic roles, as I saw them, from three in the first edition – open markets, steady capital flows, and lender of last resort in crisis – by adding two more: management of exchange rates and international coordination of monetary and fiscal policy. I also argued against one view of political scientists, that if a hegemon was no longer in a position to lead, as appeared possible in the 1980s for the United States, the world might remain stable because of what were called "regimes," that is, institutionalized habits and practices left over from an earlier hegemonic period.

But before we get to the 1970s, I must mention my riveting year at five black colleges in Atlanta, Georgia, in 1967–8.

27

Atlanta
1967–1968

One *way to* break away from the academic administration involved in being chairman of the faculty was to go on leave. Seven years had passed since our last leave in 1960–1. My wife and I thought that having enjoyed the fleshpots of Europe the last two times, it was time to go for a hardship post in a developing country. My daughter Randall objected. This would be her first year in college and she would prefer us not to be overseas. Mrs K. then had an inspiration: how about teaching for a year in one or more black colleges? I asked the Rockefeller Foundation what it thought of my teaching for a month in each of nine black colleges. They said it was a stupid idea. Far better, they said, was to go to Atlanta University Center, which consisted of four undergraduate colleges, a graduate school, and a theological seminary, sharing the same campus. The Foundation was interested in having the colleges and schools work more closely together, and perhaps an outsider who taught in the colleges and the graduate school over a year could help. Vivian W. Henderson, president of Clark College, was an economist. It was suggested that I try to work it out with him. This I did. I was to teach two courses each term, one at each of Morehouse, Spelman, Atlanta University, and Morris Brown, live in Clark in an apartment at the top of a dormitory, and organize a center-wide faculty seminar in economics. We went south in the fall of 1967, and had a wonderful year despite the tragic assassination of Martin Luther King Jr in April 1968.

In the summer of 1968 I wrote an extended account of the year, complete with exhibits in the form of memoranda, clippings, letters, and the like. Here I can set out only a few highlights.

There was already a great deal of northern white interest in the various black colleges, both the forty or so private colleges belonging to the United Negro College Fund, and the public institutions in most states. The Woodrow Wilson Fellowship Foundation, supported by the Ford Foundation, sent young scholars there to teach for a few years. The Chase Manhattan–United Negro College Fund had a program of bringing economists to various colleges for a week at a time for lectures, classes, seminars, and discussions. Walter Heller came to Atlanta on that program from Minnesota, to which he had returned after having been chairman of the Council of Economic Advisers under President Kennedy. Paul Samuelson gave an extra lecture at the Center on the occasion of a scheduled lecture at Georgia State University in Atlanta, and Ken Galbraith paid his way on from Vanderbilt in Nashville to Atlanta to give another. At one stage I asked Milton Friedman to come, mentioning these names, and he suggested that Atlanta was getting a rather high-powered group of visitors.

The four undergraduate colleges organized a trip to Washington for economics majors, visiting the Council of Economic Advisers, Federal Reserve, World Bank, Bureau of Labor Statistics, Joint Economic Committee, and Brookings Institution, and met a lot of prominent economists (Andrew Brimmer, James Duesenberry, Joseph Pechman, Emile Despres, *et al.*), and were given a party by a Brookings group. The students talked about it for months afterwards.

In addition to teaching at Atlanta, my wife and I visited a number of other black colleges in the South for lectures or seminars: Tuskeegee, Tuscaloosa, Tougaloo, North Carolina A. and M., Miles College in Birmingham and Benedict in Columbia, South Carolina.

Atlanta

The highlight of the year was stair-climbing. We lived on the top floor of Brawley and I climbed the three flights at least three times a day: once to get the newspaper, again for lunch and dinner, and a fourth time if we went out in the evening. In addition, my Spelman class twice a week was on the fourth floor, and getting the mail at Clark involved more stairs. On average, I climbed perhaps twenty flights of stairs a day.

Of Walter Heller's week in Atlanta I recall the following: first, his marvellous appeal to the students with his reminiscences about Kennedy; second, my debate with him, about which a student later said either: "Man, that cat cut you good," or "Man, you cut that cat good." My recollection as to which is faulty, but the remark meant he liked it. A third recollection is of the occasion when Heller had a free noon on Wednesday and agreed to talk at a luncheon at Georgia State University. At the last minute, he was called to Washington for the day to testify before the Congress, and asked me to substitute. I said I couldn't because I had a one o'clock class. Georgia State said it would get me a substitute. My substitute was Bon Ho Koo, a Korean trade specialist, who is now the president of the Korean Development Institute in Seoul. I substituted for Heller, Bon Ho Koo substituted for me. My books were balanced, but I never learned whether Heller gave a lecture for Dr Koo.

One Monday, I noted a squib in the *Atlanta Constitution* about the president of a bank who had given $250,000 for a chair in money and banking at Emory University, his third such gift in the state, and that he planned to give more. I called up the bank to find out the name of the president. It was Mills B. Lane Jr. I was probably the only person in the state who did not know the name of the president of the Citizens and Southern Bank. I wrote a letter suggesting that he consider giving a similar amount to the Atlanta University Center. It apologized a bit, since I did not want to be viewed as an intrusive northerner, but pointed out that banks in the South needed blacks both as customers and as tellers. To my surprise, on Wednesday I received a reply from Mr Lane saying he would do it. The details took weeks or months to work out and did not concern me. Two

Atlanta

years later, my friend Lester V. Chandler of Princeton, became the Mills B. Lane Jr Professor of Money and Banking for a year in Atlanta University Center.

In 1969, between terms, I went back to Atlanta for a week to see my colleagues of the year before, and to check up on students for whom I might write letters of recommendation for jobs and graduate school. I stayed in Pascal's, a motel on Hunter Street (now Martin Luther King Boulevard). On the first night I encountered Benjamin Mays, whom I had met in the spring of 1967 before he retired as president of Morehouse College, and once or twice more in 1967–8. Later in the week, when Vivian Henderson came to my room for a drink, we saw Dr Mays in the hall again. He and Henderson chatted for a minute or two, and then he turned to me: "Young man," he said, though I was nearing sixty to his eighty plus, "you may think I have assignations in this motel. That is untrue. I have taken a room here to write my autobiography away from the turmoil of my Morehouse office."

Morris Brown was the newest of the colleges, and the poorest in support and tradition. The others had all been established immediately after the Civil War, by northern money and dedicated souls. Starting primarily as high schools they had slowly been upgraded into accredited colleges. My class in Morris Brown – a few blocks away on Hunter Street and a bit east of the Theological Seminary – was at nine o'clock and followed an eight o'clock class in religion taught by a white minister. I got there early on the first day, and he was running late. I looked around and asked him where the chalk for the blackboard was kept. There was no chalk, he said. One brought one's own. And then he gave me a piece of his chalk for my first lesson. Unhappily I forgot the second time, and he gave me another piece. Chalk is what economists call a free good in most universities, liberally supplied by the administration – though I have been known to scrounge it from other classrooms in Brandeis (later). I duly learned to steal chalk from Morehouse, or Clark, or Atlanta University. One day I arrived in good time for my class, and saw the reverend instructor erasing the blackboard.

Atlanta

I protested, saying that at MIT we always had to erase the blackboard left by our predecessor. His answer was that any teacher who does not erase his own blackboard, is not fit to put his chalk back in his pocket. I followed that precept in the MIT years thereafter, often finding myself erasing the board when I arrived – unless it was a nine o'clock class, in which case the custodian (formerly janitor) had done it for me – and before I left, that is, twice, while some miscreants got off scot-free.

In 1978 in Paris, I was giving a lecture at the Sorbonne in Professor Gugliemi's class. In Europe, lecture halls have an anteroom where the lecturer waits until the precise moment to make an entrance. I was holding there with Gugliemi, when it suddenly occurred to him to slip into the hall and erase the blackboard. He explained: "In the old days, the concierge would erase the board after every class. When they stopped, some students took it over. Now, since the events of May–June 1968 ['*les évenements de mai–juin*'], I have to do it." *Autre temps, autre moeurs*.

The towering event of the year was Dr King's assassination. President Johnson had just announced on March 31 that he would not run for re-election. On April 3, one Dunbar Moody of South Africa, spending the year in the United States, at the last minute backed out of a series of campus lectures on apartheid at his wife's insistence after he had received a death threat. The twenty or so economics majors and faculty were *en route* home from their successful trip to Washington when the news of the assassination came over the radio. They had just gotten through Raleigh at the time, which was lucky as the Raleigh police immediately closed the streets to avoid rioting.

The next morning when I went down for the newspaper it had not been delivered, so I walked over three blocks to Hunter Street to get one. On the way back I met a student who was not in my classes but whom I knew. We chatted for ten or fifteen minutes about his academic plans. When I got home for breakfast, my wife was nearly frantic with worry about the delay in getting the newspaper, fearful that I had been caught up in some kind of racial disturbance. I recall the conversation as proof of some success in raising the academic sights of the Center.

Later in the morning there was a parade from the campus to the City Hall in which Ivan Allen, the white mayor, took a leading part. I had heard from some students that whites were unwelcome, and watched from the porch of the small residential building that housed my office, but some white faculty of longer service in the colleges than I insisted on marching in honor of a Morehouse graduate. The memorial service in the afternoon on the Morehouse campus, led by Dr Mays, was attended by all, and drew a national attendance through television.

Some weeks later I was called up by an Atlanta banker wondering how he and other white businessmen in the city could break the hidden barrier that separated most whites from most blacks.

In the next years I became a trustee, and later trustee emeritus, of Clark College, keeping closely in touch so long as Vivian Henderson was alive, and gradually drifting away from the distant meetings after his death. Another trustee was Vernon Jordan, who took the leadership first of the United Negro College Fund (UNCF) and then of the National Urban League before moving into private law practice in Washington.

28

Kiel and Rome
1970–1971

*M*IT *had installed* a sabbatical policy some time in the 1960s. After I had been back from Atlanta for a year or two, Dean Bob Bishop pointed out that I had taken leave in 1967–8 rather than a sabbatical, and that I was due one of the latter under the rules. To piece out my research on Western Europe after Geneva in 1954, and Oxford and Paris in 1960–1, I chose to try to spend half the academic year in each of Germany and Italy. The German area of choice for study seemed to me to be Kiel, the site for the Institut für Weltwirtschaft (Institute for World Economics); it had been established by Krupp in 1913, to commemorate the twenty-fifth accession to the Imperial throne of Kaiser Wilhelm II and to underline the mutual interest of the two men in yachting, and Krupp's interest in building dreadnoughts made from his steel plate. The Institute was located on the bank of the Kieler bay, next to the yacht club that had been built for the 1936 sailing Olympics. Near it was a *Haus Welt Klub* (World Clubhouse), which had an apartment also fronting over the bay where we lived.

The library was splendid in many ways, especially its five indexes – by author, title, subject, and two more that I cannot recall. Its collection, unlike those of most German universities, had survived both wars intact. The drawback was that it had grown to such an extent that its shelves were on rollers to economize space, and it had its own cataloguing system, which meant that readers were not allowed in the stacks to browse, but could browse only in the catalogues. The head of the Institut was Herbert Giersch, whom I had met when he was a colleague of Egon Sohmen at Saarbrücken, and who had been a member of the West German Council of Economic Experts, taught at Yale, and was a leading German economist. He had succeeded Eric Schneider, who in turn had followed Frederic Baade, and Bernard Harms. I read German economic history intently for four months, using it later in a series of seminars on "Germany overtaking Britain in the nineteenth century" at Edinburgh in 1974, which appeared in two parts in the *Weltwirtschaftliches Archiv* in 1975, and for the German section of a historical study on financial centers, published in Princeton Studies in International Finance in 1974. Both rather long papers are reproduced in *Economic Response: Comparative Studies in Trade, Finance, and Growth* (Cambridge, MA, 1978).

After a holiday at Christmas in the Vorarlberg, Austria, for which most of the family joined us from the United States, we went briefly to Geneva again and then to Rome, where the Bank of Italy allowed me to read in its library and to take out books. MIT has long had a close association with the Bank of Italy, through Paul N. Rosenstein-Rodan, a friend of the president of the republic, Luigi Einaudi, and later through Franco Modigliani. Modigliani in particular used to bring a series of young Italian economists, either high-level students or Bank of Italy employees, to MIT. We lived in a *pensione* in Monte Verde, run by a Russian refugee, the Contessa Olga Fersen, who was a friend of friends. I would take the number 75 bus to the Bank each day and home in the evening. The Bank of Italy library was not that deep, but my reading capacity was limited so that I could take advantage of only a limited number of standard works. Again the emphasis was on financial history in a comparative context.

It was on one of these occasions in Italy that I got a first taste of the British art of the terse ironic review. In the huge plaza of

Siena, I ran into a group of economic and financial historians who had been conferring in Prato, the town outside Florence that houses the archive of Francesco di Marco Datini, a fourteenth-century merchant who left 150,000 letters, invoices, and other papers. I was introduced to Leslie Pressnell of the University of Kent, whom I did not know. He mentioned that he had just read *The World in Depression*, adding: "It rather ripples along, doesn't it?" A further example in my modest collection is the remark of Quentin Skinner, the political philosopher, after a seminar of mine at the Institute for Advanced Studies in Princeton: "It came across the footlights very well."

It will be recalled from my study of sugar beets in Belgium that economists enjoy doing economic analysis as they get about. Rome was the scene of a great failure of mine in this connection. One drove back and forth from the city to the airport to meet an occasional plane. The route lay along the *annulare*, or circumferential *autostrada*. Seated on chairs or sometimes old car seats placed in the shade were women. I suggested to my wife and daughter that these might be taking a traffic count, as members of the League of Women Voters did from time to time in Lincoln. They hooted. This was the redlight district of Rome, or part of it, which had dispersed from downtown to bring their business to the customer, as in a suburban shopping mall. With technological change, the agglomeration of shopping that used to account for concentration in the central city had given way to dispersal, as long explained by location theory.

At about this time, MIT adopted a 4-1-4 plan, with one term completed before Christmas, a month (January) of inter-term, and then a second term from February through May. The inter-term had a number of purposes: to save heat, especially after the 1973 oil price rise of the Organization of Petroleum Exporting Countries (OPEC); to finish the first term before the holidays, so as not to have final examinations and term papers hanging over the festivities; and to allow graduate students to catch up on and organize their research without the interruption of classes. It was wonderful for faculty members, who could do their own research or go away. It seemed to me, however, to be a bit hard on undergraduates, many of whom took off for skiing or tropical swimming, although they were paying tuition. I tended to take off in January, accepting visiting assignments at Edinburgh in 1974, the University of Toronto at Scarborough in 1976 and Brigham Young University in 1978. The Edinburgh assignment was great fun, and gave me access to British official documents in the Command series. We had an apartment overlooking Arthur's Seat and a golf course, and were astounded to see Scotsmen playing golf at 8:30 in the morning in the dark in the rain. The Toronto stretch I did alone, without my wife, and I improved the shining hour by writing a long paper on "Commercial policy between the wars," for volume VIII of the *Cambridge Economic History of Europe* on the development of policies in industrial economies. I turned in the essay to the editor in February 1976. The completed volume finally appeared in May 1989. As one who gets assignments in on, or ahead of, time, I have strong feelings against editors who fail to impose discipline on the laggards, and allow the most dilatory contributor to set the pace. The Brigham Young experience was fun for the opportunity it gave us to see Utah, the universities and national parks, but a disappointment in that it was the one year in the decade with insufficient snow for skiing.

I have twice visited the European University Institute in Badia Fiesolana, outside Florence, Italy: once in 1984, and once on an earlier and longer occasion that is difficult to pin down in time. On one of these visits, Mrs K. and I struck up an acquaintance with Professor René David, a retired French professor of international law, who was a superb story-teller. He had been wounded in the First World War by a bullet in his leg and one in his spine. The pension authorities, who used a scheme of payments worked out in the Napoleonic war, had no trouble with the leg wound. There was a rate for that. The spine posed a problem, however, because people with spine wounds in Napoleon's time all died. As a result there was no rate. The issue was solved by paying Professor David at the rate for soldiers driven insane by the war. He had thus been the only certified idiot teaching law in France.

Kiel and Rome

I tried a story of my own about the meeting in the Hague in August 1929 between M. Chéron, the French minister of finance, and Philip Snowden, the chancellor of the exchequer of Britain, over German reparations. At one stage, Snowden, irritated by the Frenchman, called one of his proposals "ridiculous and grotesque," which the interpreter translated as *"ridicule et grotesque."* This proved to be a very poor translation, despite its transliterative quality, because the expression is acceptable in Parliament in Britain, but not in the Chamber of Deputies in France. "I know," said Professor David. "I was in London at the time, and the interpreter apologized profusely in the press the next day. ' "Ridiculous," ' the interpreter said, 'means laughable or amusing, and "grotesque" means unusual or original. I should have translated "ridiculous and grotesque" as *"amusant et originale."* ' " Professor David topped me every time in a delightful way.

29

Professor of Economics Emeritus and Senior Lecturer

Shortly after I retired for the first time in 1976, the age of retirement was changed from sixty-five to seventy. I was not unhappy that the seventy-year rule did not apply to me, however, as one could teach part-time as a senior lecturer for five more years until the age of seventy, and concentrate that teaching into one full-time term, taking the other term off. This would have been unfair to dissertation writers if I had had many, but my interest having shifted from trade to history, and MIT not being the sort of place that attracts students of economic history, there was little or no hardship there.

For a retirement present I was offered an electric typewriter which I hastily refused: they are user-unfriendly. If one grazes a key, it prints, whereas with my mechanical machines, five times out of ten one can pull back in making a mistake before harm is done. Instead I asked for a picture of the Department, something of a public good because others could acquire them too. There were twenty-two members present (plus one visitor whom no one quite knew how to ask to leave), and six absent for one reason or another. The front row consists of Evsey Domar, Paul Samuelson, myself, Cary Brown, the department head, Franco Modigliani, Sidney Alexander, and Bob Bishop. The photographer, on lining us up on the Sloan School steps, asked me to get into the back row as I was too tall. I protested: "It's *my* picture."

By this time my wife was beginning to be a little tired of being a camp-follower, an attitude that is fully understandable. But the first half-year away, I manipulated her by wangling an invitation from Carl Kaysen, the director of the Institute for Advanced Studies in Princeton, to go there for four months. My wife was born in Princeton, had a sister and brother-in-law living there, and a number of cousins. It was irresistible to her, and I found it very enjoyable. One walked to the Institute from the comfortable apartment and back, made use of the Princeton Firestone Library, accessible by bicycle, and had much better secretarial service – in my case mostly typing of corrected versions of papers originally two-finger-typed by me – than one was used to at MIT.

In these four months we did the paste-up job on *Economic Response*, mostly old papers on comparative economic history, or as I prefer to think of it, comparative historical economics, and I wrote most of *Manias, Panics and Crashes: A History of Financial Crises*. I say historical economics rather than economic history since I have continually been interested in how general are economic theorems or laws, how well they fit case 2 if it is evident that they fit case 1 neatly. This was true of "Group behavior and international trade" of 1951, also reproduced in *Economic Response*, of *Economic Growth in France and Britain*, of the behavior of different countries in the 1930s depression, and of the development of financial centers. The reason why one can write a lot in such places as the Institute, and later the Center for Advanced Studies in the Behavioral Science, where in the spring of 1981 I wrote nineteen chapters of *A Financial History of Western Europe* (London, 1984), is that there is no commuting, no interruptions from students or administrative duties, and superb secretarial assistance. These things make up a scholar's heaven.

Manias, Panics and Crashes grew readily out of *The World in Depression* as I tried to compare earlier financial brouhahas with 1929–32. I was helped by having Martin Mayer, the financial writer, call my attention to the work of Hyman Minsky, of Washington University in St Louis, which I had not known, but who had produced a model of economic and financial instability beautifully applicable to historical data. *Manias* has a serious message as it offers an alternative to the classic monetarist doctrine that markets are always right and governments mostly wrong, and to the theory of rational expectations that also believes that markets get prices right. It pushed the examples of instability back only to 1720, the year of the collapses of the Mississippi and the South Sea bubbles, ignoring the tulip mania of 1636. Appearing in 1978, it has had "legs" as a book, selling a few hundred copies a year steadily, and still attracting attention a decade after its publication, an interval after which most monographic literature is thoroughly dead. The reason, of course, is that the model of instability has considerable generality as it applies in the years after 1976 (when the writing of *Manias* was mostly done) to shopping centers, condominia, luxury apartments, office buildings, oil exploration, Third World debt, savings and loan institutions, collectibles, racehorses, etc. It was especially relevant to the collapse of the stock market on Black Monday, October 19, 1987. On this account I wrote a new edition in the summer of 1988 which appeared a year later.

Retired folk are fair game for organizers of *Festschriften*, symposia, colloquia, and conferences, and each invitation to contribute to one or another stimulates the thought processes. There are those that need no stimulation, and write for the desk drawer. I had understood that Alexander Gerschenkron was one such, but the two volumes of his collected papers – *Economic Backwardness in Historical Perspective* (Cambridge, MA, 1962) and *Continuity in History and Other Essays* (Cambridge, MA, 1968) – for the most part contained papers that had earlier seen the light of day. Unless such papers are collected, however, they tend to be fugitive, as compared with papers in the established journals that have to pass the scrutiny of referees. Accordingly I have taken the opportunity late in the 1970s and again in the 1980s to package groups of papers that can be said to have some

Professor of Economics Emeritus

cohesion. These include *Economic Response* (1978, already mentioned), *International Money* (London, 1981), *Multinational Excursions* (Cambridge, MA, 1984), *Keynesianism vs Monetarism and Other Essays in Financial History* (London, 1985), *Marshall Plan Days* (London, 1987), and *The International Economic Order: Essays on Financial Crisis and International Public Goods* (Brighton, 1988). *Multinational Excursions* is a collection of various pieces on multinational corporations that the editor of the MIT Press and I had a hard time finding a title for until we hit on this combination. I am not entirely clear what it means but it sounds good. As a diversionary note, I may say that I wanted to call *Manias, Panics and Crashes*, *Manias, Bubbles, Panics and Crashes*, but Martin Kessler, the Basic Books editor, objected. Having two substantives in a title is normal, three is just about acceptable, four is too many.

In the spring of 1978 I accepted an appointment at the Ecole des Hautes Etudes Politiques in Paris to teach one course and one seminar. Near to the Ecole was the Maison des Sciences de L'Homme which gave me an office and access to a library. I met Fernand Braudel, and gave a seminar on financial crises. But the whole experience, except for some good reading, was a distinct unsuccess. My French is good for reading and tourist conversation but I am poor at lecturing in the language. I found myself tightening around the middle as the time approached for the lecture or seminar, though I made myself do it. The apartment we lived in was well located on the rue Saint-Jacques near the Pantheon, but it was cramped, ill-furnished, and unpleasant. My wife thought she could spend four months happily as a tourist in Paris. In common with other American wives, she ran out of things to do after six weeks. Other wives went home and left their husbands. We had rented our house so she had to stay. It is an experience we would forget if we could.

In spring 1979 we went to Texas. The invitation emanated not from Walt Rostow, as it happened, but from an MIT graduate PhD, Hussain Askari. I was to teach two courses in the spring term, one on financial history and the other on the multinational corporation. (Most economics departments have their

Professor of Economics Emeritus

regular staff to teach regular subjects and ask visitors to present topics rather on the borderline of the economic meat-and-potatoes, such as international trade or international finance. I taught economic history of Europe at MIT in the fall term in most of the years after my first retirement, but changed in the fall of 1978 to try financial history. I offered this again in Texas. In the spring of 1980 I wrote it up as a book at the Stanford Center for Advanced Studies in the Behavioral Sciences.

Texas was a success. We had a large apartment, if perhaps somewhat skimpily furnished with rented stuff. We loved exploring the countryside – as far in the spring break as Big Bend National Park on the Rio Grande, and Santa Fe in New Mexico. The LBJ library was of little use to me because it was concerned with American history, but the regular collection was superb, since in the days of the oil boom, before the bust, the university raked in a lot of oil royalties which it could use for facilities, including libraries and personal collections, but not faculty salaries. We saw a good deal of the Rostows, the Magees, the Askaris, Wendell Gordon, the institutionalist in the tradition of the Texas economist Clarence Ayres, and Nicholas Georgescu-Roegen, who was also visiting that term from Vanderbilt. Mostly, however, as New Englanders we saw how the other half lived. People on the street would say good morning to complete strangers. One young man said about me, "You can tell he comes from New England. He wears tweeds and walks fast."

A couple of years later, the Magees, Stephen and Nanneska, undertook to collect a number of my book reviews, with emphasis on the light-hearted ones. There was an introduction, a collection of fifty reviews reflecting the wit and wisdom of CPK, plus a bibliography of the lot down to 1982. No publisher they sent it to had any difficulty in turning it down. I remembered, however, that the brilliant reviewer, Alexander Gerschenkron, had tried himself to peddle a book of his reviews to no avail. It seems to be an art form that has strongly diminishing returns to scale.

I happen to like some of the reviews that the Magees delegated to also-ran status, and will not resist setting forth one.

Professor of Economics Emeritus

I agreed to review a book on *The World Bank and Foreign Aid* (Washington, DC, 1973) by my good friend Edward Mason of Harvard and Robert Ascher, not knowing that it ran to a thousand pages. When it came I started the review by calling attention to a hymn ("Oh God, Our Help in Ages Past"), the fourth verse of which starts, "A thousand ages in Thy sight are like an evening gone," adding that a thousand pages in my sight were like three weeks shot to hell, and that instead of reading the book through I would select five sub-topics on which they might be graded, and sample those. (Many reviewers actually do this; none that I am aware of actually says he does it.) Mason did not appreciate the wit. I may add that I was moved at Mrs Marguerite Mason's memorial service in Cambridge, that this hymn was chosen to be sung.

The spring of 1980 we stayed home, more or less. There was a Fred Hirsch memorial lecture in Warwick, England, in March, a lecture in the University of New Brunswick at the end of that month, near enough to my daughter Randall in Maine to combine with a weekend spent with her family; and one in Edwardsville, Illinois, near my St Louis son in April, at the University of Southern Illinois. In May I gave the Mattioli lectures sponsored by the University Luigi Bocconi and the Banca Commerciale Italiana. I had met Signor Mattioli in 1972 (I think) when I was touring Italy for a paper for the Center for International Affairs at Harvard to replicate for Italy what we had done for France. (In this case my qualification was ignorance, or a fresh point of view.) But calling on Signor Siglienti of the BCI, I learned that the head of the bank, Raffaele Mattioli, wanted to meet me. It turned out that he collected economists, and already had Galbraith and Rostow in his collection. I found him delightful. He had strong scholarly interests which led him to celebrate the centennial of Italian independence in 1960 by commissioning a series of Italian economic histories, one overall and a great many regional ones. I had worked through a number of these in Rome in 1970. When therefore I was invited to give lectures in 1980 in memory of Signor Mattioli I was pleased to do it. Although the lectures were supposed to be on the history

Professor of Economics Emeritus

of economic thought, I asked whether I could change the focus slightly to "Economic laws and economic history," taking four rather general laws of economics and seeing how they applied to historical cases. Scholars are notorious for accepting a specific commission and then doing their own thing. I perhaps have done it less than most. One of the most egregious examples occurred in Lloyd Reynolds's series on comparative economics, where one scholar agreed to do a comparative study of a certain function, which I do not name, and then wrote about it with reference to only one country.

The lectures were enjoyable at the time but have since given me almost continuous frustration because for nine and three-quarter years after having been given, they still had not been published. The first Mattioli lectures, given by Franco Modigliani in 1977 on inflation, appeared finally in 1986; the second by Lord (Richard) Kahn in 1978 appeared in 1985. Franco Modigliani may have contributed to the delay on his, by giving the lectures from notes and taking time to write them up, but I sent a typed version of my lectures in advance, answered every communication from the bank in a week, and found it incomprehensible that the bank should have allowed the official in charge to be so dilatory; perhaps he was a close friend of Mattioli whom the bank could not sidetrack for sentimental reasons. I announced the lectures as "forthcoming" in 1984. The Cambridge University Press announced them several times. Booksellers wrote to ask about them. Even the university and the bank stated in the invitation to the lectures in May 1989 by Karl Brunner and Allan Meltzer that the book had been published the previous March. Three Mattioli lecturers died after giving their lectures without seeing them published: Erik Lundberg, Lord (Nicholas) Kaldor, and Karl Brunner. Under my 1984 contract concerning publication, if the lectures were not published within two years I had the right to withdraw them and seek another outlet. That is hardly a remedy when one expects that publication is months away and hesitates to go back to square one. However, a copy finally came from Milan by courier in February 1990, nine and three-quarter years after the words were uttered.

Professor of Economics Emeritus

The American Economic Association typically held its meetings between Christmas and New Year's Day, disrupting family holidays. From time to time it would experiment with other dates, such as immediately after Labor Day, and one such experiment took place in 1980.

I received a letter from Elton Hinshaw, the secretary of the AEA, in spring 1980 saying that it would be well if I were to be present in Denver on September 6 for a purpose which he was unwilling or unable to state, but would be to my advantage. It was obvious to me what was happening. I was about to be made a distinguished fellow of the Association. This category had been added in the 1960s when it was seen that some of the leading members of the profession would not make president because there were too many of them. Specifically, if I recall correctly, the idea was pressed by Gottfried Haberler, as president of the Association, because of his realization that Edward Chamberlin was unlikely to attain the same post. It started out as a sort of a consolation prize, and in 1980 I still regarded it in that light.

The officers of the Association are chosen by an electoral college, consisting of the Executive Committee and the Nominations Committee, based primarily on nominations from the latter. They meet at the end of March, and when a president is chosen, the secretary telephones immediately from the meeting-place to obtain his or her consent to run – unopposed as it happens since one distinguished economist years earlier had been defeated twice for president and was unwilling to run a third time with opposition. The need to know is less critical for other posts, such as vice-president or member of the executive committee, but if a candidate for president cannot run because of other commitments, for example a sabbatical, it is necessary to find an alternate candidate before the two committees disperse.

In the spring of 1983, my wife and I were visiting our daughter in Machias, Maine, when the telephone rang. My daughter answered. A man asked to speak to Professor Kindleberger and Randall said, "This is she." It happened that Elton Hinshaw instead wanted me. He had called Lincoln, MIT, and, unable to locate me, had spoken to my son in Cambridge who

Professor of Economics Emeritus

knew my whereabouts. My daughter, I may perhaps explain, was teaching history at the University of Maine in Machias at that time. As for me, the lightning had struck twice. I had been nominated as president-elect.

The presidency of the Association involves one busy year as president-elect of preparing the program for the annual meeting and a second year where the duties consist primarily of presiding over the Executive Committee, giving the presidential address, and handling a certain amount of correspondence from disgruntled members. The president-elect governs, the president reigns. The convention for which I prepared the program was held in December 1984 in Dallas. As president in 1985, I gave the address in December of that year in New York. Two more years as ex-officio member of the Executive Committee follow. The whole sentence is a four-year one. Most presidents have been prepared for the task by service on the Nominations Committee, three years on the Executive Committee, and a one-year term as vice-president.

One episode occurred when I was on the Executive Committee in the early 1960s. In those days in addition to the Clark medal, awarded every other year to the most outstanding economist under forty, there was a Francis A. Walker medal, awarded at five-year intervals, for the most distinguished member economist of all. Later the Walker medal was dropped because with the Nobel Memorial Prize in economics established in 1968 on the 300th anniversary of the establishment of the Bank of Sweden, and perhaps because of the distinguished fellowship, it was clearly redundant. In 1962 it was alive and well. That year there were two candidates, Alvin Hansen and Jacob Viner. The Nominations Committee had voted seven to six for Hansen. The matter then went to the electoral college of the two committees. Edward Mason of Harvard was president in the chair, Gottfried Haberler was president-elect. I fail to recall the others present, except for Allen Wallis, a vice-president, Richard Musgrave, I believe a member of the Executive Committee, and Harold Williamson, the secretary and treasurer. Ballots were passed around and filled out. Williamson as secretary read the votes aloud as he unfolded them. One for Hansen, one for Viner, another for Viner . . . The count ended up as thirteen for Viner, and twelve for Hansen. Wallis leaned across the table to me and asked, "Why did Mason vote for Viner?" He had had all the votes tabulated in his computer mind and correctly guessed what had swung the totals. The next morning at breakfast with Musgrave, Mason walked by, and we put the question to him. He replied that with his election and Haberler's, both of Harvard, it would have been too much for Hansen of Harvard to win over Viner of Chicago. Spread the muck, share the wealth.

I am not sure in which of these years it was that I committed an appalling gaffe. It was at a retirement party at Harvard for Edward Mason. I thought I might be called upon for a word or two and had decided to say that Mason was *par excellence* the economist of solid judgment, to such as extent, for example, that judgment in economists should be measured on the Mason scale, as temperature is measured in terms of Fahrenheit, or electricity in volts (named after Alessandro Volta). Such a judicious economist as Dick Cooper, I proposed to say, would weigh in at 0.93 Mason. It would have done well except that I started off on the wrong foot. The cocktail hour had been long, and the wine with dinner plentiful. Arthur Smithies as toastmaster called on me first, before I had had time to get my act together, and I started, saying, "Ed Mason is not brilliant but" . . . Cries and catcalls. "Go back to MIT. Get lost." With some difficulty I got to the central message.

Some months or years later, I managed to turn this damaging performance to good account. I was asked at Stanford, at the retirement party for Edward S. Shaw, to speak for the profession, while Arthur Laffer held forth on behalf of Shaw's students. I began by saying that my record at this sort of occasion was abysmal and told the Mason incident on myself. Then I recounted a story that I had found risible, of two Salvation Army lasses, taking a shower after a parade. One said to the other, "My, Mabel, you have a large navel." The other said, "Next time, Gertrude, you carry the flag." I then wound up, "Ed Shaw,

Professor of Economics Emeritus

you are brilliant – and you have always carried the flag." It did not make much sense, but it struck Moe Abramovitz as so amusing that he reminded me of it a year later when it had slipped my mind.

My embarrassment over the Mason party was matched perhaps at a cocktail party at Richard Musgrave's years ago when I met a young Swedish woman whose name I failed to catch. "Tell me," I said, making conversation, "Are all Swedes megalomaniacs?" "What do you mean?" she asked. "I was thinking of Per Jacobsson and Gunnar Myrdal." "Gunnar Myrdal is my father," she replied. She was Sissela Bok, philosopher, and wife of Derek Bok, then dean of the Harvard Law School, later president of Harvard. I hope I have made my peace since with Mrs Bok, with whom I was a lunch guest of Abraham Sachar, the first president of Brandeis University, and to whom I sent a copy of the memorial essay I wrote about her father for the *Scandinavian Journal of Economics*. But I should stay more sober and be more wary.

In spring 1981 I spent four months at the Center for Behavioral Studies at Stanford, California, as already noted. My wife, at this stage, was reluctant to travel long distances to strange places and sit around while I worked, but she agreed to come late and leave early, staying two months in all away from her real work, which is children and grandchildren. By this time Emile Despres had died, but his widow, Joanna, found us a place to live in her apartment complex, near enough to walk through a residential area and fields to the Center on the outskirts of the Stanford University campus. I was perhaps a little unfortunate in having few economists of my sort there – non-mathematical, non-statistical – and no European historians, but that may have mandated less diversion from writing. There was a marvellous team of word processors, plus part of the time of a secretary. Since I typed out my own copy, the secretary was needed only to provide the accents on a typewriter that the Xerox 360 word processor lacked. When I left, there were flowers for the word-processing room, and a bottle of meat seasoning called "Accent" for the secretary. I have never been asked to say which I

Professor of Economics Emeritus

preferred, the Institute in Princeton or the Center at Stanford. Economists do not allow the answer "both," which I would like to give. The Center has the advantage of focusing on social science as contrasted with Princeton where the historians and social scientists are something of a minority in comparison with the mathematicians and physicists. If I could get my old lady to accompany me to Princeton longer than she will to Stanford, that would settle the issue. But both places are scholarly Nirvana.

In 1981 the MIT kissing finally had to stop. The Internal Revenue Service (IRS) says you must take your pension, postponed from age sixty-five to seventy, and the rules do not allow the university to hire their pensioners. I taught for a year at Middlebury College, Vermont, driving up the 200 miles most Mondays and returning Wednesday evenings, and crowding the two courses each term into two and a half days. A house went with the chair, and I stayed there Monday and Tuesday nights, plus an occasional week when Sarah came with me for the foliage, cross-country skiing, or to explore the countryside. Middlebury furnished some money to finish the typing of *A Financial History of Western Europe*, perhaps my *chef d'oeuvre*. There was one review that was excessive, but when I mentioned this to Donald McCloskey who had been the editor of the journal, he said, "He owed you one." The reviewer in question had been harsh about *Economic Growth in France and Britain*.

The incident reminds me of my first meeting with Anna Jacobson Schwartz, who wrote a powerful attack, from her monetarist perspective, on *The World in Depression*. I had never met her, but of course knew her work with Gayer and Rostow on England in the nineteenth century, and with Milton Friedman on the monetary history of the United States. In 1975 I attended a conference on the "Organization and retrieval of economic knowledge," put together by Mark Perlman of the University of Pittsburgh, sponsored by the International Economic Association, and held at Kiel. The topic arose partly from my suggestion to Perlman, the editor of the *Journal of Economic Literature* at the time, that the riches of the library of the Institut für Weltwirtschaft were insufficiently known, and that something should be done about it. He contributed a note on the subject in the *Journal of Economic Literature*, and then proposed the conference.

I arrived in Hamburg, tired from an overnight flight, was driven up the autobahn to Kiel at 150 kilometers an hour, not a restful mode of travel, took a nap, and then went for a swim in the hotel pool. I tripped and splashed a lady, who I later learned was Anna Schwartz. One day at table, she was sitting on the other side of Mark Blaug, who remarked to me pleasantly, "Your book on the depression was well reviewed, I believe." "Not everywhere," I answered, looking pointedly at Mrs Schwartz, who was listening. Later in the conference, Mrs Schwartz and I became friendly. When the conference broke up, and I said goodbye, she remarked, "Better luck next time." I found the words ambiguous: Write a better book? Get a different reviewer? Find me in a gentler mood?

Some friends thought I should have replied to the review. Absolutely not. Egon Sohmen was, I suspect, my most contentious student, and I never could persuade him not to respond to criticism. Let the market decide. There are cases of intellectual market failure, to be sure, but sharp replies, even to mistaken interpretations or errors of what the author said, are idle. Opinions differ. Thank God.

I wrote above that I thought one review of *Financial History* was excessive. This brings up Samuelson's Law of Flattery. No matter how thick the praise is laid on – to a point sometimes that the praiser comes close to retching – the recipient thinks, "True. How clearly he sees things." Samuelson and I have discussed this law, which is based largely on a single case – a dangerous social-science practice – but extensible plausibly to the world as a whole. The names of the protagonists will be withheld. There are enough narcissistic economists to enable the reader to decide for himself who the recipient was.

30

Retirement

From 1983–4 to 1986–7, I taught part-time at Brandeis. This consisted of one course each term, usually one on the economic history of Europe and the other on multinational corporations. The latter was by far the more popular, as each student rather looked forward to the time when he or she would command such a company. The appointment was a delight: fifteen minutes from my house by car, from nine to ten-thirty on Tuesdays and Thursdays. There was a brown-bag faculty seminar on Thursdays that kept one over. If there were a particularly enticing opportunity away, such as the Marshall lectures at Cambridge University in the fall of 1985, one could reschedule one class and have virtually a week off. Ultimately, however, I tired of teaching the same undergraduate courses, and when my wife had a stroke in the fall of 1986 I stopped. I can get away now only when my wife comes too, goes to her sister, then in Princeton, now in Lexington, or have a daughter move in. This enabled a trip to Singapore and Berlin in 1988, and to Copenhagen and Seoul in 1989, around the world counter-clockwise and clockwise (if one is facing the North Pole), in each case the dates chosen to make two trips into one somewhat longer one.

Research is driven not only by *Sitzfleisch*, but also by

serendipity and luck. One always learns from students, especially graduate students who are required to write term papers. For *Financial History*, I produced not only a clutch of cartoons, my only venture into iconography, but also epigraphs, one for each chapter. It was fun, and I found myself running competitions for some chapters, replacing one I regarded settled by a better one later. One for chapter 3 on bank money was a quotation from Thomas Mun's *England's Treasure by Forraign Trade*, lifted from a student paper as I had never read Mun. Its inclusion, however, induced Horst Claus Rechtenwald of the University of Erlangen-Nurnberg in the Federal Republic of Germany to ask me to write an introduction to the facsimile edition of Thomas Mun's other book *A Discourse of Trade*. I proceeded to read *A Discourse* and *England's Treasure*, and found myself quite caught up in the financial world of the seventeenth century. The introduction is now published in German, as the series of facsimile editions of classic economic works is the project of a German publisher. But it led me to pursue a few lines of inquiry. One economic historian of whom I asked a question asked me in turn, "Are you planning to write about the world distribution of silver in the mercantilist period?" I had not thought of the idea before, but decided to pursue it. The result is a long pamphlet entitled "Spenders and hoarders: the world distribution of Spanish American silver, 1550–1750." The emphasis is on disequilibrium in balances of payments. Peru, Mexico, and Spain could not hold on to silver, as the United States today is unable to hold on to dollars; and India and China in the two centuries after 1550 (and before, too) could hardly acquire enough precious metal for hoarding, like Japan, Taiwan, and Germany hoarding dollars today. Studies running to eighty pages or so are hard to get published, being too long for articles, and too short for books. It might have made a two-part article, like "Germany's overtaking of England, 1806 to 1914," or a "study" of the Princeton International Finance Section, as opposed to the shorter "essays." In the end I persuaded the Institute of Southeast Asian Studies of Singapore to publish it as a separate pamphlet, given the relevance of the

Retirement

hoarding issue to that part of the world.

Apart from this pamphlet, I have published four books within roughly my seventy-eighth year. The list is deceptive. One consists of the 1980 Mattioli lectures inordinately delayed. Another is a collection of older essays on financial crises and the role of the lender of last resort – *The International Economic Order*. A third is the second edition of *Manias, Panics, and Crashes*, pasted together in the summer of 1988. And a fourth is a facsimile edition of letters written to the State Department from the field in 1946 and 1947, together with two or three 1945 letters from Germany at the end of the war to my wife. This came about in an odd way.

When I was in GA in the State Department in 1945–7, I had no record of what I did when I was in Washington, as I kept no diary, nor any records. When I was away from my desk, however, I would write long letters to GA, detailing what I was learning, daily, some letters being as long as ten pages single-spaced. In August 1946 I took a trip to OMAUS in Berlin, the Allied Council in Vienna, with brief stops in Frankfurt, Paris, and Brussels, the last the seat of the Inter-Allied Reparations Agency, and between August 3 and August 31 wrote some twenty letters. (The word "some" emphasizes that there is no letter numbered 9 – lost or omitted by oversight – and two letters numbered 19.) When I got back to Washington, I collected the letters and hung on to them. The following year, as a member of the American delegation to the Council of Foreign Ministers in Moscow, I wrote more letters to GA. On leaving the Department in 1948 I liberated both lots. In due course I began to lend the letters to historians interested in the nitty-gritty details of United States economic policy toward Germany and Europe. I had them reproduced and deposited in the Truman, Eisenhower and Johnson libraries. When Charles Maier of the Harvard history department asked me to contribute a paper to a symposium on Germany and the Marshall Plan, I accepted, subject to the condition that I be allowed to do so in the form of a memoir, based largely on these letters and including some refutation of the McCarthy-like charge that I had

Retirement

been a Morgenthau plant in the State Department. The paper was written in 1984, and I obtained permission to include it in *Marshall Plan Days*, which came out in 1987, before the appearance of the symposium, which is still awaited in mid-1990.

It occurred to me that the letters might be worth publication by themselves, and I made a few desultory inquiries about the possibilities to no effect. In due course I learned that Professor Ernest May of the Harvard history department had suggested the project to the Arno Press. This was a publishing house, along with a handful of others, that specialized in the reproduction of documents of various sorts for libraries. The editor there who was interested in the idea later transferred to a similar firm, Meckler of Westport, Connecticut, which brought out the letters in facsimile, along with excerpts from letters to my wife, which added detail of modest historical interest. The book had a preface by Walt Rostow, and a long historical background introduction by Günter Bischof, then completing his PhD in history at Harvard. The finished volume, *The German Economy, 1945–1947: Charles P. Kindleberger's Letters from the Field*, appeared in May 1989.

This about winds up where I stand as an economist. I have one or two writing commitments, and now that our move to a retirement place is finished and we have settled down, I may take on more. Especially I may take on a large project, with no expectation of finishing it – occupational therapy, or perhaps, like Penelope's web, something to pass the time, weaving by day and unweaving by night. The pipeline is still full of papers for this conference and that *Festschrift*. It was said of Harry Johnson when he died of a second stroke that, if you were to judge by the literature, you would not be aware of his death for three years because the papers kept coming out. The same, at a more modest level, would occur if I were to shuffle off this mortal coil tomorrow.

I would emphasize in concluding that an economist's life is a good one. Unlike a dean or a college president, one can measure output in printed words. I should perhaps be ashamed of a life of intellectual hit-and-run, of taking up a topic – foreign

Retirement

exchange, international trade, capital flows, economic development, the multinational corporation, political economy, economic history, financial crises, financial history – skimming the cream, and moving on. No great depth of perception, but some ideas. An easy flow of words, if not of equations, with the reverse side of the coin being perhaps inherent sloppiness. But fun.

Appendix A

Curriculum Vitae

Born:	October 12, 1910, 11 West 8th Street, New York, NY
Parents:	E. Crosby Kindleberger, 1875–1950, lawyer Elizabeth Randall McIlvaine Kindleberger, 1878–1959, housewife
Married:	May 1, 1937, to Sarah Bache Miles, 1910– , housewife
Children:	Charles P. Kindleberger 3rd, 1940– , city planner, St Louis, Missouri Richard S. Kindleberger, 1942– , journalist, Boston, Massachusetts Sarah Kindleberger, 1946– , kindergarten teacher, Concord, Massachusetts Elizabeth Randall Kindleberger Rosen, 1949– , historian, Machias, Maine
Education:	Kent School, Kent, Connecticut, 1924–8 University of Pennsylvania, 1928–32, AB 1932 Columbia University, 1933–7, AM 1934, PhD 1937

Appendix A

Military service: Office of Strategic Services, Washington, DC, 1942–3
Enemy Objectives Unit, Economic Warfare Division, US Embassy, London (on detached service of OSS), 1943–4
Captain and Major, Army of the United States, Twelfth Army Group, European theatre, 1944–5

Non-academic positions: Office boy, National Economy League, New York, NY, March–July 1932
Office boy, Johnson and Higgins, marine insurance brokers, New York, NY, 1932–3
Research economist, International Research Division, US Treasury Department, Washington, DC, July–September 1936
Research economist, Federal Reserve Bank of New York, New York, NY October 1936–June 1939
Research economist, Bank for International Settlements, Basle, Switzerland, July 1939–July 1940
Research economist, Board of Governors, Federal Reserve System, Washington, DC, July 1940–July 1942
Adviser, Office of Finance and Development, Department of State, Washington, DC, June 1945–November 1945
Chief, Division of German and Austrian Economic Affairs, Department of State, November 1945–June 1947
Adviser, European Recovery Program, Department of State, June 1947–July 1948

Academic appointments, full-time: Associate Professor of Economics, MIT, 1948–51
Professor of Economics and Ford

Appendix A

International Professor of Economics,
MIT, 1951–76
Professor of Economics Emeritus and
part-time Senior Lecturer, MIT, 1976–81
Visiting Professor of Economics, Atlanta
University Center, Atlanta, GA
(on leave from MIT), 1967–8
Visiting Professor of Economics,
Middlebury College, Middlebury, VT, 1981–2

Academic appointments, part-time:
Columbia University, 1949–50
Fletcher School of Law and Diplomacy,
Medford, MA, various years in the 1950s
School for Advanced International Studies,
Peterborough, NH, summer 1950
Institut des Hautes Etudes Internationales,
Geneva, Switzerland, summer 1954
Harvard University Summer School,
summer 1955
Visiting Erskine Fellow, University of
Canterbury, Christchurch, New Zealand,
summer 1966
Edinburgh University, Edinburgh, Scotland,
January 1974
University of Toronto, Toronto, Ontario,
Canada, January 1976
Brigham Young University, Provo, UT,
January 1977
Ecole des Hautes Etudes Politiques, Paris,
France, spring 1978
University of Texas, Austin, TX, spring 1979
Visiting Professor of Economics,
Brandeis University, Waltham, MA, 1983–7

Research appointments:
Palais des Nations, Geneva, Switzerland,
1953–4
Merrill Center, Southampton, NY,
summer 1956

Appendix A

Visiting Fellow, Nuffield College, Oxford University, fall 1960
Independent research, Paris, spring–summer 1961
Center for International Affairs, Harvard University, support for travel and research in Europe, summer 1964
Institut für Weltwirtschaft, Kiel, Germany, fall 1971
Bank of Italy, Rome, spring 1972
Institute for Advanced Studies, Princeton, NJ, spring 1977
Center for Advanced Studies in the Behavioral Sciences, Stanford, CA, spring 1981
Gunnar Myrdal Visiting Professor, Institute for International Economics, University of Stockholm, Stockholm, Sweden, fall 1982
James McDonnell Professor, World Institute of Development Economic Research (WIDER), Helsinki, Finland, summer 1986

Affiliations: Phi Beta Kappa
American Economic Association, President 1985
Royal Economic Society (UK)
Economic History Association
Economic History Society (UK)
American Academy of Arts and Sciences
American Philosophical Society

Honors: Bronze Star, 1944; Legion of Merit, 1945
Dr Honoris causa, University of Paris, 1966
(*Festschrift*), *Trade, Balance of Payments and Growth: Papers in Honor of Charles P. Kindleberger,* J. N. Bhagwati, R. W. Jones, Robert A. Mundell, and J. Vanek, editors, 1971

Appendix A

Dr h.c., University of Ghent, 1977
Harms Prize, Institut für Weltwirtschaft, Kiel, 1978
Dr Sci. h.c., University of Pennsylvania, 1984
Bicentennial Medal, Georgetown University, 1989

Other service: Occasional consultant to Economic Cooperation Administration, Federal Reserve Board; US Treasury; Federal Reserve Bank of New York; Committee for Economic Development
Trustee and trustee emeritus, Clark College, Atlanta, Georgia
Member, President's Advisory Committee on International Monetary Arrangements, 1965–6
Chairman, MIT Faculty, 1965–7

Appendix B

Bibliography

Books written by Charles P. Kindleberger
International Short-Term Capital Movements, New York: Columbia University Press, 1937
The Dollar Shortage, New York: Wiley and MIT Press, 1950
International Economics, Homewood, IL: Richard D. Irwin, 1953, 1958, 1963, 1968, 1973 (and with Peter H. Lindert) 1978, 1982
The Terms of Trade: A European Case Study, Cambridge, MA: MIT Press, 1956
Economic Development, New York: McGraw-Hill, 1958, 1965 (and with Bruce Herrick) 1977, 1983
Foreign Trade and the National Economy, New Haven, CT: Yale University Press, 1962, 1975
Economic Growth in France and Britain, Cambridge, MA: Harvard University Press, 1964
Europe and the Dollar, Cambridge, MA: MIT Press, 1966
Europe's Postwar Growth: The Role of the Labor Supply, Cambridge, MA: Harvard University Press, 1967
American Business Abroad: Six Lectures on Direct Investment, New Haven, CT: Yale University Press, 1969
Power and Money: The Politics of International Economics and the Economics of International Politics, New York: Basic Books, 1970
The World in Depression, 1929–1939, Berkeley, CA: University of California Press, 1973; revised and enlarged, 1986
America in the World Economy, New York: Foreign Policy Association, 1977

Appendix B

Economic Response: Comparative Studies in Trade, Finance, and Growth, Cambridge, MA: Harvard University Press, 1978

Manias, Panics, and Crashes: A History of Financial Crises, New York: Basic Books, 1978; revised and enlarged, 1989

International Money: A Collection of Essays, London: Allen & Unwin, 1981

A Financial History of Western Europe, London: Allen & Unwin, 1984

Multinational Excursions, Cambridge, MA: MIT Press, 1984

Keynesianism vs Monetarism and Other Essays in Financial History, London: Allen & Unwin, 1985

Marshall Plan Days, London: Allen & Unwin, 1987

International Capital Movements (the Marshall Lectures), Cambridge: Cambridge University Press, 1987

The International Economic Order: Essays on Financial Crisis and International Public Goods, Brighton: Wheatsheaf/Harvester, 1988

The German Economy, 1945-1947: Charles P. Kindleberger's Letters from the Field, with a Preface by W.W. Rostow and an Historical Introduction by Günter Bischof, Westport and London: Meckler, 1989

Economic Laws and Economic History: The Raffaele Mattioli 1980 Lectures, Cambridge: Cambridge University Press, 1990

Historical Economics: Art or Science, New York: Harvester Wheatsheaf, 1990

Books edited by Charles P. Kindleberger
  with Andrew Shonfield: *North American and Western European Economic Policies*, London: Macmillan, 1971; *The International Corporation*, Cambridge, MA: MIT Press, 1971
  with Tamir Agmon: *Multinationals from Small Countries*, Cambridge, MA: MIT Press, 1977
  with John S. Chipman: *Flexible Exchange Rates and the Balance of Payments: Essays in Memory of Egon Sohmen*, Amsterdam: North-Holland, 1980
  with Jean-Pierre Laffargue: *Financial Crises: Theory, History and Policy*, Cambridge: Cambridge University Press, 1982
  with Guido di Tella: *Economics in the Long View: Essays in Honor of Walt W. Rostow*, 3 vols, London: Macmillan, 1982
  with David B. Audretch: *The Multinational Corporation in the 1980s*, Cambridge, MA: MIT Press, 1983

Index

Those persons designated "prof." were teachers of CPK. Associates given their military titles, or marked EOU (Enemy Objectives Unit), GA (Division of German and Austrian Affairs), or MIT (Massachusetts Institute of Technology), have, in frequent cases, since moved to different careers. Publication dates are given only for books written by CPK.

Abramovitz, Moses 32, 36, 104, 202
Academic jobs for economists in the depression 43
Acheson, Dean 123
air force generals 72, 85
Air Intelligence (British) 74
Alexander, Sidney S., MIT 193
Alexandria, VA 106
Allom, Donald, squadron leader 78
American Business Abroad (1969) 178, 216
American Economic Association 65, 136, 200; presidency 201
American Economic Review 130
American Embassy, London 70
American Institute of Banking 42
Ames, Winslow 37–8

Anderson, Fred, general 85, 93
Angell, James W., prof. 31, 32, 39
Ardennes attack 96–8
area bombing 72, 76
Askari, Hossain, MIT 196–7
Atlanta 182–7
Atlanta University Center 182
Austin 196–7
Australia, MV 20
Austrian economic problems 117–18

Babington-Smith, Constance, flight officer 77
Babson Institute 138
Bachman, Jules 38
Bagehot, Walter 180
ball-bearings, as target system 76

Index

Ball, George W. 75
Ball, Joseph, senator 125
Baltic Sea 21
Banca Commerciale Italiana 198
Bank for International Settlements (BIS) 49, 51, 52–7
Bank of Italy 189
Banning, Derek, lieutenant 81
Barcelona 59
Barnes, Harry Elmer 14
Barnett, Harold J. ("Barney"), EOU, GA 68, 88, 112, 131
Basle 53–7
Bastogne 98
Baum, Warren C. 68
Baxter, James Phinney 67
Beckhart, Benjamin Haggott, prof. 34–5
Behn, Sosthenes 116
Belair, Felix 118
Belgium 124
Bellagio 175
Bergson, Abram 104, 154
Berkner, George 141
Bernstein, Edward 172–3
Bernstein, Peter L., EOU 92
Beyen, J.W. 54–5
Bhagwati, Jagdish, MIT 152
Biemiller, Andrew 14
Bigot, security clearance 83
Bird City, SS 21; crew 21–4
Bishop, Robert L., MIT 170–1, 188, 193
Bissell, Richard 129, 132
black colleges 183
Blaug, Mark 205
Bloomfield, Arthur 130
Board of Governors of the Federal Reserve System, *see* Federal Reserve Board
Bohlen, Charles 118, 122
Bok, Sissela 202

bomb-damage assessment 80
bombing, strategic 74–82, theory of 71–2; tactical 83–9
Bond, Horatio 80
Bonesteel, Charles H. ("Tic"), colonel 122
book reviewing 41, 202
Bowie, Robert R. 153, 179
Bradley, Omar N., general 48, 92–3, 95
Brandeis University 206
Branson, William H., MIT 152
Braudel, Fernand 196
bridges vs marshalling yards as tactical targets 83–8
Brimmer, Andrew 183
Brookings Institution 183
Brown, E. Cary, MIT 170, 193
Brown, Henry Phelps 154
Brown, J. Douglass, MIT 64
Brunner, Karl 199
Bryce, Robert 64–5
Burgess, W. Randolph 32, 43
Burns, Arthur F., prof. 31, 127
Burns, Arthur R. and Evelene, profs 32
Bush, Vannevar, MIT 171
Busser, William F. 16
Butler, Harry A. 37
Byé, Maurice 140
Byrnes, James F. 113, 115

Cairncross, Sir Alec 114
California, SS 19
Canada 63–5
capital theory 75
carpetbagging 116
Casey, William 86
Caves, Richard 135
Center for Advanced Studies in Behavioral Sciences, Stanford, CA 203

219

Index

Center for International Affairs (CFIA), *see* Harvard University
Chacholiades, Miltiades, MIT 152
Chaddock, prof. 34
Chamberlin, Edward 49, 200
Chambers, Whitaker 44
Chandler, Lester V. 185
Chase-Manhattan/United Negro College Fund (UNCF) 183
Château d'Oex 57–8
Clark College 182–7
Clark, John M., prof. 31
Clark, Mark, general 117–18
Claxton, Philander P. 130–1
Clay, Lucius D. 113, 115, 118
Clayton, William L. 48, 103–5, 115–16, 121–2
Cleveland, Harold van Buren ("Van") 121, 128
Coe, V. Frank 43–5
Cohen, Ben 110, 118
Collado, Emilio Gabriel ("Pete") 45–6, 50, 103–4
Colm, Gerhard 62, 113
Colm–Dodge–Goldsmith report 113
Columbia University 29, 31–42; course on the economy of Europe 137; dissertation requirement 40; doctoral examinations 33–4
Columbia University Press 40
Cooper, Charles, MIT 155
Cooper, Richard N. 202
Copenhagen 21, 23
Coppock, Joseph D. 158
Cosby, Arthur 27
Council of Foreign Ministers (CFM) 118–20
Council on Foreign Relations 121, 152
crimes, academic 138

Currie, Lauchlin 144

David, René 191–2
Delta Psi fraternity 14, 29
Department of State, *see* State Department
Despres, Emile 29, 46, 47–50, 57, 65, 66, 67, 102, 104, 177, 183
Despres, Joanna 203
Despres–Kindleberger–Salant article 173, 176–7
Deutsch, John J. 63–4
Deutsch, Karl W., MIT 148
deWilde, John C., EOU, GA 70, 112
Diaz Alejandro, Carlos F., MIT 152
Dillon, Douglas 122–3
Dollar Shortage, The (1950) 134
Domar, Evsey D., MIT 193
Donaldson, E. Talbot 8–9
Donovan, William J., general ("Wild Bill") 67
Dornbusch, Rudiger, MIT 139
Downes, Prentice G. 9
Downie, Jack 146
Dulles, Allen W. 57
Dulles, John Foster 118
Durand, J. Dana 63
Duroselle, Jean-Baptiste 153
Durr, Clifford J. and Virginia F. 107–10

Ecole des Hautes Etudes Politiques 196
Economic Commission for Europe 112
Economic Development (1958) 136, 152, 216
Economic Growth in France and Britain, 1851–1950 (1964) 138, 160, 164, 194, 216

220

Index

economic history 138
Economic Laws and Economic History (1989) 199, 217
Economic Response (1978) 189, 194, 217
Economic Warfare Division, US Embassy, London 51
Eddy, George A. and Eileen O'Daniel 41, 50, 107
Edey, Maitland A. 9, 100
Edgerton, Harold, MIT 2
Edinburgh University 191
Eisenhower, Dwight D., general 92, 98
Eliot, Thomas H. and Lois Jamison 106–8
Elliott, J.H. 65
Elliott, William Yandell 149
Enemy Objectives Unit (EOU) 51, 74–89
Enke, Stephen 135, 152
Episcopal High School 104
Episcopal Seminary of Virginia 104
Europe and the Dollar (1967) 216
European University Institute, Badia Fiesolana 191
European winter of 1946–7 121
Europe's Postwar Growth (1967) 176, 216

factor-price-equalization theorem 147
Fairbank, John K. 2
Fairbanks, Rev. Rollin J. and Phyllis M. 131, 176
Federal Bureau of Investigation (FBI) 120
Federal Reserve Bank of New York 27, 47–51
Federal Reserve Board 51, 61–3
Fei, John, MIT 157

Financial History of Western Europe, A (1984) 194, 207, 217
Findlay, Ronald, MIT 152
Fischer, Wolfram 179
Fitzroy, Herbert Keith ("Fitz") 14, 37
Fletcher School of Law and Diplomacy 139
Focke–Wulf airplane company: plant at Bremen 77; production at Marienberg 78; production of steering coupling 79
Ford Foundation 155, 160
Foreign Trade and the National Economy (1962) 154–5, 216
Fowler, Henry H. ("Joe") 172
Fox, Bert 142
France 91; see also Paris
free lunch 158–9
Freedom of Information Act 126
Freeman, Ralph E., MIT 170
Friedman, Milton 32, 46, 180, 183
Futcher, Palmer 6

GA (Office of German and Austrian Economic Affairs, Department of State) 112–20
Gadon, Hyman, MIT 157
Gaevernitz, Gero von Schultz 57
Galbraith, John Kenneth ("Ken") 3, 45, 75, 111, 183
Gardner, Richard 104
Gardner, Walter R. 61–2, 66
Geneva 24–6, 145–8
German Economy, 1945–1947, The (1989) 114, 208–9, 217
Germany, postwar: food problems 118; Level of Industry Agreement 114; moratorium on foreign investment 115–16;

Index

occupation currency and currency reform 115; property problems 116–17; *see also* monetary reform, Germany
Giersch, Herbert 118
Glover, Mrs Charles C. 27
Goldsmith, Raymond W. 113, 154, 175
Gordon, Aaron 43
Gordon, Kermit 142–3
Gordon, Lincoln 122
Gordon, Wendell 197
Graduate School of International Relations, Geneva 24–5; lecturers in 1931 25
Graham, Frank D. 128–9
Gray, Gordon 90
Greek language, study of 12–13
Gross, Ernest 114
Gugliemi, J. 186

Haberler, Gottfried 140, 200, 201
Hackney, Dr and Mrs Sheldon 111
Hahn, Pyung Chun 150
Hall, Max 154
Handsfield, Hugh W. 6
Hansen, Alvin H. 49, 63, 65–6, 201–2
Hardcastle, Y. Fitzhugh and Edith 166
Harr, prof. of banking 15
Harris, prof. of banking 15
Harris, Selig 12
Harris, Seymour E. 130, 133, 136
Harrison, George L. 27
Harrod, Roy 140, 142
Hartwell, R. Max 162
Harvard Business Review 35
Harvard University: Center for International Affairs (CFIA) 153–4, 174; micro-sociology 132–3; summer school 149
Harvard University Press 149–50, 164
Haus Welt Klub 188
headmasters, school 7–8
Heller, Walter W. 183–4
Hemingway, Ernest 163, 176
Henderson, Vivian W. 182, 185, 187
Hermberg, Paul 62–3
Herrick, Bruce, MIT 137
Hersey, Arthur 36
Hilldring, John, general 130
Hinshaw, C. Elton 200
Hirsch, Fred 134, 198
Hirschman, Albert O. 123
Hirschmeyer, Father 149–50
Historical Economics (1990) 217
Hitch, Charles 80–1
Hoeffding, Oleg 79
Hoffman, Michael 148
Hoffmann, Stanley 153
Höffner, German colonel 86–7
Honerkamp, Rosalene, EOU 94
Hoover, Herbert 116
Hughes, H. Stuart 9
Hughes, Richard D'Oyley, colonel 69–70, 82, 83, 93, 100–1
Humphrey, Don D. 118, 139
Hymer, Stephen H., MIT 152, 177–8

Ingersoll, Harold, lieutenant-colonel 95–6
Innis, Harold 65
input–output theory 75
In Search of France 153–4
Institute des Hautes Etudes Internationales, Geneva 147

Index

Institut für Weltwirtschaft (Institute of World Economy), Kiel 188–9
Institute of Advanced Studies, Princeton 194
intellectual profiles 8
Interallied Reparations Agency (IARA) 39
interdisciplinary research 176
International Capital Movements (1987) 217
International Economic Order, The (1988) 208, 217
International Economics (1953) 134–6, 152, 178, 216
International Money (1981) 217
international politics 178, 180–1
International Short-term Capital Movements (1937) 39–40, 216
Italy, bombing of railroads in 84–5

Jackson, William, colonel 90–2
Jacobs, George, GA 119
Jacobsson, Per 51, 55, 203
Jamestown 18
Jay, Peter 162
Jenner, William, senator 126
jobs in economics in 1930s 43
Johnson and Higgins 28–30
Johnson, Harry G. 3, 151–2, 155, 158
Johnson, Howard W., MIT 171–2
Johnson, Lyndon B., president 172
Joint Economic Committee of Canada and the United States 63–4
Jones, Ronald W., MIT 135, 152
Jordan, Vernon 183

Kahn, Lord (Alfred) 199
Kahn, Mark, EOU 68
Kaldor, Lord (Nicholas) 199
Karasik, Munroe, GA 113
Katz, Barrie 67, 88
Katz, Milton 176
Kaysen, Carl, EOU, MIT 82, 85, 88, 194
Kazekevitch, Vladimir 35–6
Kennan, George F. 122
Kent School 6–11, 18
Kerr–McGee Oil Company 140–1
Kervyn de Lettenhove, Albert, MIT 146
Kessler, Martin 178, 196
Keynes, John Maynard 125
Keynesianism vs Monetarism (1985) 217
Kiel 185–9
Killian, James, MIT 129, 168, 171–2
Kilroe, Frank E. ("Jim") 37
Kindelberger, John ("Dutch") 52
Kindleberger, family members 4–5, 56, 161–3, 166, 182, 198
"Kindleberger surplus" 124
"Kindleberger's law of alternatives" 87
King, Martin Luther, Jr 183, 186
Kipper- und Wipperzeit (debasement period) 139
Kirkpatrick, Lyman, captain 90
Kissinger, Henry 153–4
Komiya, Ryutaro 149
Koo, Bon Ho 184

Laffer, Arthur 202
Lane, Mills B., Jr 184–5
Lary, Hal B. 143, 147
Lattimore, Owen 109
law 16
Lawrence, Oliver 74

Index

lawyers vs economists in war 71
League of Nations 143
Leigh-Mallory, Sir Arthur, air chief marshal 85, 86
Leningrad 21, 23
Leontief, Wassily 75
Leventhal, Harold 117
Levy, Walter J. 122, 124–5
Lévy-Leboyer, Maurice 175
Lewis, W. Arthur, model 174
Linder, Staffan Burenstam, MIT 164–6
Lindert, Peter H. 135
Lingelbach, William, prof. 16
Lippmann, Walter 121
Lisbon 59–60
Litvinov, Ivy 107
Livingstone, S. William and Mary Walton 106–11
Lodge, Henry Cabot, senator 125
Loeb, Arthur 14
London 73, 89
Lovett, Robert 122
Lundberg, Eric 199
Lutz, Friederich 128
Luxembourg 95–8

Mabon, John Scott 6
McCarthy, Joseph, senator 126
McCarthyism 45, 126
McCauliffe, general 98
McCloskey, Donald N. 204
MacDougall, Donald 140, 162
McGee, Dean 140–1
Mackintosh, William 63, 65
Maclaurin, W. Rupert, MIT 129
McClelland, George, prof. 17
McIlvaine, Fannie Randall 14
Madrid 59
Magee, Stephen P. and Nanneska, MIT 152, 140–1
Maier, Charles 203

Maison des Sciences de l'Homme 196
Manias, Panics, and Crashes (1978) 48, 139, 194, 217
Marget, Arthur W. 119
Marshall, George C. 48
Marshall (Alfred) lectures 206
Marshall Plan 121–6
Marshall Plan Days (1987) 114, 217
Mason, Edward S. and Marguerite 67, 104–5, 198, 201–2
Massachusetts Institute of Technology (MIT) 129, 132–44, 149–59, 167–73
Matthews, H. Freeman ("Doc") 113, 119
Mattioli, Raeffele, lectures 198–9
May, Ernest 208
Mayer, Edward A., EOU 68–9
Mayer, Martin 194
Meade, James E. 62, 143, 165
Meier, G.M. 48
Meltzer, Allan 119
Merrill Center 150
Merrill Foundation 142
Meyer, André 172–3
Middlebury College 204
Mikesell, Raymond F. 140
Milan 198–9
Miles, Francis T. 10, 17, 119, 131, 153
Miles, Jeanie W. (Mrs William H. Walker) 46
Miles, Louis Wardlaw 39, 153
Miles, Sarah Bache (Mrs Charles P. Kindleberger) 38, 211; *see also* Kindleberger, family members
Miller, Robert T. 10
Milward, Alan S. 128

224

Index

Ministry of Economic Warfare (MEW), UK 74
Minsky, Hyman P. 195
Mitchell, Wesley C., prof. 31
Mitford, Jessica 109
Modigliani, Franco, MIT 157, 189, 193, 199
Molotov, V. 119
Monetary reform, Germany 113–16
Montgomery, field-marshal 95, 97
Moody, Dunbar 186
Moore, Ben T. 121
morale, and bombing 76
Morehouse College 182, 187
Morgenthau, Hans 147–8
Morgenthau Plan 46
Morse, Chandler, EOU 51, 66, 68–72, 106, 109
Morris Brown College 182, 185–6
Multinational Excursions (1984) 196, 217
Mun, Thomas 207
Mundell, Robert A., MIT 152
Murgatroyd, S. 39
Murphy, Charles 96
Murphy, Frank 69
Musgrave, Richard 201–3
Myint, Hla 140
Myrdal, Gunnar 112, 146–7, 165, 203

National Bureau of Economic Research 31
National Economy League 27–8
Nelson, Mrs John M. 38
nepotism 20
New York stock market 10–11
New Zealand 167–8
nicknames 21, 81

Nitze, Paul 122
Nuffield College, Oxford 161–3
"numbers game" 78–9
Nurkse, Ragnar 56, 146, 154

O'Daniel, Eileen, *see* Eddy
Office of Military Government, US (OMGUS) in the US zone of occupation in Germany 103
Office of Strategic Services (OSS) 49, 61, 67–72
Ohlin, Bertil 134, 155, 164–5
Oklahoma City University 140–1
Oliver, Covey T. 104
Olmstead, J. Warren 158
"Operation Octopus" 88
Organization for Economic Cooperation and Development (OECD) 175
Ostrander, F. Taylor 25
Oxford University 160–3

Palais des Nations Library 143
Palmstierna, Jacob 164
Panama Canal 19, 20
pantheon of remote bosses 77–8
Paris 160–1, 163–4
Parker, William N. 179
Parks, Rosa 110
Patterson, S.H., prof. 15
Patton, George S., general 7, 92, 95–6
Pauley, Edwin 104
Pechman, Joseph 183
Pennsylvania, University of 12–17, economics training in 25
Perlman, Mark 204
Phillips, William 123
philosophy courses 13
Pincus, Irwin Nat, EOU 96

Index

Pitts, Jesse R. 153
Playfair, Edward 66
poker 20–1
Polish intelligence 77
Polish well-to-do refugees 59
Poor, Wharton 28
Potsdam Agreement 113; first-charge principle 120
Power and Money (1970) 178, 216
Prebisch, Raul, thesis of 142
President's Advisory Committee on International Monetary Arrangements 172–3
Princes Risborough 80
Princeton University 194; Woodrow Wilson School 125
prisoner-of-war interrogation 77, 99–100
Provo 191
purchasing-power parity 43, 125–6

Rabi, Isadore 141–2
Rappard, William 147–8
Raymond, Robert 47
real bills 34
Rechtenwald, Horst-Claus 207
recruitment into economics 15–16
Reddaway, Brian 151
Research and Analysis Branch, OSS 67
Reynolds, Lloyd W. 154–5
Rhinelander, Philip 8
Richardson, H.W., prof. 25
Riddleberger, James 113
Riefler, Winfield W. 62
Robbins, Chandler and Sarah 107
Robey, Ralph W., prof. 29
Rockefeller, David 172–3
Rockefeller Foundation 175, 182
Roelker, Nancy 153

Romilly, Decca, *see* Mitford
Roosa, Robert V., EOU 91, 172–3
Roosevelt, Archibald 27
Rosenstein-Rodan, Paul N., MIT 189
Rostow, Walt W., EOU, GA, MIT 68, 70, 79, 88–9, 112, 131, 196–7
Rothschild, lieutenant 100
Rubin, Seymour J. 113
Ruggles, Richard 79

Sachar, Abraham 202
sailors 21–2
Saint Anthony Hall, *see* Delta Psi fraternity
Saint Gobain plant visit, MIT 144
Salant, Walter S. 32, 48, 70, 177
Salant, William A. 70, 85, 113
Salera, Virgil 135
Samuelson, Paul A., MIT 50, 54, 65, 133, 136, 183, 193, 205
"Sandy boys" 97
Saxe, Joe W. 153, 175
Schumpeter, Joseph A. 165–6
Schwartz, Anna J. 11, 180, 204–5
Seminary Hill, Alexandria, VA 106–11
Shapiro, Ascher, MIT 170
Shapiro, Eli, MIT 33
Shaw, Edward S. 202
Shultz, George P., MIT 127
Sibert, Edwin, general, G-2 90, 92–5, 98
Siepmann, Charles and Jane 107–8
Sill, Father Frederic H. 6–7, 10
silver, distribution of Spanish 139
Simkovitch, Vladimir G., prof. 32–4

Index

Singer Sewing Machine Co. 116
Skelton, Alexander ("Sandy") 63
Skinner, Quentin 190
Sloan fellows 144
Sloan, Pat, prof. 25
small-arms factories 96
Smith, Bedell 118
Smith, James, senator 125
Smithies, Arthur 202
Sodersten, Bö 164
Sohmen, Egon, MIT 140, 152, 205
Sokolsky, George P. 45, 117
Solow, Robert M., MIT 170
Souder, Ralph W., prof. 31–2
Spaatz, Carl, general 92–3
Sproul, Allen 47–8
Standish, Alexander, colonel 90, 98
Stanford 202
State Department: Finance Division, Office of Finance and Development (FN, OFD) 103–5; Division of German and Austrian Affairs (GA) 112–20; adviser on Marshall Plan 121–7
Stevenson rubber plan 21
Stockholm School of Economics 164–6
Stone, Lawrence 161–2
Struik, Dirk J. 42
Students International Union, Geneva 24
stuttering 41–2
sugar beets 99
Supreme Headquarters, Allied Expeditionary Force (SHAEF) 88
Surrey, Walter S. 113, 126
Swarthmore College honors examinations 156–7
Sweezy, Paul 65, 89

tactical bombing, *see* bombing, tactical
Taft, Robert, senator 126
tanks 68–9
target systems 74
Taussig, Frank William 142
Tedder, Arthur William, air marshal 84
Terms of Trade, The (1956) 142–3, 152, 216
Thorp, Willard L. and Clarice 104–5, 122, 150–2
Thorpe, Rosemary 142
Tilly, Richard 175
Toronto 191
Townes, Charles, MIT 171–2
Treasury Department, *see* United States Treasury Department
Triffin, Robert 176
Tripartite Monetary Agreement 39
trips: 1940 (bus, train, Geneva to Lisbon) 57–60; 1943 (ship convoy, New York to Cardiff) 72–3; 1944 (hitchhiking, Cherbourg to Chartres) 94
Truman, Harry S., president 104
Tufts, Robert W. 123
Turner, Sir Mark 84
Tyson, James, EOU 81

Ultra 77, 97
United Negro College Fund 183, 187
United States Senate 125–6
United States Strategic Air Force (USSTAF): A-2 (intelligence) 101–2; A-5 (planning) 69
United States Strategic Bombing Survey (USSBS) 75

Index

United States Treasury Department 43–6
University of Canterbury, Christchurch, New Zealand 167–8
University of Pennsylvania, *see* Pennsylvania

Vandenberg, Arthur, senator 125–6
Vandenberg, Hoyt, general 88, 96
Van der Tak, Herman 143
Vanek, Jaroslav, MIT 143, 148, 152
van Zealand, Marcel 55
Vaughn, William Preston 5
Verity, Charles, group captain 74
Villard, Henry Hilgardt 33
Viner, Jacob 45, 63–4, 128, 129, 201–2
Vinson, Frederick M. 104–5
von Mises, Ludwig 58

Walker, Francis A., medal 201–2
Walker, William H. 10
Wallace, Don 128–9
Wallace, Marcia 157
Wallis, Allan 32, 46
Warburg, Eric M., colonel 86, 101
Warsh, David 3
Washington DC, visit of Atlanta University Center to 183
Wedseltoft, Paul 21–2
wheat, national responses to fall in price of 137–8

Whimperton, Mr 53, 59
White, Harry Dexter 44–6, 63, 66, 115, 118
Whitin, Thomson ("Tom") 129
Wiesbaden 100
Wieser, Dr 54, 56
Wiesner, Jerome, MIT 140, 169
Wilcox, Clair 156
Wilcox, Francis 125
Williams, Bill, brigadier 97
Williams College 49
Williams, John H. 50, 87
Williams, Roger 19, 28
Williamson, Francis 117
Williamson, Harold 201
Willis, George 47
Willis, H. Parker, prof. 34–5
Willis, Parker B. 35
Wood, Barry 8
World Bank 45
World in Depression, 1929–39, The (1973) 179–80, 216
World Institute for Development Economic Research (WIDER) 1–2
Wylie, Laurence 153
Wyzanski, Charles 169

Young, Allyn 49
Young, Ralph 15

Zacharias, Jerrold, MIT 140–1
Zecchi, Antonino and Novella 53–4
Zimmerman, Sir Alfred 25
Zuckerman, Lord (Solly) 84–6